# Your Library Is the Answer

# Your Library Is the Answer

## Demonstrating Relevance to Tech-Savvy Learners

Christina T. Russo and Cathy Swan

## LIBRARIES UNLIMITED

AN IMPRINT OF ABC-CLIO, LLC
Santa Barbara, California • Denver, Colorado • Oxford, England

**Library of Congress Cataloging-in-Publication Data**

Russo, Christina T., author.
  Your library is the answer : demonstrating relevance to tech-savvy learners /
Christina T. Russo and Cathy Swan.
    pages cm
  Includes bibliographical references and index.
  ISBN 978-1-59884-933-2 (pbk : alk. paper) — ISBN 978-1-59884-934-9 (eBook)
1. School libraries—Aims and objectives—United States.   2. School libraries—
United States—Evaluation.   3. School libraries—Information technology—United
States.   4. Internet in school libraries—United States.   5. Online social networks—Library
applications—United States.   6. School librarians—Effect of technological innovations
on—United States.   7. School librarian participation in curriculum planning—United
States.   I. Swan, Cathy, author.   II. Title.
  Z675.S3R87 2015
  027.80973—dc23          2014037460

ISBN: 978-1-59884-933-2
EISBN: 978-1-59884-934-9

19  18  17  16  15        1  2  3  4  5

This book is also available on the World Wide Web as an eBook.
Visit www.abc-clio.com for details.

Libraries Unlimited
An Imprint of ABC-CLIO, LLC

ABC-CLIO, LLC
130 Cremona Drive, P.O. Box 1911
Santa Barbara, California 93116-1911

This book is printed on acid-free paper (∞)

Manufactured in the United States of America

Excerpts from "Generation M2: Media in the Lives of 8- to 18-Year-Olds", (#8010), The Henry J. Kaiser Family Foundation, January 2010. This information was reprinted with permission from the Henry J. Kaiser Family Foundation. The Kaiser Family Foundation is a non-profit private operating foundation, based in Menlo Park, California, dedicated to producing and communicating the best possible analysis and information on health issues.

Excerpts from Lemov, Doug. *Teach Like a Champion: 49 Techniques that put Students on the Path to College.* San Francisco: Jossey-Bass, 2010 and Wagner, Tony, Robert Kegan, Lisa Lahey, Richard W. Lemons, Jude Garnier, Deborah Helsing, Annie Howell, and Harriette Thurber Rasmussen. *Change Leadership: A Practical Guide to Transforming Our Schools.* San Francisco: Jossey-Bass, 2006 are reprinted with permission.

# Contents

# Introduction

Could you meet the Pizza Hut challenge? Pizza Hut announced that it would hold 140-second interviews for the position of manager of digital media. Wow—140 seconds to sell yourself! Pizza Hut advertised for someone who could "communicate clearly in a short amount of time, be on the cutting edge of social space, be super passionate, and quick on their feet" (Wong, 2013). This person must be knowledgeable about a variety of social media platforms and information outlets, as well as have the ability to think creatively and motivate others. What they need is a school librarian. Yes, a school librarian not only can do all this, but can do it seamlessly. A six-word memoir, a six-second video, or a 140-character tweet poses no problem for these tech savvy professionals, who actively participate in and construct new media daily. They not only can meet the Pizza Hut challenge, but can exceed it because of their disposition, breadth of knowledge, and responsiveness. They are a perfect fit for the fast-paced, media driven, connected marketplace.

But the real question is whether students are ready. Nearly 50 percent of all known occupations will be obsolete because of computerization and automation in the next few years, according to Carl Benedikt Frey and Michael A. Osborne in *The Future of Employment: How Susceptible Are Jobs to Computerization?* With the advent of Web 3.0, quantum computing, "tap and pay," and a host of other technological innovations, curiosity and creativity define the new marketplace skills.

An excellent school librarian possesses, models, and teaches the 21st-century "habits of mind" necessary to meet the challenges of computerization and automation, as well as exceeds the Pizza Hut challenge:

- Innovative, imaginative, and creative
- Communicates effectively
- Thinks critically and flexibly, using metacognition
- Adapts

- Multitasks
- Questions (with intent)
- Persists
- Is accurate
- Collaborates
- Takes responsible risks (Costa, 2008)

These habits of mind are natural catalysts for 21st-century learning and a positive school environment: culture, climate, conditions, and the integration of cutting-edge technology, as well as employment viability.

Librarians are transformational leaders because of their natural curiosity, creativity, and analytical reasoning. They imagine new solutions, propose new ideas, and institute new practices to construct powerful learning experiences for the "connected" students to excel at college and in the global marketplace.

Creativity, content, and connectivity knowledge highlight the importance of their multidimensional role: information broker, technology integrator, collection developer, cataloger, curator, researcher, mashup developer, collaborator, creative risk-taker, organizer, analytical decision maker, and, most important, passionate, innovative teacher. Study after study supports the role of the school librarian as a positive force in 21st-century learning and student achievement (Francis, Lance, and Lietzau, 2010; Lance, Rodney, and Hamilton-Pennel, 2005; Todd and Kuhlthau, 2005).

As information, communication, and technologies (ICT) experts, they teach questioning, gathering, selecting, evaluating, interpreting, synthesizing, and communicating in a variety of formats and on a range of platforms, all while modeling creative and critical thinking. Not only do they do this, but they do it strategically, collaboratively, ethically, and efficiently.

As coteachers, they see "learning as an act of social participation . . . through the belief that interactive, digital, and networked forms of media are supporting new forms of engagement with knowledge and culture with unique learning dynamics" (Jenkins et al., 2006).

Although the vast majority of school librarians can easily meet the Pizza Hut challenge and are on the cutting edge, the question of relevancy sometimes rears its ugly head. The following scenarios illustrate why relevancy is sometimes questioned and intensify the need to examine the role of school librarians for educational reform and lifelong learning.

During an accreditation site visit to another school, a school librarian overheard two members of the evaluation team express very different views of the role of librarians in their school. One teacher stated, "librarians are like blacksmiths"—they are no longer important. The teacher further exclaimed, "Students have access to the Internet—it's a waste of money to buy books and magazines for a library." Another teacher stated, "I collaborate with my librarian all the time. We work together on all kinds of assignments. Our library is always busy—kids use it constantly."

How do two educators have such differing points of view on the role of librarians as instructional partners and teachers, the integration of library resources for learning, and the use of tax dollars for the purchase of library books, databases, and other vital resources for students? Is there a difference in the demographics or the educational philosophy or mission of these two educators' schools?

Upon examination, the two schools systems are very similar socioeconomically. So what caused such a different reaction? That is the $64,000 question. Not knowing the librarians or their institutions, one uses digital forensics to cull for answers.

The differences are very apparent by an examination of the two libraries' digital presence—their library's homepage. Upon preliminary examination, each has a mission statement that "fosters lifelong learning and provides physical access to materials in all formats" (ASSL: American Association of School Librarians, 2008). Upon closer scrutiny, only one library's website is directly linked on the school's home page, provides evidence of the integration of emerging technologies (new media) for engaging learners, and reaches out through numerous communication channels, including social media, ongoing collaborative learning activities, community outreach, and 24/7 access to resources and librarians. One library's program is dynamic, connected, and student-centered. It merges the best of traditional and innovative library services. It adapts emerging technologies for instruction, communication, collaboration, and to create an intuitive digital presence on the web. It is clear that the librarians at this school are guides and collaborators in and for learning. But not at the other school. Understandably, the two educators would have conflicting views of their library's role in 21st-century learning.

Toward the end of the accreditation visit, during the findings and recommendations session, it was suggested that the library at the school under review adopt the AASL Standards for the 21st-Century Learner in Action. Some members of the committee questioned the inclusion of these standards and professional guidelines. Why did dedicated educators question the inclusion of the AASL's professional standards? They go hand in hand with Common Core State Standards (CCSSs) and Partnership for 21st Century Skills (P21), as illustrated by the AASL's CCSS crosswalk (www.ala.org/aasl/standards-guidelines/crosswalk). The answer is simple: Although all school librarians are dedicated to providing the best possible instruction and services, sometimes they do not quantify and qualify learning outcomes—gains in reading comprehension, 21st-century literacies, results on high-stakes tests, or the new knowledge obtained. They fail to measure 21st-century college and career readiness skills.

The amalgamation of quantitative and qualitative data validates the values and vision of a school library program and its vital role in educational reform and learning. Objective measurements and empirical evidence of learning outcomes provide librarians with the essential documentation to personalize instruction for each learner and are the best way to compete for education dollars to advance library programs. Learning outcome data is the key to relevance.

The second event that crystallized the need for all school libraries to engage and evolve came during a state library panel discussion on partnerships—community and schools. It was very apparent during this lively and revealing discussion that some public librarians and college librarians do not feel that school librarians are responsive community partners. How could this be? Schools librarians are innate collaborators and communicators.

It is natural to seek community partnerships to advance learning, share resources, coordinate events and activities, and to form networks (Fitzgibbons, 2000). It is incumbent upon librarians and technology integration teachers to prepare students to live, work, and thrive in a quickly evolving technological landscape—to communicate, collaborate, and create. The key to a successful learning experience is engaging the entire community so that each learner can meet the Pizza Hut challenge.

# Part I

# Advocate and Manage

# Chapter 1

# *Leadership*

Excellent educational leadership is like a mind-blowing science fiction novel. Think H. G. Wells's *The Time Machine*, Ray Bradbury's *Fahrenheit 451*, or Suzanne Collins's *The Hunger Games*. It requires imagination, adaptability, and a sense of purpose. Just like in sci-fi, responsible risk-taking, critical thinking, and creative problem-solving skills are essential for success.

Science fiction isn't called the literature of change for nothing. It is visionary and complex, as well as transformational. It features problem resolution that wows us with the outcome. Exceptional leadership is the same.

Excellent school librarians are exceptional educational leaders who know how to wow. They are visionary problem solvers who love challenge. Finding answers is in their professional DNA. By the very nature of their profession, they are collective leaders. Their overlapping roles as instructional partner, information specialist, teacher, and program administrator uniquely qualify them to be change agents.

The National Institute on Educational Governance, Finance, Policymaking, and Management "developed a comprehensive description of an effective school leader. Consistent with the observation that the job of a school leader is multidimensional, the forum identified areas in which school leaders must have skills: (1) instructional leadership; (2) management; (3) communication, collaboration, and community building; and (4) vision development, risk taking, and change management" (North Central Regional Educational Laboratory, 2000). This description fits librarians to a T! They instruct, manage, collaborate, and build community and are flexible and adaptable.

It is by building respectful interprofessional relationships with a sense of "team-ness" (Harada, 2011) through visibility and credibility that librarians make a difference. Collaboration is not only necessary to effecting change, but is an essential 21st-century skill. Fostering team-ness through responsive exchange of ideas, exceptional communication and listening skills, and—most of all—collegiality is what librarianship is all about. Yes, with their sense of team-ness, school librarians do extraordinary things!

Excellent school librarians visibly lead by transforming school libraries into 24/7 knowledge centers and learning labs. They set in place the tools (communication, informational, digital) necessary for learning and collaboration to take place anytime and anywhere. They understand that time and location need no longer be considerations.

As information specialists and collection developers, librarians are credible information brokers. Librarians provide others the opportunity to get verifiable, important, actionable, good, reliable, accessible (VIAGRA) information. Transformational leaders empower others to take ownership and succeed—they are highly functional members of their learning community.

Maybe the following scenario will shed some light on how collective leadership—leading through team-ness—works. Members of a district's information, communication, and technologies (ICT) team share a common vision of trusting and opening access to emerging technologies, including social networks such as Facebook, Twitter, and YouTube, believing that it engages students in the learning process, allowing them to become responsible, ethical users of information and technology, and promotes 21st-century skills, including "habits of mind." They believe that Internet filtering limits educational opportunities and that banned sites are as much a disservice to constitutional rights as banned books are.

It is the ICT team's desire to regain open access to the Internet for all users: students, faculty, staff, and community. The state set up tighter filter controls for Internet access, blocking numerous Internet sites, including all social media sites. The school, which has integrated many of these sites for instructional, communication, and learning purposes, seeks to reopen access to all online resources, with the exception of pornography. In essence, the school wants a free-range digital environment again.

But first some background information is necessary to understand how the team functions and the dispositions of its members. Members of this ICT professional learning community (PLC) have strong personalities—to say the least. They are creative thinkers who not only think outside the box, but create a new box—or eliminate the box altogether. They are responsible risk takers by nature, content experts with a fervent dedication to learning. Each is always willing to go the extra mile.

Are they perfect? Absolutely not. They have certainly been known to falter on occasion. But they always pick themselves up and start again. They are persistent; some might say relentless. They get things done! They know that persistency is a habit of mind—an essential disposition for 21st-century life.

They understand that a productive team shares a focused and actionable vision for excellence. And they know that before vision can become a reality, the team has some challenges to overcome:

- Defining the outcome: What do you want to achieve, and why?
- Formulating essential questions to guide discussion and action
- Extensively analyzing the current state of affairs (e.g., state, district, school)
- Conducting scientifically based research
- Crafting and implementing a theory of change
- Setting SMART (specific, measurable, attainable, realistic, timely) goals
- Building coalitions (e.g., students, faculty members, administration members, staff, community)
- Petitioning the state for autonomy

First, the team uses Understanding by Design (Wiggins and McTighe, 2005) to define outcomes. They then craft essential questions: How do 21st-century learners learn? What do we want our students to know, understand, and be able to do or demonstrate as

21st-century learners? How does the Internet affect student learning? Does open access to the Internet affect student engagement and motivation? Do social networks affect learning? If so, how?

After contemplating and researching the answers to these questions, the team is ready to move from vision to practice. Next, the team extensively analyzes current state, district, and school policy and regulations to ascertain any potential obstacles to regaining local control over the Internet filter.

They craft a theory of change and begin implementing it by setting SMART goals. They strategically plan a timeline of next steps to gather quantitative and qualitative evidence.

For the theory of change to progress, the team begins to unify various coalitions. The team sets out to make all stakeholders aware of the current state policy and the need to change it. To accomplish this, the PLC meets with student groups; addresses the issue at faculty meetings, departmental meetings, and district meetings; speaks with parent–faculty association (PFA) members; attends board of education meetings; and meets with a variety of community groups. Because of their strong, evidence-based practice, the team rallies all coalitions behind their cause.

The next step is petitioning the state commission on educational technology for autonomy in Internet filtering. To get ready to meet with the commission, members decide on strategies for overcoming the commission's resistance to change:

- Student exemplars
- Learning outcomes—qualitative and quantitative evidence
- Testimonials from students, faculty, administrators, parents, and community members
- Action research data
- Survey results
- Scientific-based research
- Student tech team and teen advisory group (TAG) input

While the team is deciding on strategies, librarians are formulating ideas about how they can make a difference and use their expertise to help the team accomplish its goal. The librarians think of numerous ways they can take on leadership roles and contribute to a team. The UbD and the information search process work at many levels.

Traditionally, the librarians have been asked to do research—which is all well and good. (Actually, it's great!) But the rest of their skill set allows them to do much more than that. Being a program administrator, an excellent school librarian possesses facilitating skills. Productive teams need an assertive facilitator who can move the agenda forward to bring resolution. They understand the value of a well-written agenda—and that includes topics, priorities, presenters, and schedule.

Furthermore, as consummate communicators, school librarians are well versed in all the latest communications tools and gadgets for productivity and idea exchange. Excellent librarians not only know how to get the word out, but they are able to focus the discussion in any venue—especially on social media. Ongoing, open communication is important for team decision-making and consensus building. As analysts, librarians understand the power of data, including how to analyze it, graph it, and link it to standards and student outcomes. Changing opinion is even easier when using real-life, credible results and data.

As teachers, school librarians know how to perform action research, design effective learning activities, and integrate emerging technologies. As educators, school librarians know educational theory and put it into practice. As 21st-century thinkers, excellent librarians understand the need for multiple literacies and habits of mind. And as a literacy (reading) coach, a librarian realizes that online venues require different skill sets. Furthermore, as media specialists, librarians understand that "the medium *is* the message."

Yes, librarians are a powerhouse of expertise. And librarians have a home court advantage: Because they are already viewed as collaborators, all stakeholders have a sense of parity. Librarians exude team-ness.

The librarians on the team take a critical stance for change, commanding a leading role. They volunteer to do what they do best—multitask. They volunteer to take on multiple responsibilities, and not just traditional ones, either.

Using a shared leadership model, each member of the team uses his or her expertise as a 21st-century learning leader to make meaningful contribution(s) to the process. Librarians, being information specialists, do comprehensive, scientific-based research on open access to the Internet; on the use of social media for learning; on using emerging technologies as a learning tool; on 21st-century student engagement and motivation; and on 21st-century literacy-transliteracy. After exhaustive research, the librarians supply the team with credible information and data to help it move forward.

Librarians and technology integration teachers set up online communication channels to move the discussion forward and to warehouse evidence. They design a survey on digital technologies usage and post it on the library home page. This survey includes questions on usage patterns: frequency, social, school, entertainment, profiles, and safety issues. The librarians analyze results, connecting data to learning goals and vision. Their vision is to create a supportive, collaborative, engaging, 24/7 learning environment through open and unfettered access to the Internet through "power standard development," Understanding by Design, the integration of emerging technologies, project-based learning, and real-world applications. The technology integration teacher also crafts and posts a national survey on the use of emerging technologies as an instructional tool. Posting results from surveys on the library website gives transparence to the discussion.

School librarians provide the team with action research data from various information and digital literacy projects, such as the Healthy and Balanced Living: My Personal Wellness Project. The action research from such projects demonstrates how open access to information affects learning and 21st-century literacies. Librarians and technology integration teachers collect student exemplars produced using emerging technologies, conducting video interviews of students and faculty about open access and learning. A librarian edits and produces the resulting film, uploading it to a secure online site for the team's review to elicit comments and suggestions. After the review process, a librarian produces the final cut, preparing the film for presentation to the commission.

To prepare for the commission, team members continue meeting. The team meets (in person and digitally) to assess, act, debrief, and reflect on next steps. Each member brings his or her own piece of the puzzle. The team amasses the evidence. Evidence-based practice not only is for instruction but also is critical to insight change. Just like in a sci-fi story, the plan of attack has been formulated and is now set in motion.

Again, team members meet with key district stakeholders: administrators (district and school-based), curriculum leaders, teachers, students, parents, and community members. Active listening and authentic conversation help move the vision closer to reality. To provide a basis for meaningful conversation, they present highlights of results from the surveys, the action research data, and the film, as well as professional literature, fostering an active interchange of ideas and thoughts. The vision comes one step closer to fruition.

The team selects three strong school leaders to represent them (the ICT director, a high school librarian, and a technology integration teacher) to meet with the state commission. These three key members of the ICT team present the commission with scientifically based research and data; student, teacher, and administrator testimonials; survey results; and, most important, exemplary student work created using valuable blocked resources and social media.

As instructional leaders, the ICT team lobbied for the fundamental right of students, faculty, and staff to use digital media to create, communicate, and work collaboratively. The commission granted the school system autonomy over filtering and access to social media (Google Apps, Facebook, Twitter, YouTube, etc.) and other Internet sites routinely blocked by the state filtering system. This evidence-based petition was strategically planned and designed by members of the ICT team (administrators, librarians, and technology integration teachers) to ensure rigor and relevancy for 21st-century learners. Because of the team-ness approach, all members of the ICT participate in decision making and policy development through various leadership avenues—the Tech Council, the Curriculum Leadership Council (CLC), and the Information and Communication Technologies (ICT) team, as well as in professional development activities.

This shared leadership model proved advantageous when a school librarian was approached at a professional conference by a member of the Commission on Education Technology, who asked about the upcoming filtering meeting. He asked whether the librarian were a member of the contingent coming to address the commission. Although the school librarian was not among the three representatives, she had been involved in the discussions and plans for petitioning the state about filtering. Thanks to ongoing departmental communication and shared leadership practices, this librarian was able to have a productive, face-to-face, evidence-based discussion on the topic with the state commissioner. She was also able to support an open access position thanks to her knowledge of American Libraries Association (ALA) standards and the ALA's position statement: "[B]y embracing values over filters, we are expressing trust in our children, that they will judge wisely when the opportunity for misjudgment presents itself. By stressing values over filters, we send the clearest message to our children: As is true in the real world, you can go anywhere you wish, and it is ultimately up to you to decide what is right and wrong and face the consequences of your judgment" (ALA, *Especially for Young People and Their Parents*, n.d.).

Action leadership, coupled with a commitment to a shared vision and ongoing, open communication, produced a sense of team-ness. This translated into open access to emerging technologies for learning.

Excellent school librarians know that making change happen really isn't science fiction. But, like the elements of a great sci-fi novel, it takes critical thinking, creative problem solving, and persistency—as well as risk taking—to wow.

# Chapter 2

# Mission and Core Values, Beliefs, and Expectations

John Lennon's lyrics in *Revolution* are really asking: What is your plan before I commit to action? For most school libraries, the plan of action is their mission statement. A library's mission statement unambiguously delineates and articulates the purpose of its program and equivalently reflects the core values, beliefs, and expectations of the school it serves. A functioning mission statement is succinct, measurable, and compelling, as well as memorable. It can be communicated effectively in a variety of online and offline venues: on the school website, the library's homepage, on the library wall, in an interview, in a meeting, in a short video clip, in a presentation, in a lesson, in a pamphlet, or on social media. The wording is vitally important, because it needs to connect to the imagination, emotions, and intellect of all key constituents. Creativity plays a role. As Dr. Seuss said, "think and wonder and wonder and think." You are creating an image of "library." You are really selling your library brand through your mission statement. Does each word suggest a visual image or Pinterest—a "digital scrapbook"? Can all your stakeholders visualize it? It is important to write your mission statement to construct an image that will connect at a visceral level. In a 1996 *Wired* interview, Steve Jobs said, "creativity is just connecting things" (Wolf, 1996). Realizing a memorable mission statement is really about thinking and wondering and wondering and thinking about what "things" you are connecting and how you are connecting them.

A mission statement is an organic document that seamlessly connects who, what, when, where, why, and how. This can be achieved formally and informally through essential questions: "Does the statement connect to you personally or emotionally? Does the statement describe an inspiring purpose? Does the statement describe the organization's responsibility to its stakeholders? Does the statement define a domain? Does the statement describe the strategic positioning in a way that identifies specific advantage(s)? Does the statement reflect the culture of the organization? Is the statement clear and easy to understand?" (edbarrows, 2009). Also, does the statement instill and inspire "habits of mind" or disposition for college readiness and a career in the 21st century?

An excellent mission statement is evolutionary. It takes time to craft a personally memorable and quantifiable plan of action. Brainstorming is the key to the development and design of a cohesive and coherent mission statement. A responsive mission statement evolves through creative collaboration.

It is not only important for librarians to routinely evaluate the library's mission, but it is equally important that all stakeholders (students, faculty, staff, administration, parents, and the community) have the opportunity to be involved in the process. It is an opportunity to apply the ALA's *School Library Program Health and Wellness Toolkit: Advocacy.* It advises one to "identify the school library program's stakeholders and their agendas. For each stakeholder group, know their issues, concerns, priorities, and needs. This is about them and what they need. It is not about what is best for the library and what you want them to want" (ALA, 2013).

It is a statement of advocacy, accountability, and transparence. It explains "Why I need my library" or "Why I love my library!" The following student YouTube video demonstrates this point: www.youtube.com/watch?v=HMb9d2rGydE.

The use of overarching guiding questions centers the reflection process and is a top-notch assessment tool for evaluating a library's raison d'être. Guiding questions not only bring focus and clarity to any process, but also guarantee rigor, reliability, and validity. Good questions anchor thought, purpose, and discussion around the role of the library in the educational institution it serves. They help to identify what patrons want and how they want it. Focus questions authenticate the process and build consensus.

There are endless ways to connect with all stakeholders to ascertain answers to these guiding questions, both formally and informally:

- Face-to-face
- Student organizations and clubs, as well as athletic teams
- Use of digital technologies
- Instructional time
- Coplanning
- Professional Learning Communities
- Faculty meetings
- Department, team, or grade-level meetings
- Administrative meetings
- Parent and teacher associations meetings
- Focus groups
- Advisory meetings
- Board of education
- School volunteers
- Community-centered organizations
- Alumni associations

Personal connections play a major role in the success of any action plan. Therefore, the first and probably the most important question to ask is, does the library have a personal or emotional connection to you? In *Learning from Lincoln: Leadership Practices for School Success*, Harvey Alvy and Pam Robbins expound upon this idea. The authors explain that "Compelling mission and vision should have personal meaning to all those who may be affected by the idea" (Alvy and Robbins, 2010: 11). All stakeholders must feel personally connected with and find value in the library's instructional program and services.

Building an environment of trust is vital to connecting with all stakeholders, but especially with students. Visibility is the key to making the personal connections to build trust. By coteaching, mentoring, collaborating, and attending club meetings, athletic practices and games, visual and performing art events, and student governance meetings, librarians foster trust. These are invaluable venues for a librarian to ascertain the "issues, concerns, priorities, and needs" of students and infuse them into the library's mission.

But question with stealth! Direct questions may be too intimidating, turn students off, or elicit "canned" responses from some students. Asking the right questions in the right way goes a long way to achieving "actionable" answers.

Direct questioning does work with many students, such as a library's TAG (teen advisory group), book club, R.E.D. (Read Every Day) team, or tech team. These students have a vested interest in the library. This is a great place to start the dialogue in person or virtually. Their advice and answers are invaluable. Questions can be tweaked to elicit more responses from other students.

The acknowledgment of partnerships to accomplish the mission is paramount to success. An effective library program is achieved through vigorous collaboration. Outreach works wonders.

Student to student is also an effective way to ascertain whether the library is accomplishing its mission to and for students. A library's TAG (teen advisory group) team or tech team is an effective liaison between the student body and the library and to measure mission success. Students asking students provides validity, as well as candor to the process.

PLCs or members of the library's advisory board can also play a significant role in obtaining sincere answers to guiding questions from students, as well as other faculty members. They are a crucial arm in crafting changes to the mission statement that reflect shifts in school culture and climate.

If all stakeholders agree that the mission statement is inclusive, makes them feel personally and emotionally connected, describes the purpose of the library, and inspires them to action, then you have a well-designed mission statement.

Maybe the following analysis will illustrate this. The library's mission statement reads, "In support of the [school] mission, the library program's mission is to help each student excel and achieve maximum potential by creating a 21st-century learning environment, fostering a love of reading, and promoting the effective use of information and communications technology. Through collaboration, the library faculty partners with the larger community to empower students in becoming lifelong learners, responsible citizens, and industrious problem solvers" (NCPS, 2013).

This school library's mission statement "connects things." It creates a visceral and visual image. It effectively and seamlessly answers who, what, where, why, and how. "We are the [school name] library (who). We serve [name of school] students (where). The difference we make is that we foster a love of reading and promote the effective use of information and communications technology (what). We exist to empower students to become lifelong learners, responsible citizens, and industrious problem solvers (why). We accomplish this through collaboration and creating a 21st-century learning environment (how).

All stakeholders are clearly able to understand this library's mission. It connects at personal, intellectual, and emotional levels. This mission statement is a simple, emphatic affirmation of the library's purpose and vision of 21st-century learning. It promises to help, expresses responsibilities, defines domain, describes strategic positioning through collaboration, identifies advantages to all stakeholders, and reflects a culture of excellence. All can easily understand it and value it. It is a concise, proactive statement that can be easily communicated.

Another way of evaluating a library's mission statement is how it supports and connects to the overarching school or institution's mission statement: Is there unity of thought and vision? Does it facilitate the achievement of the school's mission? The example library's overarching school's mission (core values and belief) statement reads, "[School] is committed to preparing all students to meet the challenges of living in an increasingly global and diverse society. We believe that students learn best in an environment that fosters respect for themselves and others. This allows students to be active participants in their learning, to identify and solve authentic problems, and to effectively share their learning with the appropriate audiences. In partnership with parents and the community, we strive to inspire students to the habits of mind and character that will make them lifelong learners" (NCPS, 2012).

If we reexamine the example school library's mission statement and overlay it on its school mission statement, we can see a clear corroboration. Each statement's goal is to enable all students to become respectful, independent, lifelong learners and problem-solvers with parents and the community. The library's mission is symbiotic with the school's mission. It scaffolds the school's core beliefs through specific, relevant, and attainable action.

How does a school library achieve its school's mission, core beliefs, and expectations? This is accomplished through leadership, a standards-based curriculum, setting S.M.A.R.T.E.R. (specific, measurable, attainable, relevant, time-bound, evaluate, re-evaluate) goals, establishing a student-centered environment, transparency, and outreach.

The library is the knowledge lab—a learning center for curricular and cocurricular activities within the school and for the community. Its vision to provide a challenging and differentiated learning experience and an engaging 24/7 educational environment for the "community of learners" encapsulates the American Association of School Librarians' belief that "[t]he mission of the school library media program is to ensure that students and staff are effective users of ideas and information . . . and the development of students' core competencies for lifelong learning" (AASL, 1998: 1).

The Beatles song *Revolution* asks to see the plan. What is your plan of action? Is it measurable, compelling, and personal? Will it improve student learning outcomes and create a positive school culture and climate? If so, then everything will be definitely be "all right." It just might start a revolution—a learning revolution!

# Part II
# Socialize and Engage

# Chapter 3

# Environment

A positive school environment is like the scene from *The Wizard of Oz* when Dorothy sees the Emerald City for the first time. Everything goes from mundane monochrome to unbelievable, vivid colors. Everything seems right. There is a sense of wonder and harmony. Yes, harmony! The very sound of this word conveys both meaning and context. One has only to say it or read it and understanding occurs. Edgar Allen Poe's *The Bells* (1849) clearly demonstrates this.

> Hear the mellow wedding bells—
> Golden bells!
> What a world of happiness their *harmony* foretells!
> Through the balmy air of night
> How they ring out their delight—
> From the molten-golden notes,
> And all in tune

Harmony in this poem connotes not only a sense of sound, but accord, agreement, and concinnity. You instinctually understand the varied meanings of this word.

Unfortunately, this is not so with the word environment. Environment does not necessarily conjure up a universal sense of what it is or its unique properties. There is no homogeneous understanding. Environment means different things to different people—nature, setting, location, milieu, world, atmosphere, surroundings, situation, ecosystem, climate, conditions, ambience, even mood and feeling. So defining a positive school environment is contextual and multidimensional.

There are three mutually decisive factors in creating and understanding a positive school environment: climate, culture, and conditions. Together, they define a safe, student-centered learning setting.

Climate is usually defined in terms of social, academic, psychological/affective, and physical elements. These include, but are not limited to, interpersonal relationships, learning, teaching, leadership, engagement, safety, behavior, management, accountability, communication, decision-making, and collaboration. Many educators refer to this as the "feel" of the school.

Culture is commonly described as a set of shared attitudes, values, ideas, learning expectations, artifacts, and practices that are embedded within the learning community. This is, in essence, the school's character.

Conditions refer to the coordination of activities: span of control, resource allocation, task and time allocation, as well as processes and procedures. These are tactical controls.

All three factors have to be in sync in order to build trust, creating a positive educational environment in which all learners feel safe to take responsible risks, to solve problems, to innovate, to create, and to thrive.

Librarians synchronize all three elements by coalescing process, policy, procedures, and product through

- Vision and expectations
- Multiple roles
- 21st-century pedagogical approaches
- Plurality of learning space
- Information, communication, and technologies
- Collegiality
- Planning and organization
- Professional learning communities (PLCs and networks)
- Professional development activities
- Transparency

Because of the multidimensional role of a school librarian, a librarian is in the unique position to transform school culture, climate, and conditions into a cohesive and comprehensive learning environment. School librarians are involved in every aspect of the school life through "shared thinking, planning, and creating" (Montiel-Overall, 2005).

Vision guides the synchronization for a positive school environment. "A *vision* means an image of what the school can and should become. It is deeply embedded in values, hopes, and dreams . . . and is clear, compelling, and connected to teaching and learning" (Peterson, 1995). A shared understanding of the five "components of a vision," as defined by the North Central Regional Educational Laboratory (NCREL) in *Critical Issue: Building a Collective Vision* provides educators with a blueprint to carry out its vision. The components of vision are imagination, articulation, connection, implementation, and realization.

The following vignette about one high school's preparation for a regional accrediting association visit demonstrates the understanding of the components of vision. Members of the Information, Communication, and Technologies (ICT) team—librarians (department chair and STEM—science, technology, engineering, and math) and technology integration teacher (humanities and social sciences)—are strategically involved in the accreditation process as cochair, as a steering committee leader, and as district professional development representatives. They facilitate the development of a launch plan: target goals, schedules, communication, and strategies.

Because of the library department chair's leadership and technology expertise, she is selected to cochair the visit by the school principal. She creates a blog and a self-study website to manage the visit. The website includes timetable and timeline, events calendar, survey and report findings, evidence, steering committee information, resources, rubrics, standards, and contact information. This fosters transparency and builds trust—a key factor in creating a cohesive school environment.

To initiate the launch, the ICT team designs a professional learning day (PD) to define the school's vision—*A Vision of the Ideal High School Graduate. A five-question exercise.* What does a graduate need to know, understand, and be able do to be successful in the 21st century? What skills, literacies, attitudes, and dispositions are needed to succeed at college or in the workforce?

As research-based professionals, the librarians and technology integration teacher planning this professional learning day integrate the essential questions from Trilling and Fadel, *21st Century Skills: Learning for Life in Our Times* (2009) to inform the discussion. Faculty are asked to imagine the future—to think, envision, and predict what life will be like in the next five or ten years. The answers are analyzed and assessed by members of the steering committee, spearheaded by the department chair of the library. She creates a word cloud to visualize the answers.

During a homeroom period, the faculty facilitates a modified version of the five-question exercise with students. The two word clouds align: learning, creativity, problem-solving, collaboration, communication, and technology. This connection is important in developing a shared vision for the school's core values, beliefs, and expectations.

This whole-school activity provides a backdrop for consensus and setting the tone for a positive rollout. In order to increase awareness, the department chair of the library creates a core values, beliefs, and expectations poster contest and a QR code and stages a faux flash mob. This is both imaginative and creative. This sets the tone for school unity.

As a member of the assessment standards committee, the STEM librarian demonstrates the role of the librarians as teacher, instructional partner, information specialist, and program administrator by explicit documentation of numerous, rigorous, collaborative learning projects and assessments.

To strategically implement her school's vision for student success, the STEM librarian includes this statement on communications and instructional materials: assignments, rubrics, multimedia, curriculum concept maps, and course platform. She also designs and integrates challenging, collaborative structures, accountability indicators, tools, processes, and "best practices" to demonstrate the school's 21st-century learning expectations.

As members of the district professional development team, the technology integration teacher and STEM librarian design a professional development activity to identify the school's strengths and challenges for the visiting accrediting committee. The technology integration teacher crafts an array using Google—a mathematical formula on a Google spreadsheet to calculate input data—for the faculty to come to consensus on these. Streamlining the process builds immediate consensus and a positive response.

One only has to look at Nancy Everhart's list of *100 Things Kids Lose without a Library* to understand the effect a school librarian has on an institution and the positive role he or she plays in defining a collaborative learning environment (Everhart, 2011).

By the integration of a plurality of "learning spaces" (physical, virtual, formal, informal, blended, mobile, personal, networked, and social), interpersonal connections are established. Libraries are integrated learning spaces. They blend asynchronous and synchronous learning. "The reconceptualization of library space into a collaborative student learning "place" changes the essence of any library with which we are familiar, moving from a book-centered to a learning-centered space. Students are no longer simply recipients of knowledge, but they are rather also collaborators and producers of knowledge—they become active participants in their own learning and discovery process" (Weiner, 2010).

A school library forms the perfect venue to cultivate schoolwide trust. Trust is very important to the development of a positive school environment. In one school, the welcoming video, *We Trust You*, has changed the school environment enormously. The brainchild of the library department chair, this video has set the stage as the welcoming refrain during the freshman orientation. Because this engaging video is filmed throughout the school and library, it gives incoming freshmen the sense that the library is an integral part of the school—a go-to place.

At the end of each school year, a new, fun video is filmed featuring numerous students, teachers, staff, administrators, and librarians, providing the incoming ninth graders with important information about how the library can help them succeed. This is combined with a chant of "we trust you." This short video conveys the sense of community and a commitment to "team-ness"—we are all in this together. That so many members of the learning community willingly participate in the production of this yearly video testifies to the importance of the library to the school. There are no rules or "can't," but rather a positive affirmation of what the library can do for you. It is an authentic expression of the school's core values, beliefs, and high expectations. It is a shout-out to trust.

This video is a great promotional tool for the library, an invaluable school artifact—and, most important, it clearly communicates community. By the end of the video, students know "we trust you." Trust is fundamental to building connections/relationships, breaking down barriers, and providing a positive physical and virtual learning environment.

Delivery on the message is as important as the message. This video is not just lip service for incoming students, but the library's modus operandi. The librarians work continually to instill a sense of community, collegiality, and trust.

School libraries are evolutionary and revolutionary learning spaces. Building a constructive school environment is an evolutional process, as well as a revolutionary one. It takes leadership, time, and "focus" to build capacity and make large-scale, systematic changes.

School librarians are evolutionary thinkers who welcome change. Sometimes the progression is slow and incremental, and sometimes it is fast and immediate, but however it develops, it creates a paradigm shift in a school environment.

"Libraries are now 21st-century 'learning space'—principally a gathering and discovery space . . . for broad educational engagement and activity, rather than simply a place to research. . . . The librarian has become an 'embedded' resource, helping library patrons navigate the print and digital space" in person and virtually (Parker, 2013).

With the integration of social media and emerging technologies, a librarian is no longer a "sage on the stage," but a "guide on the side"—acting as a go-between for learners and learning outcomes. Collaborative learning "enhances student satisfaction, builds self-esteem, and promotes a positive attitude" (University of Oregon, 2013). This fosters a positive school environment.

Peer teaching is powerful and strengthens student involvement and responsibility. Instruction through a "relatable source" is integral to developing a cooperative learning venue. For example, at one school, TAG (teen advisory group) students designed, wrote, managed, publicized, and implemented an interactive scavenger hunt using QR codes and audiovisual clues to assess library knowledge and informational skills on use of instructional portals, social media, databases, and the online card catalog.

Student-to-student directed instruction attest that librarians trust students to make positive contributions to the school. Peer-to-peer instruction engages students in the learning process, forming connectedness and helping establish a positive school environment.

Many libraries have integrated the "learning commons" model. A learning commons is a "common or shared, learning 'space' that is both physical and virtual . . . it is designed to move students beyond mere research, practice and group work . . . it allows students to explore, experiment, collaborate, create, share and celebrate their learning" (Loertscher and Koechlin, 2012: 20). This model brings students to the forefront in the learning process. They feel connected, vested, and valued.

According to Jody K. Howard in *The Relationship between School Culture and the School Library Program: Four Case Studies*, three themes must be present for libraries and librarians to effect positive change: a collaborative culture, the leadership style of the principal, and high expectations of students and staff.

Howard describes a collaborative culture as the integration of cross-curriculum collaborative projects, cooperative curriculum planning and decision making that encompass vertical planning to facilitate student skill development, the inclusion of formative assessment to evaluate learning and effectiveness of instruction, the establishment and participation in PLCs, rigorous curriculum, sound instructional methodology, a mentoring program, and a goal of having every student succeed (Howard, 2010).

School librarians and technology integration teachers are consummate collaborators who work diligently to provide a collaborative and harmonious school environment through

- A welcoming, inviting, and safe atmosphere
- Unfettered and unfiltered 24/7 access
- Inclusive policies and procedures
- Decision making
- Equity and respect
- Interpersonal relationships and outreach
- Leadership

- Coteaching
- Standards-based curriculum
- High expectations for all
- Professional learning communities (PLCs)
- Evidence-based strategic planning
- Assessment and ongoing evaluation through data mining

The following scenario illustrates this. Just after reading a short account of a successful Read and Feed activity, a school librarian receives an e-mail from the culinary arts teacher about the school café—its own mini CIA (Culinary Institute of America). Usually, only faculty are served. Serendipity! Why not serve students?

After giving it some thought, the librarian proposes a collaborative literacy project among English, career and technology education (CTE), special education (SPED), and the library. Everyone thinks it is a great learning opportunity to integrate the Common Core State Standards and the school's core values, beliefs, and expectation.

The Read and Feed Challenge is on its way. The boy and girl from each ninth grade English class who read and review the most books will go to the café.

To make this possible, the librarian contacts the Parent–Faculty Association for funding. Parental and community awareness is crucial for establishing a positive school environment.

The review question is agreed upon at an English PLC meeting. Why this book? Students are given a choice of review format—oral, recorded, or visual—as well as media: OPAC; NoodlBib or EasyBib; Google Drive; Aurasma, an augmented reality app; Word document, infographic; blog post; mobile devices; e-mail; or face-to-face presentation to a librarian, English teacher, SPED teacher, member of the teen advisory group (TAG) team, or member of the R.E.D. (Read Every Day) team—or any other alternative a student can think of.

The CTE teacher, students, and the librarian design a healthy, student-friendly menu and decide on table decorations and invitations.

After dining on a delicious meal prepared by CTE students, the winners of the Read and Feed challenge complete a peer-to-peer survey on the quality of the service, menu, and food. This gives CTE students invaluable feedback. This is real-world. Think Yelp, a crowd-sourced app that allows you to find, review, and rate local businesses, such as restaurants and entertainment venues.

To promote the project and create an environment of readers, this librarian

- Gives a brief introduction about the project to each ninth-grade English class and the CTE class
- Creates QR codes
- E-mails each ninth grader
- Use the library's Facebook page to stimulate enthusiasm
- Announces the program over the school's PA
- Creates a poster
- Requests that the school newspaper and television station cover the project

To scaffold student learning, this librarian

- Creates or finds online tutorials and promotional videos for Aurasma, etc.
- Conferences with students
- Asks the R.E.D. and TAG team to set up mini workshops on how to use a variety of online resources to create reviews and to listen to reviews (peer-to-peer assessment)

To assess, this librarian and teachers collaboratively

- Read, listen to, or watch reviews
- Review the peer-to-peer café surveys
- Design an anonymous survey for students to assess the project
- Debrief

To make the celebration special, this librarian

- Has graphic art students design a certificate of accomplishment
- Asks the school newspaper and television station to cover the project
- Asks that the district's webmaster to photograph the celebration and add a photo to the district's website
- Invites the principal, superintendent, assistant superintendent, English teachers, and PFA president to the celebration

Because of the active participation in this literacy initiative by students, teachers, and administrators, climate, culture, and conditions coalesced to form a positive school environment.

Librarians communicate high expectations through choice, decision making, rubrics, and respectful, active engagement. High expectations make a student feel valued, safe, and connected. According to C. Rubie-Davies in the *British Journal of Educational Psychology*, "teachers who create supportive learning environments and have affirmative and respectful attitudes about their students' interests and motivations are more likely to enable students to experience positive self-perceptions and high achieving learning" (RMIT University, 2014).

Jody Howard's study on the relationship between school culture and the success of a library's program depends on the school's principal. A school principal's leadership is paramount to the success of a positive school environment: "[T]eacher leaders provide valuable insight and ideas to principals as they work together toward school improvement. . . . the community ultimately will build trust" (Stronge et al., 2008). Librarians are in the unique position to provide valuable insight in the workings of the school to its principal.

A school environment depends on growth, passion, and sense (GPS). Librarians always navigate in the right direction.

# Chapter 4

# Social Bookmarking

What tools are your students using to track and organize their research? Are they scribbling notes on note cards? Are they cutting and pasting chunks of text from the Internet into Word documents or Google docs with little regard for the metadata (e.g., author, date created, date modified, file size) they will need later to build their bibliography?

Today's librarians can help students work quicker and smarter, increasing their ability to track and share resources by teaching and encouraging the use of a cloud-based social bookmarking system. Social bookmarking enables collaborative research (both with classmates and with site members around the world), web discussion, annotation, and tagging. Some services automatically generate citations in various formats, and students can search social bookmarking sites by entering relevant tags yielding far fewer results than a search engine.

For example, search D-Day in Google, and you'll have 4 billion options to choose from. Some will be government documents, but few will originate from the deep web databases of peer-reviewed scholarly resources. Students generally check links found on the first, and sometimes second, page of results, finding resources that may or may not be relevant, let alone trustworthy. Students should be taught to vet each source for such things as currency, accuracy, bias, authority, audience, and scope before taking notes, but unless that is a required step, most students will take the position that "it's on the Internet, so it must be true!"

But let's look at the same search in an online bookmarking service such as Diigo, where the student can search tagged sites for D-Day. Such a search will yield fewer than 400 resources that have been reviewed and recommended by others interested in that same topic. Although there are no guarantees (Diigo reviewers are other Diigo users of any age and expertise), tagged sites tend to be more relevant and can include titles from databases that can be searched with a user name and password. Tagged pages often include public sticky notes and annotations left by other readers. Members can also search for a history or social studies Diigo user group where more expert information can be found.

Just a few years ago, a search for the top social bookmarking services led to specialty sites such as Del.icio.us, Digg, Diigo, and Zotero. Today, the landscape has changed, signaling the fusion of social networking and social bookmarking. In April 2014, the eBiz/MBA Guide listed Facebook, Twitter, Pinterest, Google+, Tumblr, and Reddit as the top six, with Digg coming in at eighth and Delicious a distant thirteenth (eBiz, 2014). Despite the power of Diigo and Zotero, they didn't even make the list. Why? Because social networking sites that can double for bookmarking appeal to young users who prefer one-stop shopping, allowing them to do schoolwork and socialize all in one place where they are invited to tag, like, tweet, post, or e-mail favorites to friends, classmates, colleagues, or groups. For this reason, social networking sites should have a place in the curriculum where educators can work with students to teach them to use them safely, responsibly, and ethically.

There are no strictly social networking sites, however, that match the power of a fully integrated information management system dedicated first to the task of bookmarking, making it social only within the context of the research. In this chapter, we'll examine two of the best: Diigo and Zotero. These and similar services are generally accessible on desktops, laptops, tablets, and smartphones.

# Diigo

Diigo (www.diigo.com) is a privately owned company made up of a 12-person team with a broad range of backgrounds. The company's self-described goal is to develop more effective ways to "discover, process, manage, and share online information more productively and effectively." Diigo is an acronym for "Digest of Internet Information, Groups, and Other stuff," and the Diigo team will tell you that the "other stuff" is a big deal, giving them license to go in any relevant direction as they constantly develop new "stuff" for Diigo users. Diigo's online interface electronically replicates the old-school research practice of finding and printing a resource, then highlighting and annotating relevant passages and writing notes and comments on note cards. Diigo refers to itself as a social information network (SIN) rather than a social bookmarking site and describes its service as a personal research tool, a collaborative research platform, a social content site, and a knowledge sharing community.

Because Diigo users store and manage their bookmarks in the cloud, it's easy to organize, annotate, retrieve, and share resources. Diigo is optimal for a green movement in a school, encouraging online reading and note taking by offering options for color-coded on-screen highlighting and electronic sticky notes for personal annotations and reflections. These features eliminate the need to print every article of potential worth, providing huge savings in print costs (e.g., ink, paper, printer maintenance).

To get started, go to www.Diigo.com and sign up for a free account. Teachers can upgrade to a free educator account at www.Diigo.com/education, or your district IT administrator can apply for a free Diigo district domain (Diigo, Special Offerings for Educators, 2014). Select the browsers and mobile devices you will use, and download the Diigo toolbar, highlighter, extension, browser, or app on each. Although each of these tools and extensions is slightly different (the Diigo iPad app lets you highlight using your finger), they are all easy to learn how to use. Saved resources on any device are automatically saved to your online library with highlighting and annotations intact. Sharing to your social networks lets others see your highlighted passages as well. And becoming a Diigo educator is easy—just fill out the application found on the Education upgrades page at https://www.diigo.com/teacher_entry/educationupgrades.

On many browsers, Diigo will appear as a blue lowercase d in the upper corner of your computer screen. Every time you launch your browser, Diigo will be ready, making adding resources to your bookmark library a snap! There is no need to constantly log onto the service—when you find a web page you want to include in your library, just click the blue d on the menu bar to access the Diigo toolbar.

Diigo behaves like some browsers' bookmarking feature, saving selected sites to the user's online library at Diigo.com. But that is where Diigo starts showing its true power. Lists on Diigo can be labeled private or public and, if shared, become searchable by other Diigo groups and community members. You can add a description, highlight passages, add sticky notes, create tags or select from tags suggested by Diigo, and, if you don't have time to read a page now, mark it as **Read later**.

Diigo hosts more than a thousand groups within more than a dozen categories, such as Government and Politics, Health and Wellness, Travel, and Cultures and Communities. In the area of education, registered users can select from hundreds of international collaborative groups, including Diigo Educators, EdTech Talk, Discovery Educator Network, Classroom 2.0, Literacy ICT, and Google in Education. Specialty groups in all curricular areas are easy to find using the search function on the Communities page. Inside the Diigo communities, you will have daily opportunities to hear about new ideas, get links to new products and applications, enter discussions on widely varied topics, and establish collaborations with teachers around the globe. Groups you've joined will always be available on the My Groups page, eliminating the need to search each time. New groups can be formed on any topic and benefit from the full array of resources, notes, and reflections of all other Diigo members with like interests. Furthermore, teachers can create a private group to allow students to share resources with classmates or those in other class sections.

Web pages come and go. If you're concerned that the Web page you are bookmarking might not be there in the future or will undergo regular updates, the cache option offers a unique solution. Caching will archive the site in your Diigo library, allowing you to always retain a copy even if the site is taken down. (Note that free accounts have limits on how many web pages can be cached per year.) Let students know that caching is especially crucial when bookmarking an online journal, news feed, or blog, because these tend to change frequently while maintaining the same URL. Using Diigo, users who want to track changes in a web page over time can cache the same page again and again.

The Diigo toolbar lets users take a screenshot, share the page, and search for similar sites within the Diigo community. Click on **Annotate** for a multicolored highlighter or to add sticky notes that can be private or shared. Your highlights and annotations will remain with the article for future use by you and those you share with. This allows students to share vetted resources and to learn from comments and annotations left by their classmates or others in the community. The Chrome extension for Diigo lets users annotate screenshots, adding words, shapes and arrows. Users can also blur parts of images to protect sensitive information, and screenshots can be saved as images or e-mailed (Diigo Blog, 2014).

Diigo's Share This Page function supplies a URL that can be copied and pasted into an e-mail, a blog, or an instant message. One click lets you post to Facebook, share on

Google+, or tweet. For today's students, this Share bar presents a familiar interface that needs little explanation.

Today's students live in a visual world and should be encouraged to use photos, drawings, symbols, graphs, charts, maps, tables and other forms of relevant imagery and graphics in their work. Diigo can facilitate the process by displaying a tiny disk icon when you mouse over a web-based image that allows you to click and save the image to Diigo. However, if the disk icon doesn't appear (and it doesn't always), the user can right-click the image for an option to save to Diigo. As with articles, Diigo will automatically record the URL and the title of the page. The Filter option in your Diigo library lets you select **Images** to see your saved graphics.

Locating and retrieving a bookmarked resource from your Diigo library is as quick and easy as saving. On your browser's Diigo toolbar, click the dropdown menu and select **My Library**—or simply log on at www.diigo.com. Your bookmarks are displayed chronologically, and you can sort them, choosing lists or selecting tags. Clicking on individual Diigo resources will display title, URL, and the additional information you added when you bookmarked the site, including your description, tags, blocks of highlighted text, and sticky note annotations. You can also return to the original online article by clicking on the title—or access your cached file if you requested one. Additionally, you can elect to view public sticky notes that might have been added to the same article by other Diigo members, a practice that often yields insights and perspectives to enhance your own thinking.

Users can benefit from the collective knowledge of Diigo members around the world by searching with keywords or tags. A Diigo keyword or tag search will give you access to annotated resources that have been selected by community members interested in the same topic.

## *Diigo in the School Library*

On Diigo's Educators FAQ web page, the company states: "The 21st century calls for knowledge workers who can effectively utilize the vast array of information that resides on the Internet and who are capable of processing the information collaboratively with others." Today's project-based learning gives educators the opportunity to teach students the "skills of finding, organizing, synthesizing, and presenting information, as well as the social skills of working in groups, all of which are necessary in the knowledge-based economy" (Diigo Help, "FAQ," 2014)

### *Create a Diigo Class Group*

All Diigo members can create Diigo groups, but those who have a Diigo Educator account can use the Teacher Console to create class groups that offer a protected environment through preset privacy settings that prevent group members from communicating with members in the outer Diigo community. Class groups don't require students to set up individual accounts, and e-mail addresses are not required for group formation.

Groups can be formed using student names, or the class roster can be uploaded all at once. And although these groups are completely private, you also have the option to enter aliases, such as a student number, rather than real names. Diigo will automatically generate student names and passwords from your input. On the Teacher Console, you can select moderators, add or subtract group members, and suspend and restore memberships. Work done in private Diigo groups will not be searchable, and no messages can be exchanged outside the group. Go to http://groups.diigo.com/create to set up your first group.

An effective 21st-century education means learning to collaborate across spaces. This poses a quandary for educators: On the one hand, we want students to be safe, but on the other, we want them to collaborate and communicate locally and globally with the knowledge that sharing resources is a good thing. For high school and higher education, teachers can ask students to create their own individual accounts outside the educator's environment. These accounts are not restricted and will allow students to communicate with individuals and groups in the worldwide Diigo community who share like interests. Despite fears of "stranger danger," this affords educators the opportunity to once again address privacy issues, because with one click, student bookmarks and annotations will become part of a vast social network. Kids today are accustomed to instant public exposure thanks to social networks that strive to minimize what is kept private. For our students, sharing has become the norm, with privacy being a notion that they shrug off as insignificant. It's up to schools to remind them of the risks and to teach them to think critically before sharing publicly.

## Group-based Collaborative Research

Classes coming to the library for research can take advantage of Diigo's group-based collaborative research structure to create shared lists, pool resources, share thoughts and insights, and send e-mails or messages to group members. And work need not be limited to library time. Diigo's cloud-based access gives all group members 24/7 access. Several classes and teachers can join together in group discussion forums where all involved teachers can be designated as moderators. Creating a new list for each research project will help maintain organization, sharing resources will increase efficiency and eliminate redundancy, and working online will ultimately save hundreds of pieces of paper as students learn that working in the cloud environment, a critical 21st-century skill, eliminates the need for printing.

To learn more about using your Diigo Educator account with student groups, go to http://help.Diigo.com/teacher-account/getting-started. Find more answers at http://help.Diigo.com/teacher-account/faq.

Let's look at an example of how a Diigo student group can become a powerful resource for collaboration and learning:

Several junior classes were merged into one Diigo group and asked to identify one or more professions that most interested them. Within this group of approximately eighty students, subgroups were formed to research, identify and save resources to Diigo library folders created for each profession. Students worked both in the library as well as independently and asynchronously to build career resources. They were encouraged to highlight relevant passages on each web page, to add sticky notes with their thoughts, comments or questions, and to discuss and write about their choices in the discussion forum. Each page added to the folders was tagged with the name of that profession and students were able to set Diigo to alert them when a new resource was added. Although most students had a number one choice, they were asked to explore the resources of three different professions in order to open their minds to various options. The final product was an essay on a chosen profession asking students to identify their reasons for the choice they made. They were also asked to include secondary choices and to reflect upon each.

This project was conducted within a Diigo Educator group. Had students been working in the public Diigo domain, they would have been able to use tags and keywords to search worldwide resources for web pages added and annotated by experts in the various professions. They might have found Diigo groups for their chosen profession where they could ask questions and receive a broad range of answers. Although some teachers might find this public option frightening, others might view it as an opportunity for students to broaden their perspectives as they gather information from people of all ages and from all cultures. The decision to allow students to enter the public domain of Diigo is often a matter of the district acceptable use policy and network rules. Teachable moments and life lessons are lost when kids are locked into private groups. Teens need to learn the responsible, ethical, and safe way to enter public web spaces. To go there with them as part of their education will help them understand the dos and don'ts of navigating the public Web. In this way, we can teach kids to consider the possible consequences before they click.

Diigo's ability to function with licensed databases, where librarians encourage students to do most of their research, can be a bit cumbersome. Because of the password-protected nature of these subscription databases, Diigo's functionality becomes inconsistent. The good news is that your highlighted text and sticky notes stay with your Diigo list. The bad news is that these same highlights and annotations may not reappear when you go back to the article a second time. Users wanting to get back to the original article will also be prompted to sign in. This makes sense, because these databases come with a high price tag. Once logged in, the student will sometimes, but not always, be taken directly to the article. In many cases, you may have to search for it again.

In the public web, Diigo automatically transfers the article's name and URL to the list, while in subscription databases, the URL that Diigo posts is most often the login page rather than the article. Returning to the article will often mean copying and pasting the web page title into the database search. Students can avoid this necessity and save time and effort by taking two important steps when accessing resources on databases. First, they must manually add the title of the resource to the description window when it is first bookmarked, along with crucial bibliographic citation data. Then they should be reminded to read, highlight, and annotate thoroughly so that they won't have to refer back to the original web page. If there is still a need to go back to the web page at a later date, the student can log in, then copy and paste the title that was manually added to the Diigo Library into the search window of the database. Annotations and highlights that were originally added will appear in the Diigo library but won't be visible when returning to the database.

Another option on first view is to use the Capture command to take a screenshot that will remain with the Diigo list. In some cases, it might be possible to cache the page. Diigo's functionality differs slightly from one database to another, but the above advice will help to make the best of any inconvenience.

The Diigo development community continues to work to maintain the edge. Remember that the "o" in Diigo stands for "other stuff." (For example, Diigo has recently enabled the annotation of PDFs and added functionality to Safari and Android applications.) To keep up to date with new stuff and community news, check the Diigo blog: http://blog.Diigo.com.

# Zotero

Zotero (www.zotero.org) is a different kind of social bookmarking site and a perfect complement to Diigo. It bills itself as a citation management tool. "Free and easy to use," Zotero helps you "collect, organize, cite, and share" your research sources (Zotero Home, 2014). It is produced by the Center for History and New Media of George Mason University and funded by the Andrew W. Mellon Foundation, the Institute of Museum and Library Services, and the Alfred P. Sloan Foundation. Zotero is free and open-source, with a community of developers who maintain and upgrade it often based on suggestions from users. Designed as an add-on for the Firefox web browser, the Zotero extension can be found on the bottom right of the browser screen when installed. Zotero has released a standalone version for Firefox on Windows, with extensions for Chrome or Safari and plugins for Word and LibreOffice. Zotero has won awards from PC Magazine, Northwestern University's CiteFest competition, and the American Political Science Association (Puckett, 2011, 3).

Zotero manages bibliographic and reference materials by extracting metadata from an online resource, typically with a single click, to create footnotes, bibliographic and in-text citations from books, articles, documents, web pages, artwork, films or sound recordings, among other things. Not all sites make metadata available, but when a site does so, a capture icon will appear in the address bar. Note that when the Zotero extension is added to your browser, the icon will not appear until you navigate to a site that offers metadata. After metadata has been gathered, the icon will disappear until another site with metadata is accessed. The icon can take several forms depending on the file format. When searching for a book on a site such as Amazon or Google Books, the user will be able to click on a Zotero book icon that automatically appears on the address bar. With this one click, Zotero will gather title, creators, publishers, dates, and other metadata needed to cite this item. Searching for an author often yields a collection of resources.

In this case, Zotero users will see a folder icon. By selecting this icon, the user can check off all or some of the resources in the folder prompting Zotero to gather metadata from all those selected. Websites such as Amazon, Google Scholar and Google Books, Wikipedia, publishers' websites, newspapers such as the *New York Times*, and library catalogs make metadata available to Zotero. Resources or items can also be added by ISBN number, digital object identifier (DOI), and PubMed ID. Each time an item has been successfully added to your Zotero library, a message will appear to let you know which item or items have been added. Be aware that many primary documents don't allow Zotero to collect metadata. In that case, the user can insert that information manually.

One of the more extraordinary features of Zotero is its ability to generate bibliographic or in-text citations as well as footnotes in your chosen bibliographic style. A dropdown menu will offer the most common choices. If you can't find the style you require, go to the Zotero Style Repository (Zotero Style Repository, 2014) for thousands of other choices. Users also have the option to create and save their own styles. To create a bibliography, simply drag and drop the title of the item from the middle column of the Zotero library window into any text field, such as a Word document, Google doc, e-mail body, or blog compositor. Another option is to right-click on a resource or multiple selected resources and choose the option to "generate a bibliography from selected item(s)." The generated file can be copied, saved to the clipboard, or printed.

For users of Microsoft Word, LibreOffice, or OpenOffice, Zotero offers plugins to add their toolbar to documents. This allows the insertion of a dynamically linked bibliography that automatically updates and alphabetizes as new resources are added to Zotero. Other options include style selection and the ability to create in-text citations or footnotes. At any point, you can select a different style, and your Word, LibreOffice or OpenOffice document will immediately reflect those changes. Just as quickly, you can also convert in-text citations to footnotes.

Zotero can preserve entire websites and will capture entire PDF files that are then fully searchable. Websites, articles, and files can be added to collections that can be easily accessed for viewing. Items in collections can be sorted, and notes added are unlimited in length and automatically become part of your searchable content. Files, in the form of Word documents or PDF documents, can be attached; these, too, become fully searchable. A useful feature of Zotero is the ability to build a set of criteria for a given search using tags and dates. An established search can be saved so that subsequent articles found by user and tagged according to search criteria will be automatically added to the appropriate collection.

Zotero can be accessed from any computer with Internet, offers cross-platform access, and can be viewed offline. Apps for mobile devices include ZotFile, ZotPad, Zotero Reader, and Zandy. Group libraries can be formed and shared, and group members can collaborate and communicate using these pooled resources. The exciting news for librarians, teachers and students is that when Zotero is installed on all library and lab computers, the Zotero bookmarking service works in all the same ways with many library databases (there are some exceptions).

But, again, not all web pages are "recognized" by Zotero: users will not see a file type icon in the address bar for some sites. This will require a bit more effort, using the

**Create New Item from Current Page** icon on the Zotero toolbar. One click on this icon will add the web page to your library, leaving it to you to gather and insert the title and all metadata into the premade form found on the right side of the Zotero library window. Zotero assists by maintaining a library of previously entered data so that as you begin typing, options will appear to choose from. To further maintain your Zotero library, the **Attach** tool (paper clip icon) will attach a copy of the web page, a link to the current web page, a stored copy of the file, or a link to the file. To any of these created items, you can also add a note with unlimited text. Selecting a **standalone note** allows the addition of an annotation not associated with any one item or resource but of general value to the list.

School libraries spend large sums on subscription databases yearly, yet they often have to struggle to get kids to use them. Even though these databases are filled with primary source documents selected by an editorial board, kids still prefer the ease of Google. Zotero can help drive more business to the library's home collection with its **Locate** button. This will locate a resource at your library using OpenURL, searching your library's physical collection as well as your subscription databases, thus speeding the process of locating worthwhile resources and encouraging students to use them. To take advantage of this service, students will find a green arrow to the right of the search window. Selecting **Library Lookup** from the dropdown menu lets the user search the library catalog. Although this requires a few extra steps, students who learn the system will benefit from your library's collection. In Jason Puckett's *Zotero: A Guide for Librarians, Researchers, and Educators*, available on Google Books, you will find a step-by-step illustrated guide to linking your library's server to Zotero (Puckett, 2011, 56). Puckett, a subject librarian at the University of Georgia library, also hosts an excellent web page on Zotero. Visitors to the site can benefit from his extensive collection of how-tos and tutorials: http://research.library.gsu.edu/zotero.

Legal, responsible use of resources means appropriate citation and attribution, yet students view the process of creating bibliographies as laborious and onerous. Imagine how thrilled they will be when they find they are able to drag the title of an item from their Zotero library to their text document, where it will magically become a correctly formatted bibliographic entry, or where they can change it to an in-text citation or footnote by adding a page number. Kids—and teachers—will want to create bibliographies just to watch it work!

# Conclusion

Bookmarking in the 21st century has become a social activity. Teaching appropriate socialization skills is an important part of preparing our students to live, work, and thrive in a technologically driven world. Kids should learn to benefit not only from the bookmarking aspect of these web-based services, but also from their collaborative and communicative features. Teaching students to work in these environments in an ethical, responsible, and cybersafe way will enable them to profit from the collective intelligence of whatever group they join.

Whether you select Zotero, Diigo, or one of the many other social bookmarking ser-vices available, take the time to get to know what each can do for you. Consider a com-bination of services to benefit from the strengths of each. Students will appreciate the highlighting and note-taking capability of Diigo and the bibliographic generator offered by Zotero, so why choose only one? Whatever your choice, social bookmarking is an important tool for students and teachers working and researching in your school library.

# Part III

# Communicate and Collaborate

Chapter 5

# Collaborative Technologies and Cloud Computing

*The AASL goals ask librarians to work to ensure that all members*
*of the school library field collaborate to connect learners with ideas and*
*information, and to prepare students for life-long learning, informed*
*decision-making, and the use of information technologies.*

AASL Governing Documents, 2014

## Cloud Computing

For years, teachers and students struggled with moving computer-generated documents back and forth, from school computers to those at home and back again. Work begun at school had to be e-mailed as an attachment or, if the file was too big to e-mail, moved on a flash drive—a device easily forgotten in the computer or misplaced. Even with a flash drive, it was a tricky business to get the final version of a piece of work, especially a slide set or video, back to school and ready to submit on time. When dealing with images, there were tricks to getting them to show up both on a Mac and a PC. When it was a video that had been burned to a CD or DVD, there were endless issues with how the file had been processed to play on all computers. Teachers were constantly being asked for extensions because a transfer from home had failed!

"Cloud computing" makes file transfer a nonissue as all work takes place on the Internet. Schools that shifted to the cloud were spared endless stories of why a deadline couldn't be met because the technology had failed to transfer correctly.

The advantages to cloud computing far outweigh any negatives that worry schools. Yet many are fearful that working, saving, and communicating online will expose students to a broad and anonymous audience, inviting intrusions into student privacy and possible contact with negative influences. A simple and powerful solution to this dilemma is for schools to find cloud-based collaborative technologies by means of which students can work and interact safely. Many of today's collaborative technologies offer specialized educators' domains with added security options that let schools store work remotely on secured servers selecting the level of permissions extended to staff and students. Some allow settings to be varied by subgroup, dependent on things like grade level. Although the first inclination of many schools is to keep cloud-based student work completely private, there are valid reasons to select a hybrid plan where privacy

35

settings can be selected dependent upon each piece of work. We'll explore some of these later in this chapter as we look at Google Apps for Education (GAFE) as a collaborative cloud-based technology.

## Collaborative Technologies

The Partnership for 21st Century Skills (Mission, 2014) states that "There is a profound gap between the knowledge and skills most students learn in school and the knowledge and skills they need in typical 21st-century communities and workplaces." In response, they ask schools to merge traditional education with their 4Cs, emphasizing skills needed to live and work in a technologically rich world where success is based on Critical thinking and problem solving, Communication, Collaboration, and Creativity and innovation.

Today's students, accustomed from a very young age (we see children in high chairs using a smartphone or tablet!) to our fast-paced technologically rich world, are no longer satisfied only to page through books and magazines in search of information. Today's libraries can no longer rely strictly on print materials to connect students with resources. Instead, they must offer the 21st-century tools that empower and challenge kids to learn and to want to learn, appealing to their desire for the socialization and constant communication necessary to engender a collaborative response to problem-solving.

A decade ago, educators had to work hard to find, vet, and cobble together the various tools needed to make this 21st-century mandate happen. But the scope of educational technologies has broadened enabling cloud-based classrooms to work collaboratively to generate authentic research products that include documents, slides, spreadsheets, drawings, diagrams, videos, and posters. They can also team up in online think tanks such as blogs, notepads, discussion forums, wikis, social networks, chat rooms, and social bookmarking. The most robust of these online environments offer many of these options in one place with a single logon. These include Google Apps, Wikispaces Classroom, Edmodo, ePals, Moodle, Schoology, Blackboard, and Collaborize Classroom to name a few. Learning spaces such as these are great places for project-, research-, and evidence-based learning where students can band together to take on and, in some cases, help to solve real-world problems.

One cloud-based learning environment with an extensive reach is Google Apps, with its dynamic suite of free cutting-edge tools and applications that can serve to expand the options in any school library. Students and teachers have easy access to these simply by signing up for a free Google account. To be more effective, a school or district can establish a free Google Apps for Education (GAFE) domain that consists of individual but interconnected accounts for teachers and students. A GAFE domain lets members create private, shared, or public documents and web pages all stored remotely in the cloud. Once a school has established an online learning environment such as this, the four Cs identified by the Partnership for 21st Century Skills become ubiquitous! User-friendly and easy to learn, Google Apps has changed the way we think about learning by creating teams of users who can easily share thoughts, concepts, strategies, and resources.

Google's 24/7 cloud access helps students who are disorganized, because cloud-based docs can always be located in the student's Google Drive. Much of the stress created by deadlines is mitigated, because students can work and submit assignments digitally from any Internet-enabled device, anytime and anywhere.

# Coteaching

To prepare students to achieve success in the 21st-century workplace, educators should strive to replicate a similar environment in our schools. This entails creating a system that permits collaboration across space. In multinational corporate workplaces today, teams are assembled with members from around the world with workflow centered around Internet technologies. Much of what used to require constant travel by team members can now be done online, using shared research, writing, and web conferencing to save on airfares and travel time.

Librarians and technology integrators can encourage teachers to work in this same way, pairing up with other educators to coteach their classes face-to-face and virtually. Students from all participating classes can be viewed as one unit, then assigned to teams made up of a cross-section. Assigned the same task by all involved teachers, students will be asked to work virtually to collaborate and problem-solve together, sometimes never meeting face-to-face. This model can be adapted to include groups from within a school or by pairing up with teachers and students from any point on the globe, working synchronously and asynchronously to gather resources, construct knowledge, hypothesize solutions, and resolve problems. Google Apps for Education, Moodle, ePals, Edmodo, and other social learning platforms afford access to millions of students and teachers worldwide.

When coteaching is structured to mimic today's real-world business model, our digital generation gains access to the tools needed to engage in significant and tangible work to address authentic problems in a constantly evolving technological landscape. In this model, critical thinking will occur even as students "communicate, socialize, share information, and do all of the things that they relish about hanging out with friends" (Boyd, 2008). Learning to navigate these environments in school will give students invaluable skills that will transfer into the workplace. When the school library becomes the hub of this activity, it will become a place where kids—and teachers—want to be.

*Chapter 6*

# Google Apps for Education

Google Apps for Education (GAFE) has created a shift unlike any other software suite, with users creating, sharing, collaborating, and storing their work in the cloud, where time, place, platform, and device become irrelevant to productivity. In this environment, the only requisite is access to the Internet. What's more, GAFE allows educators to establish a learning space for students that replicates the powerful team structure of today's corporate workplace, defining success through collaboration, cooperation, and communication. For so many of today's students, who would rather work alone or who choose to hitchhike and let other group members do the work, mastering team skills becomes a challenging imperative. Establishing a Google Apps for Education domain can make the task less arduous and more enjoyable by linking its members to all the technologies they need to be a real team—for free! Google says it best: "What better way to prepare your students for the newest technology in the workplace than by giving it to them as a part of their education?" (Google Apps for Education, 2014).

Why would any school turn down this unparalleled free offer to bring today's cutting edge tech tools to all students and staff? You can read more about how to establish a GAFE domain in your district at the Google Apps for Education training center at www .google.com/edu/training. In this chapter, we will take a closer look at the core apps that make up the Google Apps for Education domain and examine how they can transform the culture of your school library.

## Google Drive

Google Drive (http://drive.google.com) is Google's cloud storage where users can upload and organize documents, photos, and videos. In Google Drive, users can access Google's suite of applications consisting of a word processor (Google Docs), a spreadsheet application (Google Sheets), a forms creator (Google Forms), presentation software (Google Slides), and drawing software (Google Drawings). Students of any age can log on to their accounts to independently create a new document of any of these types that can be shared with group members and teachers. The document owner can define the degree to which those individuals have access either as viewers, editors, or commenters. When sharing with Google Apps for Education (GAFE) domain members, names will self-populate as the user enters the first few letters of a first or last name. For students who aren't sure of classmates' last names or how to spell them, this streamlines the task, allowing them to select the name from the popup list. Previously created distribution lists will also self-populate as you begin typing the group name, making sharing with PLCs, classmates, teams, group members, or rosters effortless. The document owner can make his work public on the web, viewable to anyone who has a link, viewable to anyone in the domain, or private. Teachers can discuss these options with students to help them make the most responsible decision. Although among educators, the knee-jerk reaction is to keep things out of the public eye, for older students, there are many instances in which publishing work for others to see and comment on is the best option. Users within a GAFE domain will have searchable access to documents that they own or that have been shared with them. If an individual document has been published to the web, searchable access to that document will be expanded to search engines, such as Google.

## Google Docs

The Google Docs toolbar and dropdown menus are similar to Microsoft Word's and will be familiar to new users. With just a few minutes of instruction, students can be taught to create a new doc, share it with team members and their teachers, and begin composing on it. After it has been shared, a team of students can collaborate on the same document from different computers in the same room or miles apart. And once a document is created, Google Docs will autosave every several seconds. Team members working asynchronously can always use the Insert menu to leave a comment, question, or message for teammates. Teachers with rights to edit or to comment can take advantage of this function to insert comments that guide student work. Comments appear to the right of the document and can be inserted without interfering with the body of work.

Learning to function as a member of a team is an important 21st-century skill that can't be overlooked in education. Although educators would all agree with this, they also acknowledge that successful group work has always been difficult to achieve. Inevitably, one student takes the lead and does much of the work while others lag behind or participate only marginally. And although giving students individual grades for their personal contributions serves to quell frustration and anger among hard-working team members, it neglects to acknowledge that in the real world, teams that have members who fail to commit often fail as a team. We need to strive for a "Three Musketeers" mentality, emphasizing to our students the "All for one and one for all!" imperative (Dumas, 1878: 74). So hitchhikers beware! With Google docs, the teacher can quickly access a document's revision history to see times and dates of all modifications, as well as who made them, allowing him or her to track who has contributed, how often each team member accessed the document, and, selecting "show more detailed revisions" will give you a sense of how much time he or she spent there.

Teachers often use revision history for catching project "hitchhikers." But it's also particularly useful if a section of the work has been inadvertently deleted or overwritten, if the author changes his mind about edits to previously written segments, or if team members need to document who contributed what. Select the version you'd like to see.

If you determine that the previous version is the one you want, you can click on **Restore this revision**. Doing this will not lose all changes made since that date and time, but will move the selected previous version to the top of your revision history. Another option is to combine the older version with the latest revision by locating the previously written sections of text that you would like to restore, and copying and pasting them back into the most recent version.

In March 2014, Google announced Add-ons for Google docs. These are third-party scripts that can be added to docs to make them more functional. Add-ons include EasyBib, to generate bibliographies; Lucidchart for flowcharts, mindmaps, and diagrams; VexTab Music Notation to add music and drum notation as well as guitar tablature to any doc; UberConference for conference calls to collaborators or viewers; and others like RhymeFinder, Twitter Curator and Table Formatter, to name a few. Google Apps Scripts gives users/developers the coding tools to build more add-ons. As such, your add-ons options will continue to grow as people around the world build and post new tools.

## Generating a Table of Contents

Teams of students conducting research in the library databases can build their research and track their resources using one shared Google document. Because a team document can quickly become long, disorganized and unmanageable, it is invaluable to teach students to create a table of contents that can be automatically generated and updated. To do this, students can select section titles from within their text to identify as headings. In the style dropdown list located next to the font settings on the menu bar, the user can select heading size 1 through 6. (To remove a heading, simply return to the dropdown and select Normal Text.) After headings are identified, the table of contents can be added from the Insert menu. It sounds hard, but in fact doing it is much simpler than explaining it. Here's an example of how this can work:

> Social Studies classes often examine concepts and issues through a lens that is known as PERSIA+GT, an acronym that stands for Political, Economic, Religious, Social, Industrial, Aesthetic, Governmental and Technological. Students are assigned in a group of four to use those parameters to research a given topic. The team can begin by creating a Google doc and typing the letters (or words) that make up PERSIA+GT vertically. As students take notes, their goal will be to insert resources for each category beneath the appropriate letter heading, but with four students working together to add their resources under each letter, including notes on articles and books, images, video links, and bibliographic data, this research document will quickly become lengthy and unmanageable, leaving students to scroll through pages of text to find the right letter heading. To organize the document, students can select the eight letters of this acronym, go to the style dropdown list, and select the size of the heading, with 1 being the largest font and 6 the smallest. After headings have been identified, the student can place the cursor at the very top of the document (above the letters) and select Insert > Table of Contents. Instantly, Google Docs will generate a hyperlinked table

of contents, making it easy to insert new resources in any category without wasting time scrolling and searching through the document. The table of contents is a useful resource that can be quickly updated when other words throughout the document are selected and given heading status. Students in this case might want to further organize by adding subheadings under each letter category. To update the table of contents, select it and click on the refresh tool that appears. The ability to generate a table of contents at the top of a document is not unique to Google Docs—Microsoft Word has the same capability. It's an efficient way to save valuable time and effort as resources continue to be added to a shared document. Google docs now offers an Add-on called Table of Contents that facilitates this process inserting the table of contents in the sidebar for easy access.

The real advantage of a Google doc is the ability to work as a team synchronously or asynchronously in the cloud. Students will appreciate not having to keep track of paper documents and note cards and will always know where to find their materials. And teachers like being able to monitor student progress from any computer and comment electronically without carrying a heavy bag stuffed with student work back and forth to school. For the school librarian, it has always been difficult to monitor student progress on a project he or she has helped to design. Classes tend to come to the library to conduct research but don't necessarily return during the final phases of the work, making it hard to assess success or know where modifications are necessary. Sharing Google docs with librarians allows them to check in to view each student or group's real-time progress. Inserted electronic comments with insights, suggested resources, and questions will serve to initiate a dialogue that allows the librarian to remain a viable part of the learning process even after the class has left the library. As a result, librarians will be able to assess the project's success in a more substantive way, using the data to inform next steps.

The efficiency of Google's cloud storage is not just good news for students and teachers. GAFE also represents savings for schools as they preserve district server space for other uses. Text-based files presently saved on the district drives can be uploaded effortlessly to the Google servers, converting each document into a fully editable Google doc format, or choosing to maintain the document's original format. In other words, a Word document can be uploaded and converted to a Google doc, or can be uploaded as a Word document. To further facilitate the process, the upload screen allows you to select the destination folder and to set the privacy level before the conversion process begins. More powerful than individual file uploading is the ability to upload an entire folder when working in Google's Chrome Internet browser. With the same ease as the upload function, Google docs can be downloaded in a variety of formats including DOC, RTF, PDF, and HTML. Google docs can be set to write in 60+ languages by going to the Settings menu. Text can also be translated using the Google translator in the Tools menu. This is not a useful tool for world language students—the translations don't guarantee accuracy—but for ESL or ELL students, translating a document into the target language will give them the gist.

## Google Slides

Google Drive allows users to generate a set of cloud-based presentation slides that work much like PowerPoint. Like Google Docs, Google Slides can be shared with collaborators working together to build one slide set. In the library, we often use Google Slides as phase 2 of a research project, asking students to use the slides as a storyboard to convert their lengthy research Google doc into a more manageable format before finalizing it as a formal slide presentation, video, or research paper. Students can use each slide to create a black-and-white barebones outline to which they can add the URLs of text-based resources, images, or videos, as well as bibliographic information from print resources. The speaker notes can be opened to write script or special notes, and reminders, suggestions, or questions for teammates can be inserted as comments. When using a storyboard approach, students can focus solely on the organization of the information they will present without taking the time to experiment with colors, fonts, or animation schemes that slow the work down and often prevent the final project's timely completion. After the lengthy Google doc has been condensed to a manageable set of slides in the storyboard, students can then go on to create the final product. Since the team has 24/7 cloud access to their slides, they don't have to worry about how, when, or where they'll work. Better yet, they don't have to find a common time to work with collaborators—work can be asynchronous. With Google Slides, cross-platform complications, especially with media files, become a concern of the past. If slides are first created in PowerPoint, they can be uploaded directly to Google Drive. But users should be advised to uncheck the box that allows Google to convert the PowerPoint format to a Google Slides format. Failure to do so may result in the loss of features not found in the Google version, including fonts, themes, and animation schemes. However, Google Drive is a good place to store PowerPoint slides for safe-keeping. Students can download them on any computer to continue working in a Microsoft environment.

## Google Sheets

Google Drive includes Google Sheets, which functions much like Microsoft Excel. A basic component of the Google Apps for Education domain, these sheets can be quickly created and easily shared using class distribution lists. When left to their own resources, students tend to overlook spreadsheets and opt for a document, to which they add a table. Opting for a spreadsheet allows data to be sorted, conditional formatting can be added, and functions can be defined. Charts and graphs can be easily generated and a growing field of add-ons can be inserted to gain even more functionality. Social studies students can generate data-rich problem-based reports; math students can learn business applications inserting data, adding formulas, and working with mathematical operators; and science students can enter findings into a spreadsheet that can be shared and manipulated with up to 50 users able to work simultaneously to quickly generate robust data sets that yield more reliable results and can be augmented by the next year's classes to create a longevity study.

Here's an example of making quick work of an arduous task. A social studies teacher has a class of 25 students studying demographics of states throughout the United States. Each student has been assigned two states with the task of finding information at the U.S. Census bureau website. In the pre–Google apps days, students had no easy way to share data, but with a shared Google sheet, kids can enter individual responses that will be instantly accessible to the entire class or a group of classes. In fact, students can watch the spreadsheet data populate as the class period progresses and classmates add their statistics. In no time, the class will be comparing and contrasting, analyzing, interpreting, restating, and predicting based on the shared data. Students can also work together to manipulate, sort, and convert data into charts and graphs for a dynamic group discussion. Other classes can add to this same spreadsheet, expanding the data field and enriching the dialog. Although this research may begin in the library with the guidance of librarians and classroom teachers, work on this cloud-based document can continue asynchronously at home. Whenever and wherever students log on, they will find and be able to edit the class spreadsheet in their own Google Drive.

There are many great opportunities to integrate Google Sheets into a lesson plan. English classes can collaborate on a project to define the attributes of each of the various characters in the book they are reading. How were the boys in *Lord of the Flies* different from one another? What attributes did they share? What were their character strengths and weaknesses? Which boys had leadership qualities? Which were the followers? Students can collaborate to add descriptors to a spreadsheet for each character, adding quotes from the book to substantiate their claim. At the end of the period, students can already be debating, explaining, citing and describing to make their point. No waiting to collate all results. It happens as fast as the students can type!

Classes working in the library can add favorite books, poems, videos into a school-wide spreadsheet to create a student-generated reading list for the entire school. The list can be sorted alphabetically for ease of use, with columns for title, author, date of publication, and reviews. Inserted comments and notes reveal themselves with a tiny triangle in the top right hand corner of a given cell. Students or teachers can "hide" comments, notes, hints, or questions in this way without affecting the body of the sheet. What an easy and effortless way to compile their own favorites list for kids to see. And it can be updated daily!

Google Sheets, like other Google documents, can be quickly and easily shared, published, and downloaded in various formats, including XLS, PDF, and CSV. Spreadsheets created in Excel can be uploaded and converted to a Google Sheet or uploaded as an Excel file. To supercharge spreadsheet functionality, check the Add-ons menu for optional tools created by third-party developers. Add-ons for Sheets include tools like Doctopus for mass-sharing of teacher-generated files based on a saved class roster and its counterpart, Goobric for using a rubric to automatically grade student work; Flubaroo to grade quizzes taken on a Google form or spreadsheet, analyze results, and send grades to students; autoCrat to produce PDFs based on spreadsheet data; Twitter Curator to find and collect tweets inside your Google spreadsheet; and g(Math) for Sheets to easily create graphs and complex mathematical formulation. For Google Analytics users, the Analytics add-on transfers data to a spreadsheet for easy manipulation and control.

Add-ons make spreadsheets—viewed by many educators as complex and confusing—more accessible to the general teaching population. And once you've downloaded an add-on, you'll find it in the Add-ons dropdown menu each time you open a new spreadsheet. No need to reinstall each time. Check the Add-ons menu often for new additions.

Just as in the other apps, Google Sheets offers revision history. In this case, revisions present themselves in a unique way, allowing views of individual changes made cell by cell, with each collaborator's work represented in a different color.

In the library, aside from using spreadsheets as an integral part of various lesson plans, they can be used by the library staff for a variety of things:

- Tracking infractions of the library and computer network rules
- Maintaining computer serial numbers
- Generating summer reading lists
- Publishing circulation statistics into the library website (these can be generated and published as graphs)
- Documenting the library program and usage
- Tracking and publishing database usage
- Assessing and tracking success and problem areas in various lessons, such as by creating an annotated bibliography required of all freshmen or a junior research project required for graduation

Data collected in Google sheets serve to inform the library program about budget, programming, and improvement. And what better way to create a budget than on a spreadsheet that can be archived in the cloud, with new sheets (tabs) added year to year?

## Google Forms

Google Forms is a survey application. A companion to Google Sheets, it offers a user-friendly and quick way to collect and graph data, opinions or other information. The American Association of School Libraries asks that "all members of the school library field collaborate to participate as active partners in the teaching/learning process as we connect learners with ideas and information" (AASL, 2014). To be effective in this process, we need to develop ways to relate to students as individuals, to know more about them as learners and to use this information to ensure that learning experiences are respectful to all. By gathering data on what students want and need, how they prefer to learn, and how they best communicate, school libraries can establish a learning environment that integrates highly differentiated technology-rich experiences allowing every student to feel respected and to be successful. Knowing the client allows the library to nurture a growth mindset in participants as they engage in new learning and practice new skills. Students who recognize that they are being heard and that their opinions are being respected will be more highly motivated to work to construct their own learning, often generating a product that adds value to their present and future life and to the lives of those around them.

A school library will succeed when it identifies as a priority the desire to keep current on what their clients like, need and want. Since student tastes, interests and preferences change as often as the technologies they use, the school library will benefit from a quick and easy way to gather data in order to keep up with the quickly shifting trends. The Google Forms application is easy and intuitive to learn, fun to use, and its various themes allow the user to appeal visually to various audiences. The look and feel of your form can also be customized with school banners, personal photography or artwork, and selection of color palette. With Google Forms, librarians can generate quick polls or surveys that can be easily posted on the library's home page. Do you want to know what books they read this month? Create a form! Do you want to know how students prefer to communicate? Create a form! Here's just a short list of the many ways these Google surveys can inform school librarians:

- Survey to create a summer reading list.
- Conduct a pre-assessment of prior knowledge to launch a research project.
- Have students complete a readiness survey preceding the use of a new technology.
- Give a post-assessment of how well the lesson plan worked for students.
- Create a peer assessment form.
- Create a directory of project URLs for easy tracking of student work.
- Gather a list of favorite poems for National Poetry Month.
- Allow students to recommend a resource for the library.
- Ask students' opinions on an author.
- Create a registration form for a library event.
- Get feedback from a library event.
- Gather information on which databases kids prefer to use.
- Ask students what technology tools and applications work best.
- Ask students to recommend technology tools to purchase.
- Gather data on which mobile devices students prefer to use.
- Ask them which mobile devices you should buy.
- Learn what's trending with your students.

Post a different Google survey on your library home page each week, even if it's only one question. Follow up with results from last week's question and you'll keep the kids coming back to see what's up in the library. Can't think of enough questions? Post a Google form to let the kids submit their ideas.

Data collected in Google forms are displayed on Google Sheets where the summary of responses automatically converts spreadsheet data into charts or graphs that display percentages. Google does the math to supply valuable feedback. When the school library leads the way with forms, inviting everyone to submit responses to weekly surveys, the entire school community will soon want to follow suit in classrooms. Teachers will use Google forms for surveys as well as for quick formative assessments. Students will use them to gather data that can be used in course projects. And as with the other Google Apps, it's possible to add collaborators so that teams of teachers and/or student groups can work together to create the same form.

Google Forms can be easily shared and distributed by e-mailing a link or the actual survey, hyperlinking from a document, or embedding it into web pages. The link can be shared with Google+, Facebook, or Twitter, or a utility such as TinyUrl (http://tinyurl .com), or Bitly (http://bitly.com) will let teachers create a shortcut that students can easily remember. An example would include the teacher's name, project abbreviation, and year. This tinyurl—http://tinyurl.com/jonestkam2014—represents a sample naming protocol for a survey that could be sent to Ms. Jones's 2014 English class reading *To Kill a Mockingbird* (tkam). The following year, this teacher can copy the form and rename it for 2015, clearing the data, updating the tinyurl, and saving time and effort.

The owner of a form can elect to share only the live form or to share both the form and the resulting spreadsheet in the event that participants can be permitted to view the results. It should be noted that for forms that ask students for confidential information, teachers need to be mindful to keep the spreadsheet containing the data private. In this case, only the form should be shared.

Google Forms offers the user numerous options for question types, including

- Short text
- Paragraph
- Multiple choice (radio button)
- Checkboxes that allow the survey participant to select all that apply
- Choose from a list (dropdown menu)
- Scale (Likert scale)
- Date
- Time
- Grid with criteria on both the horizontal and vertical axes

Most of these questions types are self-explanatory. Use a grid for questions like this: How often do you use the following technologies for school? On the horizontal, the responses will read, from left to right, "Daily," "Weekly," "Monthly," and "Never." The vertical axis will list the various technologies (e.g., desktop, laptop, tablet, smartphone), each to be considered separately. The grid can also serve to create a rubric that, in combination with the Flubaroo add-on, will do the math for you to determine the students' grades.

Google surveys can be branched from any multiple choice question by checking the box that says **Go to page based on answer**. Section headers, page titles, descriptions, and page breaks can be inserted. Images and videos can also be added. Individual survey questions can be marked as **Required**. Responses are displayed in a Google Sheet. The response summary generates pie charts and bar graphs to help the viewer diagnose the data.

The school library is the perfect place for Google forms to be showcased. Students and teachers will tell you that they appreciate the opportunity to express their views and to know that the library staff values their input. So whether you post them to your library website, send them out as an e-mail blast to the student body, or feature them on an easy-to-access computer on your circulation desk where anyone can go to register their responses, Google forms will show your school community that your goal is to make the school library a place where kids and teachers want to be.

## *Google Drawings*

Today's emphasis on graphic arts makes the Google Drawings application more important than ever. This easy to learn, fun application allows students to generate original artwork, diagrams or flow charts to insert into a Google project. Drawing tools in Google are similar to those found in Microsoft Word and PowerPoint, but these will be saved in Google Drive, whence you can easily insert them into a Google document or web page. Just as you can with other document types, Google drawings can be shared to be worked on by a team with the option to review the revision history, which will show changes made by different participants in different colors. Drawings can be exported as a JPG, PNG, PDF, or SVG files for use in other programs.

Often teachers view the use of Google drawings as irrelevant to serious content. But computer-generated graphic design is one of today's most rapidly expanding professions, and learning to manipulate drawing tools allows students the freedom to create visuals that are specific to their needs. Students can be asked to create a graphical representation of an idea, a theme, or a topic. For example, students studying the six dimensions of wellness—social, intellectual, spiritual, physical, emotional, and occupational—can be asked to represent that concept with an original graphic of their own design to be posted on the Google web page they created to write about that topic. Individual interpretations allow teachers to ask students why they chose what they drew and to get kids to think in a different way about the concepts they're studying. For example, a student might represent the six dimensions of wellness by drawing a pyramid divided into 6 levels, each labeled with one of the dimensions. When you ask him to explain how he chose to label each of the increasingly large levels (Were some of the dimensions more important than others?), you'll see immediate recognition that since all six dimensions should be considered equal to our mental and physical health, they should be represented as equal in the drawing. It seems like a small thing to quibble about the shape, but it's an important lesson in visual literacy that wouldn't otherwise be taught.

The Partnership for 21st Century Skills (P21.org) identifies creativity as one of the four Cs (collaboration, communication, creativity/innovation and critical thinking/ problem solving), a vital life skill that we often overlook as we strive for content mastery (Partnership: Our Mission, 2014). And creating something like the six-dimensions graphic requires only one class period as students learn to use the tools available and experiment with designs. This sort of activity is generally popular with both students and teachers, especially when comparing the many different graphical representations produced by the class. Reviewing each drawing with the class can be an eye-opener as students begin to see how differently each person interprets and visualizes the same concept.

So as you experiment with all the apps within Google Drive, remember to look for ways to integrate Google drawings into your students' work. Not only is it fun, but it will change their perspective on how they think of and view their world.

## Google Drive: Conclusion

Google Drive is fun to use and easy to learn, and the Google staff is dedicated to constantly adding features to enhance the applications. As such, new users need to be aware that there are often changes in the interface and added options that pop up on a regular basis. (From time to time, Google will also eliminate really cool tools and functions that work well.) This is an important consideration, particularly if you intend to create tutorials with screenshots that run the risk of being outdated by the time you share them with students. These constant changes can be a source of panic to teachers who thought they had it all figured out. Don't let it throw you when you're standing before a group of students looking for a button that was there yesterday but that has seemingly disappeared or a menu item that has been renamed! Just be ready to say what we always say to our students: "Oops! It's just Google's constant quest to make our work more dynamic! So let's figure it out together!" In today's cloud-based world, mastery of our ever-changing technologies is no longer feasible. Accept it—and roll with the changes. Teachers can be put off by this aspect of integrating technology into our work, but kids take it in stride. So let them share the fun of finding new ways of doing all the things you want them to do and discovering the new options that come with the ever-evolving Google Apps.

## Google Sites

As part of the Google Apps for Education suite, Google Sites (http://sites.google.com) offers libraries, as well as students and teachers, a user-friendly and intuitive way to publish online content. Sites offers many user benefits. First, there is no need to notify a web manager in order to create a new site. All members of your Google Apps for Education domain can simply click on Sites and create a new site. Some district planning should be done to establish organizational protocols, such as naming websites, customizing URLs, and identifying categories and tags. This will be invaluable in tracking the many new sites created daily by teachers, administrators, staff and students.

Google Drive gave us a way to create and share all kinds of documents. Google Sites offers a way to merge, publish, and share the end product. With just a few clicks of the mouse, students can integrate any of their shared or published Google docs, sheets, forms, slides, and drawings into a web page and share the site with members of the domain or publish for the world to see. Images can be inserted by file browsing or by entering the URL, a process so simple that careful instruction must be given to ensure copyright has been protected for each online resource as the students' tendency to "harvest" images at will can only lead to copyright woes later on.

Online publishing requires students to understand the concept of visual literacy, including layout, design, and other elements of look and feel. Attending to visual literacy will ensure that students select relevant images that enhance the content. They could be chosen to be an actual representation of the words on the page or could, in other cases, be symbolic of the writing. Freshmen in one English class wrote dramatic monologues based on characters in *To Kill A Mockingbird*. The teacher, in talking to students about how to select appropriate images, reminded them that a photo of the actors who portrayed the various roles in the movie will not be the best representation of the emotion experienced while reading the passage. Suggest that sometimes the best way to represent your own work visually is to stage and take your own photographs. Students who heed that advice say that the act of staging the photo made them think about their written work in a different way. Those electing to search online should be encouraged to search within Creative Commons for images that are free to be reused. The Usage rights filter in the Google Images Search Advanced Settings will shortcut the process, eliminating the time-consuming need to explore copyright policies for each image.

Google Sites makes it easy for any library to post a website that can be modified at any time by the library staff. Not having to wait for a web manager to get to updates allows the librarians to adopt a just-in-time attitude posting things on the fly as it becomes necessary. Sometimes this entails posting a link to a tutorial after overhearing a student wishing he could find one to help him with his project. Sometimes it's a quick video recorded by a librarian with a cell phone that can be instantly uploaded to the library's YouTube channel and inserted into the library's Google site. If during the course of the day you are inspired to create a Google survey, it can be posted that very day so data can begin accruing.

Since groups of students can collaborate to build a Google site, this has become the solution to publishing a pre-reading information center. Teams of students can spend the few weeks prior to reading Elie Wiesel's *Night* researching various aspects of the Holocaust that touched Wiesel's life and publishing their findings to a website that furnishes the background needed to grasp and interpret the full impact of the chapters they are about to read. Students of Fitzgerald's *The Great Gatsby* can create a website to help classmates understand life in the 1920s before reading the book. Dividing the era into subtopics, each assigned to a small group of students, makes this otherwise enormous undertaking manageable in a short period of time.

Librarians can expand research options by linking class websites to the card catalog where all students can benefit. Over time, an English department working together can create a full complement of prereading sites for all required reading, all accessible 24/7 through a school library's electronic catalog, such as Destiny. Once posts are live, teachers can ask students in the following years to continue building these sites. Before sites are made public, rubrics should signal students to scrutinize their work for inaccuracies, misconceptions, unsubstantiated facts, and insufficient attribution. These should then be addressed and corrected before the site is linked to the card catalog, where it will become part of the permanent library collection.

Video is a powerful medium for teaching and learning. Our students search video sites such as YouTube, Discovery Education, TeacherTube, and Vimeo for digital footage to enhance their websites. These can be easily added to their site using the URL for YouTube and the embed code or iFrame for other online video sources. Again, appropriate attribution is essential, and students should be cautioned that many videos are restricted by copyright and illegal to repost. They should be instructed to do their due diligence as they determine permissions and once granted, determine how to attribute the owner.

Today's world is one in which anyone can be a published author, songwriter, entertainer, musician, comedian, or actor. How many of our students own a phone or device that can create a video? A Google Apps for Education domain includes a free YouTube channel where each domain member can post original video-based work. This makes it easy for students who have written and published original poetry, dramatic monologues, short stories, creative essays or historical fiction, among other things, to then capture a performance of their work in digital form, upload it to their YouTube channel, and insert it into their Google Site using the URL. Visitors to the site will be treated to a personal interpretation by the author, which can, in turn, have a profoundly different impact on the person listening. Imagine reading a Robert Frost poem silently, then watching a video of Frost reading it himself. In most cases, this will be a very different experience as you hear things from the poet that you hadn't "heard" as you read it. Make your students aware of experiential learning and urge them to strive to create unique experiences for their audience each time they publish

Students need guidelines for posting on the web. At first, posting videos featuring yourself on YouTube can seem frightening and too exposed. But YouTube offers three settings: Private, Unlisted, or Public. To view a student's Private video, you have to ask that student to share it with you. This can be inconvenient when he also has to share it with each of his classmates and others in the domain. And if this student wants his grandparents in Florida to view it, they too would need an individual invitation. Except in the case of the video being of a very personal nature (i.e., the student's personal health goals), private is generally not the best way to go. The Public setting allows the video to be searchable using the YouTube or Google search function. This degree of exposure is often unacceptable to educators and parents, particularly with younger students. So how can we safely encourage kids to publish? The safest way to do so is to ask students to select the Unlisted option. This allows the student to post the link to their Google site, allowing anyone with the link to view the video without special permission—yet the unlisted video will not be searchable in YouTube or in a Google search. It's important to note that older students often prefer to make their videos public. If careful consideration has been given to discussing the implications of going public, and if parents have no objection, you can let them make the final decision. A student with an original piece of music might want to be discovered. As long as all parties are cognizant of the decision, publishing to the world can be very fulfilling, especially when people around the world add comments. Teaching students to publish on Google Sites gives them a way to showcase their work, to practice graphic design as they experiment with layouts, and to learn new techniques for integrating several technologies into one final product.

The Google apps featured in this chapter represent the tip of the Google iceberg. Your domain will offer a calendar and Google e-mail (Gmail) to each member as well. Each app can be turned on or off for the entire membership, or subdomains can allow the IT administrator to set permission by age level or group. Log into your Google account, and in the apps menu (the dot matrix near your name), click on More. See what's there, and then continue to Even more—Google is constantly acquiring new applications. Lucid-chart is a free online diagram software and flowchart maker. VideoNot.es lets teachers upload a video so students can view it and take notes on their own screen. YouTube, Google Maps, Google Earth, Blogger, Google+, and many more can be accessed from within the Google Apps for Education domain. And all this with a single sign-on!

The latest addition to the GAFE suite is Google Classroom (www.google.com/edu/classroom/) designed to afford teachers "More Teaching, Less Tech-ing" ("Google Classroom" 2014). Here, teachers can host their students and create assignments that distribute individual copies organized in students' Drive folders. Teachers can eliminate the paper shuffle, easily collecting assignments online and assessing electronically to provide timely feedback as well as grades. Students will always know where their work is, making it effortless to stay organized and freeing teachers from replacing lost papers. And librarians, technology integrators, and support staff can join classes to monitor student work adding valuable feedback to enhance learning.

A Google Apps for Education domain, with its abundant 21st-century toolbox, will change the way your school community works and can revolutionize the way kids—and teachers—look at the school library!

*Chapter 7*

# Online and Blended Learning

In 2004, the term Web 2.0 became a technological buzzword representing a new kind of Internet through which users could generate web content and interact with other users. Everyone was talking about Google, blogs, and wikis. Wikipedia, Flickr, and YouTube invited users around the world to upload content and interact socially. Creative Commons licensing helped everyday users select their own level of permissions for reuse, allowing anyone in the world to copy, distribute, edit, remix, or build upon others' original work. Web 2.0 resulted in a constant stream of social media sites popping up, giving us endless new applications to choose from. Web 2.0 technologies offered us a chance to communicate with the world quickly, easily, and largely for free! It was a very exciting time.

Web 2.0 initiated the shifting role and relationship of teacher and student with cloud-based options that constantly change how teachers teach and students learn. This nonstop morphing has made it hard for teachers to keep up. What's more, they're generally wary of anything that they haven't mastered. This is where the librarian and technology integration teacher can be agents for progress, tracking new and emerging online options and helping teachers use them to make the shift to the interactive web.

The term Web 2.0 isn't used much these days. The notion of an interactive web is one that we now take for granted. Our students don't remember a time when online socializing didn't exist. Still, many schools are confused by how to make social applications relevant to learning in a secure way and wonder if they really have to get involved. One has only to ask students to find the answer.

In the February 9, 2012, issue of *The Journal*, Chris Riedel reported that according to Project Tomorrow CEO Julie Evans, "today's students have their own vision for learning" (Riedel, 2012). Results from Project Tomorrow's Speak Up surveys revealed frustration among kids that there's not enough technology in schools—and that even when there is, it's not being used the way students want. Students want their learning to be socially based and untethered, without the constraints of traditional rules. One Speak Up student said, "When teachers limit our technology use, they limit our future" (Project Tomorrow, "Unleashing the Future," 2010).

Project Tomorrow proposes a 3Es model of education, pointing at how kids are leveraging online learning, digital content, and mobile learning to become "enabled,

---

On April 19, 2012, I presented a webinar for edWeb.net's Blended Learning Bootcamp online community entitled "Selecting an Online Course Platform" (Swan, 2012). Much of the information in this chapter is adapted from that presentation.

engaged, and empowered." Their vision is to ensure that today's students are well prepared to be tomorrow's innovators, leaders and engaged citizens of the world (Project Tomorrow, 2014).

Today, many schools are still wrestling with how to shift away from century-old educational practices. Connie Yowell of the Macarthur Foundation says that we need to reconceptualize what teaching and learning look like (Connie Yowell, 2012). But it's easier to reimagine education than to make 21st-century education happen. There is no quick way to move to a technology-rich learning environment, but online options offer abundant resources to help teachers take small steps toward a social and collaborative curriculum. Many believe that schools don't have to teach technology, because kids already know that stuff, but in fact, kids know what they know—their games, music, social sites and texting—yet have little grasp of the many applications that let them work and learn online. In this chapter, we'll look at how teachers can take their curriculum online. Librarians and technology integration teachers can be a powerful force for change by working with teachers and students to learn new technologies and ensure their success.

Online coursework is commonplace at the university level, where an individual can enroll to earn a degree virtually. In this model, face-to-face interaction takes place only through web conferencing. Although virtual high school courses are becoming more readily available, with new cyber and virtual high schools appearing each year, K–12 education continues to function predominantly on a five-day-a-week brick-and-mortar classroom schedule with students and teachers face-to-face. Taking a course completely online is often considered unrealistic, but numerous web-based applications let teachers create hybrid courses that combine face-to-face classroom time with online learning. This educational model extends teaching and learning time 24/7, liberating kids to work on their work when they want and how they want on any computer or mobile device from any place in the world. Many of today's hybrid courses work on the flipped classroom principle, supported by applications that let teachers and students upload media and interact asynchronously. Teachers benefit from their round-the-clock cloud-based classrooms by reserving in-school class time for face-to-face hands-on interactions. These days, it's easier than ever to create a blended learning environment for your students, no matter the circumstances.

Is your school library ready for this 21st-century teaching and learning model? If you're in a bring-your-own-device (BYOD) environment, everywhere you look, you'll see technology tools at work: iPads, tablets, iPod Touches, laptops, Chromebooks, netbooks, smartphones, and desktop PCs and Macs. Circulating among them, you'll find teachers, librarians, and technology integration teachers helping students interpret what they're finding and seeing—or learning something new from them. In this environment, students are working to construct meaning using their online course content as a guide. Teachers who for many years viewed technology integration as an add-on are starting to recognize that hybrid or blended learning can spark a new interest in learning among students. In an October 2011 Center for Digital Education article entitled "Great Online Teachers Have to be Radical Collaborators," Tanya Roscorla wrote, "Radical collaborators are those prepared to engage and motivate kids by teaching the way they want to learn."

So how can teachers get started creating a blended curriculum? There are a few simple guidelines to ease the transition—and many free services for those who want to go it alone in districts that don't offer online options. Selecting an online course platform or management system is key, and there are many to choose from. It's also possible to create your own online course environment on a website such as Google Sites by integrating apps, a blog, a Twitter feed, and a link to your classroom's online discussion forum such as the class Facebook group. But the option to build your own online course environment from scratch should come with a sticker that says "Assembly Required"—it takes time and a bit of know-how to put all the pieces together. A more user-friendly solution is to select from the numerous options that exist for creating and hosting a fully integrated online classroom where the teacher can get started just by signing up. Whatever you decide, the best part about getting started is that it's easy to choose free technologies that enable any faculty or individual teacher to host, manage, and teach a course that is collaborative and provides for content delivery, online assessment, and development of an online learning community.

For the most part, fully integrated online platforms share a set of similar attributes. Upon closer examination, you'll often find unique features that will work best for you. It's a good idea to check out several before deciding. Ask questions: How do the privacy settings work? Is the platform user-friendly? Can you subdivide students into user groups? How easily can media be integrated? Does the platform offer an interface to work with your school's electronic gradebook, Turnitin, or other district technologies? What are the options for online testing and grading? It's a good idea to make a list of what you might need before starting to shop around. Add to the list as you find modules of interest in various platforms. Successful online learning requires "interaction, not only between teacher and student, but there will also be learner–content, learner–learner, and learner–interface interactions" (Thurmond, 2004). The platform you select should provide structure for optimizing opportunities for interaction and feedback in all four categories.

## Online and Blended Learning Platforms
### *Schoology.com*

Schoology.com is a cloud-based system that requires no software or hardware to support implementation. Although it's able to be scaled for any size of district, an individual teacher can log on right away for a free account to get started. The first thing you'll notice when you enter Schoology is that it has a familiar social networking interface—much like Facebook's—so kids are immediately put at ease. Building a course on Schoology is intuitive and user-friendly. It's WYSIWYG (what you see is what you get), making it a breeze for teachers to create a course and for students to jump right in and start interacting with course content. Assignments, files, and links can be quickly uploaded and posted. Attendance, grades, private or class messaging, and a calendar help keep students apprised of their progress and up to date on assignments.

Schoology offers abundant opportunity for a key online skill—social writing. This represents a real-world hook for students. We often hear of kids who are already building a national or international following by publishing online. Although many students groan when they are asked to write in class, it seems that writing online has a social aspect that hooks them. They want to know that they're not writing in a vacuum—that what they write will matter and will elicit responses not only from the teacher but, potentially, from the world. They want to write about things that interest them. Often that means writing on Facebook about their weekend activities. But we can capture that passion for writing in blogs and forums. In class, students often struggle to fill a page! Yet, as we're finding so often, if you let them write it online in a social environment, it triggers a different response, yielding thoughtful, critical results.

Most online platforms offer notifications. If requested, Schoology will notify the teacher when—for example—something is posted to a blog or discussion forum. And students can be notified when the teacher adds a new post. It's a simple matter to adjust privacy settings as well, and they can be changed whenever necessary.

Tests and quizzes can be automatically scored and entered into the integrated gradebook. Question by question analysis is also available. Teachers are especially happy to be able to track the amount of time each student spends logged on.

Student accounts can be synced with Google Drive for access from within Schoology They can also submit docs through the assignment dropbox. Among other partnerships, Khan Academy videos can be added and embedded into your course.

## Moodle.org

Moodle.org is an online platform designed by educators to be completely open-source. It is global, multi-lingual, scalable, and customizable, using an ever-expanding selection of modules such as blogs, forums, messaging, online self-grading quizzes, and student-built glossaries. Moodle is free but is a bit more complicated—it has to be hosted either on a school server or by a hosting service. It's a good idea to sign up as a school or district rather than as an individual teacher, because you'll need savvy tech support and network administrators to back you and maintain the system.

Whether you're living in China or Russia or are teaching a language, the Moodle Language packs enable foreign character sets and displays all blocks, modules, and activities in the language of your choice. There are 86 languages to choose from, but if you find one missing, you can ask in the Moodle user forum for it to be developed.

A Moodle course is made up of up to 52 blocks in which you add content such as resources, media, and activities. Blocks can look as plain or tricked-out as you'd like. It's a blank slate, and you're the designer. Embed codes from a wide variety of applications will let you add video, audio, calendar, or other online files with ease. Get the kids to help!

Moodle enables numerous kinds of reporting. Teachers can enter and track grades, track student participation inside the course, and track activity progress. This information can be viewed by class or by individual student.

Moodle also has a vast global community where you and your students can meet up in discussion forums or one-to-one.

# Blackboard.com

If you've taken a college course in the past decade, you've probably used Blackboard. Blackboard is interested in "closing the gap between the way students live and the way students learn" and offers a broad range of platforms for K–12 and higher education. Although only offered as subscription-based in the past, Blackboard now offers CourseSites where teachers can create up to five course websites free.

# WizIQ.com

WizIQ.com is a unique multilingual platform that offers synchronous online learning through video conferencing. Teachers can share their desktops, divide students into groups that attend breakout sessions simultaneously, create virtual whiteboards, conduct live polls, and share recordings of live classes. Although there is a fee for organizations, individual teachers can sign up for a free account to "deliver real-time, interactive e-classes". WizIQ offers apps for iPad and Android and plug-ins for Blackboard Learn, Moodle, Sakai and even your own website.

# Edmodo.com

Edmodo's learning community is growing so rapidly that until recently, the company posted a live counter on its home page so you could watch the membership increasing by the second. To date, membership has topped 43 million. Edmodo, appropriate for all grade levels, offers social networking tools for safe exchanges among even the youngest students. Grade levels can be easily divided into subdomains adjusting permissions for each. Edmodo features teacher-created groups such as book clubs that students around the world can join. Group membership is by invitation only, for those with the enrollment key. Teachers can join subject-specific international communities such as World Language or Math teachers. Within each community you can post or respond to questions, find recommended resources, and network with teachers around the world. It's a great way to find classrooms for collaborative projects or to check in to see what's new on the discussion board. Your Edmodo classroom can be customized by adding apps, both free and for a small fee. Assignments can be posted as links on the course calendar, making it easy for students to find them. Both teachers and students can receive e-mails from Mr. Edmodo, acknowledging receipt of submitted work and other important messages. Quick polls are a fun way to gather opinions or answers to a simple question and let the group see immediate results. The Edmodo gradebook lets you individualize student and group progress. And kids of all ages enjoy receiving badges that can be designed and created by teachers as awards for various behaviors.

Each Edmodo course has a personal library where teachers can add online resources to increase functionality, organize in folders, store images, and connect with third-party sites such as Google Apps for Education. Add video and other media for a flipped classroom. Edmodo offers easy access with Android, iPad, and iPhone apps.

New to Edmodo is the Snapshot app that offers free quizzes and analytics based on the Common Core standards. To get started, just enter the grade level and subject and Snapshot will create a quiz for each students based on the standards you select. For some teachers, the hardest part about data is analyzing the results. Snapshot does that for you, yielding results that are ready to be integrated into your reports and evaluations.

Whichever platform you choose, you'll find a multitude of options to select from. Use a broad array of technology tools and applications to achieve smart learning and engaged students, and don't hesitate to change them up as new technologies emerge. Don't know how to use them? Let the kids figure it out and teach you! Be sure these apps are available in school, at home, and on mobile devices. Don't be afraid of social technologies such as Facebook, YouTube and Twitter. Students know how to use them and teachers can leverage their use to teach social netiquette and safe, ethical and responsible use. If those sites are blocked by your filter, don't be afraid to demonstrate to administration and network personnel the good things you can achieve by using them. But be aware of age restrictions for creating online accounts in some applications. Many of those offer educator accounts that will let you create user names for your classes. Clearly define course goals for students, keeping in mind that it's about giving students the opportunity to construct their own knowledge, to work independently and as teams, to generate and share real data online with classmates and the world, and to publish original writing, photography, music, and graphics. Teachers should become facile with 21st-century literacies and skills and determine how to teach and assess them.

The advantages of online learning are clear. The anytime anywhere component is key, allowing total flexibility and independence. Participants have the freedom to learn at their own speed and to construct their own meaning from the work. In classroom environments, students often hear only the voice of the instructor. Not so in an online environment, where rich interaction can enormously enhance the experience.

As the librarian, encourage teachers to set up an online component for their classes. And be sure to enroll in blended courses designed by teachers in your building. There will be teachers and students who doubt their ability to navigate the online learning environment, who express an unwillingness to learn new technologies, who panic over feeling lost and feel frustrated when they can't catch up. Some will find it difficult to deal with time management issues, and resent having to interact online. The librarian and tech teacher can encourage a slow and easy start that puts all participants at ease. The asynchronous nature of online work can be a difficult adjustment that, when achieved, will give students—and teachers—a set of new skills and literacies and a new confidence that will benefit them in future life.

## Teacher as Facilitator

Defining the role of the facilitator in an online or hybrid course is one that differs rather remarkably from the sage on the stage model. It's important to remember that as facilitator, you no longer hold the position of principle orator and no longer have to be solely responsible for teaching and for doling out feedback. In fact, responding to every blog post and answering every question removes the need for student–student interaction and puts the teacher right back into traditional classroom mode. In this model, the teacher as facilitator should work to keep the group organized, maintain the pace, supply the tools for communication, collaboration, and creativity and then stay out of the way, making your presence known when you want to redirect, remind, reiterate, or make kids aware of a misconception. Remember to let kids work to construct their own meaning, and be open to learning something from them!

The school library's online platform is a good place to publish schoolwide "guidelines for online learning." These could include recommendations for participating in online chats, peer review, and discussion forums. Remember to include guidelines for communicating with students in other cultures reminding them to be aware of that culture's beliefs, to avoid questions of religion and politics unless the teacher has carefully prepared the class to undertake these topics, and to avoid humor, because humor doesn't always translate well.

Today's online learning environment permits access to infinite resources on any topic. It makes no sense to limit learners to classroom and textbooks. Give kids access, step back, and watch what happens. It won't take long for teachers and students to be hooked on their new blended learning environment.

# Part IV
# Use Standards

Chapter 8

# The Core of Common Core
# State Standards

In his novel *A Tale of Two Cities*, Charles Dickens begins his story with one of the most famous lines in English literature: "It was the best of times, it was the worst of times; it was the age of wisdom, it was the age of foolishness . . . ." This is how Tony Wagner describes the current state of education in *The Global Achievement Gap* (Wagner, 2008, 46), but more to the point, is it describing the current state of school libraries? All librarians know the answer. It truly is the "best of times" because of the adoption of the Common Core State Standards (CCSSs). These progressive, rigorous, relevant, real-world learning standards define what a learner needs to know, understand, and be able to do to be successful in college or a career. They emphasize reading and text complexity, sustained research using technology, strategic use of multimedia for presentation, effective communication, coherent writing, problem solving, and reasoning abstractly and quantitatively, as well as higher-order thinking. They are really *Learning4Life* expectations and competencies. Yes, it truly is the best of times to be a librarian.

The school librarian's multidimensional role affords him or her the unique opportunity to integrate the CCSS high-level cognitive skills across disciplines and grade levels. The "first impression" of the Common Core State Standards is that they are a perfect partner for the American Association of School Librarians (AASL) standards. Yes, it is a love story in the making. One needs to look no further than the original "first impression" to understand this significance. Yes, Elizabeth and Darcy! And just like in *Pride and Prejudice*, there will be challenges, but the ending is happy.

These national standards provide librarians with the opportunity for relevancy and leadership. Just examine *A Matrix for School Librarians: Aligning Standards, Inquiry, Reading and Instruction* (Moreillon, 2013: 30–31). This matrix clearly delineates the relationship between these standards and learning through the lens of inquiry, reading comprehension, and applications.

According to the Metropolitan Life Insurance Company survey *American Teachers: Challenges for School Leadership* (2013), 62 percent of teachers believe the CCSSs are challenging or very challenging to meet. But these standards do not pose a challenge to school librarians. They are a natural fit—like hand to glove.

The CCSSs are truly a gold mine for school libraries. Yes, solid gold! These research-based "standards insist that instruction in reading, writing, speaking, listening, and language be a shared responsibility within the school" (CCSS, 2010). Looking at the English Language Arts (ELA) subheading, one can see why:

- Key Ideas and Details
- Craft and Structure
- Integration of Knowledge and Ideas
- Range of Reading and Level of Text Complexity
- Text Type and Purpose
- Production and Distribution
- Research to Build and Present Knowledge
- Range of Writing
- Comprehension and Collaboration
- Presentation of Knowledge and Ideas

In addition to the symbiotic relationship between the English language arts (ELA) standards and library science; the mathematic standards have a strong correlation:

- Counting and Cardinality
- Measurement and Data
- Ratios and Proportional Relationships
- Statistics and Probability

Not only do the CCSSs mandate a shared responsibility, but they also underscore research, media, and technology. "To be ready for college, workforce training, and life in a technological society, students need the ability to gather, comprehend, evaluate, synthesize, and report on information and ideas, to conduct original research in order to answer questions or solve problems, and to analyze and create a high volume and extensive range of print and non-print texts in media forms old and new . . . use technology and digital . . . employ technology thoughtfully to enhance their reading, writing, speaking, listening, and language use. They tailor their searches online to acquire useful information efficiently, and they integrate what they learn using technology with what they learn offline. They are familiar with the strengths and, limitations of various technological tools and mediums and can select and use those best suited to their communication goals" (CCSS, 2010).

The CCSSs' expectations for grades 11–12 in ELA and mathematics demonstrate this. For example, the ELA standard under *Research to Build and Present Knowledge* is for all students to "gather relevant information from multiple authoritative print and digital sources, using advanced searches effectively; assess the strengths and limitations of each source in terms of the task, purpose, and audience; integrate information into the text selectively to maintain the flow of ideas, avoiding plagiarism and overreliance on any one source and following a standard format for citation." The mathematics standards under *Interpreting Categorical and Quantitative Data* and *Making Inferences and Justifying Conclusions* expect all students be able to "distinguish between correlation and causation . . . evaluate reports based on data . . . and display numerical data in plots on a number line, including dot plots, histograms, and box plots" (CCSS, 2010). These learning standards inculcate AASL best practices.

The CCSSs align perfectly with 21st-century information, communication, and technologies (ICT) literacies. They require students to use "technology and digital media strategically and capably" (CCSS, 2012). This is what librarians do best. It is part of their DNA. Yes, it is the best of times for school librarians and library relevancy.

At the core of the CCSSs is an inquiry approach to performance-based learning. This conforms perfectly with school librarians' common belief that "reading is a window to the world . . . inquiry provides a framework for learning . . . ethical behavior in the use of information must be taught . . . technology skills are crucial for future employment needs . . . and equitable access is a key component for education" (AASL, *Standards for the 21st-century Learner in Action*).

The CCSSs are robust learning expectations that convey "big ideas"—enduring understandings relevant to problem solving, critical thinking, "habits of mind," and literacies outlined by the Partnership for 21st Century Skills.

The CCSSs foster self-reflection, self-assessment, and self-regulation to

- Read, comprehend, evaluate, and critique complex text
- Communicate competently
- Develop inquiry-based research skills
- Choose appropriate technology and Internet tools to produce and publish
- Produce coherent writing
- Evaluate, analyze, interpret, and predict
- Calculate and solve
- Engage collaboratively and independently
- Apply new knowledge to create, solve a problem, or answer a question (CCSS, 2010)

Yes, it is the best of times for school librarians, because these college and career readiness expectations are at the core of the AASL vision.

The CCSSs show a progression of academic growth over time—an escalation of knowledge complexity from one grade to the next. Because of the ever increasing steps in complexity, many have compared the CCSSs to a staircase. Viewed as a staircase, each pairing of tread and riser defines the depth and breadth of student learning. In essence, the CCSSs define the theoretical scope and sequence for high expectations for all learners. Each step indicates a level of complexity to be achieved. A learner has to "own" each level/step of complexity to move forward and up the staircase.

As coteachers, librarians know that it is not only important for students to reach the top level/step, but equally important for them to recognize what they need to know, understand, and be able to do to get there. The challenge for both teacher and learner is to view the staircase from the bottom looking up and from the top looking down. It is through this duality that true understanding is achieved. This duality corresponds with the backward design concept of Understanding by Design (UbD) developed by Wiggins and McTighe (2005). Backward planning articulates learning outcomes that stresses enduring understanding—"big ideas." UbD and the CCSSs are both perform-ance-based. Performance-based learning improves content acquisition, "habits of mind," and higher-order thinking skills "[u]sing project-based inquiry and embedding the new global skills calls for . . . focus on the cognitive processes of creating, generating, and producing, which is in alignment with 21st-century skills" (Spires et al., 2012).

School librarians play a pivotal role in providing performance-based learning oppor-tunities for students to effortlessly climb each level/stair successful through a tightly woven infrastructure that includes

- Rich reading culture
- Meaningful collaboration
- Intentional planning
- Engaging instruction
- Authentic applications (real-world with intrinsic meaning)
- Robust assessments
- Rigorous collection development both in print and e-content
- Equitable and unrestrained access

A key underpinning of the CCSSs is an understanding of "text complexity"—what it is, how to measure it, and how to integrate it across disciples and grade levels. Complex text includes not only print (literature and informational texts), but also data, as well as interactive media.

The Common Core State Standards define "text complexity by

1. Qualitative measures—levels of meaning, structure, language conventionality and clarity, and knowledge demands
2. Quantitative measures—word length or frequency, sentence length, and text cohe-sion (readability—Lexile score)
3. Reader and task considerations—motivation, knowledge, and experiences." (CCSS, 2010: 57)

Excellent school librarians teach and integrate complex text in numerous ways by integrating reading strategies, modeling and monitoring comprehension skills, leveling complex text, creating connections through social media, engaging in book talks, and providing writing opportunities: note taking, annotating, and summary.

Close reading of complex text demands that the reader focus and question. The reader must take time to "unpack" the text. Comprehension depends on this. School librarians integrate and model a variety of effective questioning, focusing, and reading strategies to aid students in comprehending complex texts:

- Keyword reading
- Inferring and predicting
- Levels of questions
- CRAAP (currency, relevance/reliability, authority, accuracy, and purpose) testing

- Note taking
- Interactive read-aloud
- Think–pair–share
- Comparison matrix
- Story maps
- Stance questions/response approach
- Graphic organizers

The segue from strategy or protocol to application is an easy one for librarians because they are experts in leveling text, questioning, and providing instruction in selection, evaluation, synthesis, summary, and creating. Take, for instance, the *keyword reading* strategy. Librarians think in terms of keywords, so they take to this strategy like fish to a sea. This strategy requires the selection of a short, but grade- and curriculum-appropriate, complex text. The CCSSs provide a list of text exemplars in CCSS *Appendix B* and provides sample annotated reading texts in *Appendix A*. Subtext, a digital reading app, also does this. The next step is prereading of the text by the librarian while jotting down a list of words that most signify what it is about—the keywords. This list of words is entered onto the presentation device before the class begins. During class, the text is read to the class. As each word on the list is read and stressed, it is exposed on the presentation tool. After the reading of the text, the students are asked to look at the list of words, reflect upon them, and write a summary of the reading using all the words. After the students finish writing their summary, they read their summary and look at the list words, again. Once they are finished, the students are asked to select the two or three words that best describe what their summary (the text) is about. One can see how this process easily fits in with information search process (ISP)—an advanced search strategy. Another approach is to have two students read their finished summary and keywords to each other. The librarian provides the students with a list of questions that promotes the discussion of the differences and similarities. Why did you include (person, place, thing, situation, event or description) in your summary? Why did you choose these keywords? This learning activity enhances other CCSS learning goals: higher-order thinking, speaking and listening skills, and coherent writing. It also includes Marzano's instructional strategies of summarizing and note taking, identifying similarities and differences, and cooperative learning (Marzano et al., 2001).

The *levels of questions* strategy is easily integrated into collaborative learning opportunities. Levels of questions corresponds with the Revised Bloom's Taxonomy: Can you remember or recall? Can you explain? Can you use this information (apply)? Can you compare and contrast (analyze)? Can you judge (evaluate)? Can you construct meaning (create)? These questions are fundamental to ISP and inquiry. Levels of questions also correspond with Wiggins and McTighe's (2005) six facets of understanding: can explain, can interpret, can apply, can empathize, have perspective, and have self-knowledge. Students read, question, infer, reflect, and draw conclusions using this strategy.

*Story maps* enhance literacy skills. They work especially well with current events articles. After conferring with the teacher about the project and selecting a story map graphic organizer, a librarian selects a few appropriate complex text articles. This allows for differentiation and difference in reading levels and provides choice. The librarian gives a very brief introduction to the purpose of the reading and the use and subheadings of the graphic organizer. Students are asked to read the text and take notes using the story map graphic organizer. This graphic organizer usually contains the following headings: characters/people/organizations (who), time (when), setting/place/event (where), problem/question (why), and ending/resolution/answer (how). This process goes hand in hand with analysis and evaluation skills as outlined by AASL. Students are then asked either to write about the story for retelling later or to retell the story directly to someone, depending on the purpose of the lesson, the student, and time constraints. If directly retelling the story, students are put into groups of two by the coteachers. Each student retells his or her article to the other student. This strategy incorporates numerous CCSS skills: reading, writing, speaking, and listening.

Classification is second nature to a librarian. A *comparison matrix* classifies or categorizes similarities and differences in complex text. Its purpose is to chart information for reflection. It is easy to design and demonstrate visually in person or virtually. The characteristics or details are listed down the left columns, and the categories are listed across the top rows—it's that simple. It cultivates metacognition and independent learning. This is a great strategy to use before, during, and after reading in all content areas and for all age levels.

The *CRAAP test* is an excellent reading and comprehension strategy. Although the CRAAP test was originally designed to evaluate websites, it can be easily modified to work with a variety of complex text formats. Basically, it is a predesigned list of questions that prompts the reader/researcher to evaluate a resource's validity and usefulness. These include questions on currency (timeliness or date), questions on relevance (scope/depth and breadth or audience), questions on the authority (author's background, expertise, or affiliation), and questions on accuracy (reliable and objective information), as well as GUM (grammar, usage mechanics) and questions on purpose (to inform, teach, persuade, or entertain). The CRAAP test, just like the CCSS, is really a lifelong and college readiness strategy. This evaluation process corresponds with the Association of College and Research Libraries' Information Literacy Standards: "The information literate student evaluates information and its sources critically and incorporates selected information into his or her knowledge base and value system" (ACRL, *Standard 3*, 2004). The beauty of the questions posed by the CRAAP test is that they are easy to integrate into almost any lesson, and there are a number of readily available CRAAP test worksheets and graphic organizers to choose from.

In addition, the *response approach* (global, interpretive, critical, personal), or *stance questions*, developed by Judith Langer (1994), helps students to become critical readers and make meaningful connections to what they read, thereby increasing comprehension. Students critically interpret the text through the lens of the following questions: What is the big picture or main idea of the text (thesis, subject, topic or theme)? How does the information in the text connect to various parts of the same text, to other texts (compare and contrast or similarities and differences)? What prior knowledge do I have about this topic (explicit and tacit knowledge, metacognitive and conceptual knowledge)?

*Graphic organizers* (e.g., graphs, charts, timelines, frames, clusters, diagrams, maps, webs) are great reading and comprehension tools. School librarians use a variety of graphic organizers, such as *KWL* (Know, Want to Know, and Learned), *KWL+*, *perspective chart, character analysis frame*, and *Venn diagrams*. Graphic organizers organize the thought process, clarify details, and help students make sense of the text. *A Guide to Graphic Organizers: Helping Students Organize and Process Content for Deeper Learning*, 2nd edition, by James A. Bellanca, is a great resource for all types of graphic organizers to integrate and assess for the CCSS. It is available on Google Books at http://books .google.com/books?id=gDIYahNUU44C.

Another resource is *Common Core for the Not-So-Common Learner, Grades 6–12: English Language Arts Strategies*, by Andrea M. Honigsfeld and Maria G. Dove. Again, this is also available on Google Books at http://books.google.com/books?id=lTwKAgAAQBAJ.

A *perspective chart* is a graphic organizer that can be used with a variety of genres. It helps a learner evaluate narrative and expository/factual text through the lens of characters or people, events or history, setting or geography, problem resolution, and societal issues. The reader is able to make predictions or interpret the text through a series of pointed questions—such as who is the main character? A *perspective chart* is a comprehension tool, as well as a writing tool. It certainly supports the CCSSs to "recall information from experiences or gather information from print and digital sources; take brief notes on sources and sort evidence into provided categories or use precise language and domain-specific vocabulary to inform about or explain the topic" (CCSS, 2010).

After doing a sci-fi book talk with a class, a librarian introduces the class to the use of perspective chart for literary analysis. Because most of the students have read the book or seen the movie, she selects *The Hunger Games* to demonstrate this graphic organizer. The librarian fills out the information for the protagonist on the chart before class. Using an interactive smartboard, she shows this to the class. She models how to use the chart. She uses Inspiration software compatible with smartboard technology to demonstrate how to fill out the second half of the chart. She asks student to name the antagonist(s) of the book. Not surprising, students suggest Cato, President Snow, and the Capitol government. Because the majority of the students suggest Cato, the librarian uses him to fill out the second half. Students are asked to visualize Cato and describe him. As you can imagine, the answers include ruthless, violent, strong, aggressive, brutal, devoid of conscience, and a warrior. The librarian asks the students to think about these descriptors and to select the three that best describe him. Students discuss their choices and come to consensus. Cato is a brutal warrior without a conscience. The librarian adds this to the chart. She continues this process until the *perspective chart* is finished. Students are asked to fill out a perspective chart on the science fiction book they are reading. These charts are collected and assessed by the coteachers.

In addition to informational text comprehension, literary text comprehension is equally important in the CCSSs. A *character analysis frame* is an excellent graphic organizer to document each character's thoughts, beliefs, or feelings, actions, personality, and physical traits, as well as his or her experiences, problems, and resolution (Varlas, 2012).

Numeracy is an important 21st-century skill. It is vital that a learner think, reason, and communication mathematically. The ability to infer and draw conclusion from statistics and numerical representations in tables, graphs, and charts enhances problem solving.

Librarians use a variety of entry points and formats to engage students in numeracy: picture books, ISP (information search process), data analysis, graphic organizers (charts, tables, graphs, diagrams), online drawing tools, and virtual manipulative.

School librarians use picture books to introduce mathematical concepts: counting, time, size, addition, subtraction, multiplication, division, fractions, measurement, patterns, and logic. Think *The Very Hungry Caterpillar*, *365 Penguins*, *Don't Let the Pigeon Drive the Bus*, *Chicka Chicka Boom Boom*, *Inch by Inch*, *Safari Park*, and *Math Curse*. The list is endless. Clearly, school librarians introduce the math CCSSs through literature.

In addition to the rudimentary math concepts and skills offered in picture books, school librarians integrate the math CCSSs through the informational search process (ISP) and data. ICT (librarians and technology integration teachers) instruction includes creating data, finding data, plotting data, comparing data, interpreting data, and predicting outcomes from data. It is evident that library instruction awash in numeracy from bar (candlestick) graphs to pie charts, from line graphs to point charts, from scatter graph to flow charts, and from line histogram to Venn diagrams. The use of Venn Diagrams to visualize the use of Boolean operators (And, Or, Not) are paramount to inquiry.

School librarians and technology integration teachers, as part of the information, communication, and technologies (ICT) literacies, expedite numeric comprehension through a variety of learning strategies, such as *understanding the problem*, *make a table*, *change the representative*, and *transactional reading strategies*. The goal of these strategies is to provide authentic learning opportunities that allow students to think strategically, as well as mathematically: reason and logic, estimation, comparison, quantitation, as well as classification. *Understand the problem* helps students recognize the interrelationship among numerical qualities through a series of pointed questions: What do you see? Do you see a pattern? What can you count? Do the numbers add up? What can you measure? What relationships do you see? What conclusions can you draw? This strategy helps student infer and visualize relationships.

Questioning is part of the 21st-century mobile landscape. Just ask Siri? Questioning has become part of our social context and excellent librarians harness it and inculcate as an instructional tool. This strategy forces a learner to become active participant and to question with intent or, as Tony Wagner (2008) so aptly puts it in *The Global Achievement Gap*, the "ability to be your own reference librarian." This strategy is part and parcel of a good reference interview, which is a natural component of a school librarian's toolkit. Modeling good questioning enhances students' critical thinking skills.

During an assured ICT/health experience at one school, the STEM (science, technology, engineering, and math) librarian integrates the *understanding the problem* questioning strategy. Each student inputs personal nutrition and physical fitness data onto ChooseMyPlate.gov, reviews and analyzes the various personal graphs and charts generated by this government website, identifies similarities and difference against national guidelines, and decides on a wellness concerns to do research on. The librarian models the process in-person and with online tutorials. The librarian uses her own personal data from ChooseMyPlate to demonstrate the process. She asks do you see the relationship between her data and national recommendations. What relationships do you see? Do my numbers measure up? What conclusions can you make or draw from my results/data? To aid in this process, the librarian designs a keyword document to guide students in seeing the relationship, therefore enabling themselves to ask themselves the questions.

The ICT team also integrates *change the representation* into this project. This is a "mind-on, hands-on" problem-solving strategy. Students design a variety of representations to demonstrate and communicate understanding of a problem. These representations can be verbal, graphical, or pictorial. This strategy inculcates multiple intelligences. Students apply communication skills, multimedia, and online graphical and drawing tools, as well as problem-solving competencies, to represent the six demission of wellness for the project. This strategy touches many of the CCSS ELA and math standards.

The technology integration teacher uses the *make a table* strategy to help students organize information and data. Students review personal data from ChooseMyPlate and are asked to think about the best way to organize this information graphically. The next questioned posed is how this table or graph should be plotted or set up (spreadsheet). Students are asked to input their relevant data or information onto the spreadsheet.

During the keyword and research question portion of this project, the librarian asks students what they see looking down and across their spreadsheet. What is the data telling you? Can you make a prediction about your wellness? This strategy helps student to visualize, to make real-world connections, and to think numerically. Some students need one-to-one assistance in this process. The librarian confers with students to ensure understanding and assists with application.

The STEM librarian develops a project-specific CCSS crosswalk to demonstrate project viability and the integration of these national with district and school expectations and enduring understanding. Yes, romance is in the air. It is a perfect match! And just as with Darcy and Elizabeth, the ending will be a happy one. It truly is the "best of times" to be a librarian, because the CCSSs make it so!

# Part V
# Instruct

# Chapter 9

# *Instruction*

"Libraries and librarians have been involves in the teaching process since the 19th century when Melvil Dewey introduced the concept of librarians as educators, stating that 'The time is when a library is a school and the librarian is in the highest sense a teacher.' Over time, library instruction has evolved to support changes in information formats, student differences, programmatic changes, and library services" (DeFranco and Bleiler, 2003: 11). There has been a sweeping migration from providing process and directional instruction in access and citing skills—how to find a book, locate an article online, note taking, and composing a bibliography—to a more complex cognitive instructional pedagogy for critical thinking and creativity: brainstorming, reflection, evaluation, analyzing, decision-making, problem-solving, imagining, and synthesizing. This is definitely a sea change—a "full fathom five." It is as multifaceted and complex as Shakespeare's *The Tempest*, Jackson Pollack's painting *Full Fathom Five*, Igor Stravinsky's *Three Songs from William Shakespeare*, and Sylvia Path's poem *Full Fathom Five*. 21st-century teaching is like excellent fine art: It incites a positive reaction and personal interaction.

In this paradigm shift librarians are facilitators/guides and not the directors of the learning process. They create inquiry-based blended pathways to differentiate and to guide students in the discovery of how to think, how to learn, and how to be life-long learners. It is a "hands-on/mind-on" approach. Or, as Toffler so succinctly put it, to learn, relearn, and unlearn.

Twenty-first-century learning is collaborative, customized, contextual, and connected. It occurs through questioning, responding, doing, and creating to fulfill a personal, academic, and social need.

Learning today is really about transliteration—in other words, about having the ability to "process information quickly, determine relevancy of information, process information in parallel, access information through imagery, network, communicate, and play" (Klopfer et al., 2009). This is why librarians adopt an integrated, blended/hybrid learning environment to facilitate the "gradual release of responsibility" for students to learn how to learn.

Self-knowledge, task knowledge, and strategic knowledge are paramount to becoming metacognitive. The information search process is a perfect instructional vehicle for metareasoning and cognitive processing. Jean Donham, in *Creating Personal Learning through Self-assessment*, explains, "Self-assessment is a habit of mind that engages one in metacognition and reflection. Such reflective behavior calls for intentionally reviewing our own performance based on criteria that we have internalized. We can think of it as metacognition with an evaluative bent. When we are metacognitive, we are aware of what we know and what we do not know. We are able to plan a strategy for producing what information is needed, to be aware of our own strategies as we problem-solve, and to reflect and evaluate our own productiveness" (Donham, 2010).

By thinking about what they are doing, students learn how to be metacognitive. It is a higher-order executive function that involves

- Self- awareness
- Analysis
- Evaluation
- Problem solving
- Decision making
- Revision
- Transference

Metacognition helps learners control and regulate learning through self-knowledge, task knowledge, and procedural knowledge. Excellent school librarians and technology integration teachers leverage social media, online resources (web and deep web or invisible web), digital tutorials, simulations, and interactive media to maximize metacognition. They intentional designed coherent, rigorous standards-based content to facilitate metacognition through

- Information search process
- Advanced graphic organizers
- Summarizing
- Critical reflection
- Blogging
- Vlogging
- Posting
- Journaling
- Debate
- Mind maps
- Checklists
- Content curation
- Gaming
- Book chats—in person and virtually

Many libraries adopt a 24/7 e-learning platform such as Moodle, Blackboard, Blogger, or social media, to deliver content, instruction, and give each student the opportunity for self-regulate learning. Electronically supported asynchronous learning activities give students the opportunity to work independently, as well as control task and strategy. Students gain executive management processes skills and strategic knowledge. This environment sets the stage for future "full immersion" learning or technology as an extension of mind.

A blended learning environment allows students to construct meaning through project-based inquiry. This environment fuels student engagement, self-management, and creativity because it is student-centered, metacognitive, and responsive. It integrates emerging technologies to differentiate "content, process, and product" by complexity, interest, and learning modality/styles. "Scientific research supports teaching students' comprehension strategies using direct, explicit, and systematic instruction. . . . When students experience explicit instruction on a specific skill, teacher modeling, guided practice, and independent practice, they are much more likely to become proficient at the skill being taught" (U.S. Department of Education, *What Content-Area Teachers Should Know About Adolescent Literacy*: 7).

e-learning platforms free librarians to respond and intervene when necessary. They are an excellent tool for progress monitoring and the application of interventions (RTI). "Todd argues the real role of teacher-librarian is one of instructional intervention that moves students beyond information seeking and helps them to 'transform found information into personal knowledge'" (Hay and Foley, 2009: 18).

School librarians engage students during the information search process (ISP) in high-order-thinking skills (HOTS): remembering, understanding, applying, analyzing, evaluating, and creating. The goal is for each student to achieve the highest level of thinking—creativity: designing, constructing, planning, producing, inventing, devising, composing, formulating, developing, making, publishing, programming, videocasting, filming, blogging, animating, remixing, combining, and customizing, as well as synthesizing. Students achieve creativity by finding, verifying, evaluating, analyzing, and synthesizing or combining information for authentic learning tasks completion.

Guilford (1973) in *Characteristics of Creativity*, analyzes the steps of the creative process: "preparation (skills, techniques and information), concentrated effort (finding a solution or suitable form), withdrawal from the problem, insight or illumination, and verification, evaluation and elaboration."

In *The Creativity Crisis*, Po Bronson and Ashley Merryman (2010) state, "Creativity isn't about freedom from concrete facts. Rather, fact-finding and deep research is vital stages in the creative process . . . ." Innovative school librarians use emerging technologies to leverage all aspect of creativity from the traditional artistic level where students create nonlinguistic representations using online drawing tools to illustrate ideas, concepts, or points of view to a more theoretical approach to creativity developed by Torrance (1964) (fluency, flexibility, originality, and elaboration) whereby students reflect, evaluate, synthesize, organize, and create or produce based on authentic research and tasks completion.

Free-range school libraries use social media, such as Facebook and Twitter, during the inquiry process to guide discussion, for questions and answers, for peer-to-peer evaluation and collaboration, assessment, and to help students stay on task and redirect. It is used as a virtual learning tool to enhance research on current events, scaffold learning, and provide direction. Social media allows for an organic "in-the-moment" approach to learning. It transfers the responsibility for learning to the student. It is student-centered and driven.

For example one school librarian uses a live Twitter feed for current events: elections, social unrest, and natural disasters. She has the students analyze and evaluate the sources of the tweets: news sources, blog, or reference source.

The formulation of research question(s) and thesis statements is essential to ISP, metacognition, and creativity. Online citation generators such as NoodlBib and EasyBib help prompt students to think about and create them.

A "mind map" is a great brainstorming strategy for keywords understanding. A mind map is a graphic representation, a nonlinear visualization of an idea, concept, or information. Librarians also incorporate word/tag clouds for summarizing, analyzing text, art, prioritizing, compare and contrast, reading, writing and research prompts, posters, and reflection.

A constructive or "discovery" approach to research prepares students to navigate and interpret data, information, and the multidimensional realities (real or augmented) of digital content. This methodology requires students to think deeply and to question often to construct new meaning and to resolve complex issues. Students become self-directed, metacognitive learners who develop "habits of mind" through self-discovery.

At one school, during ISP, students craft advanced search strategy using self-selected keywords, Boolean operators, truncation or wild cards, and delimiters to find information pertinent for their own needs. They evaluate and synthesize information according to self-set parameters and CRAAP test (currency, relevance, authority, accuracy, and purpose). They are asked to reflect on their learning.

Reflection is an important aspect of ISP. Self-awareness is accomplished only through deep reflection. As a collaborating teacher, a school librarian sets up mechanisms (an online self-reflection journal, forum, discussion board, blogs, wikis, apps, or nonlinguistic representations using drawing tools) to record thoughts, monitor progress, communicate and scaffold instruction. Using a blended learning environment allows students opportunity to reflect upon learning anytime and anywhere. It also gives them the ability to reach out and the librarian and teacher the ability to reach in.

"A Habit of Mind is a pattern of intellectual behaviors that leads to productive actions: persisting, thinking and communicating with clarity and precision, managing impulsivity, gathering data through all senses, listening with understanding and empathy, creating, imagining and innovation, thinking flexibly, responding with wonderment and awe, thinking about thinking (Metacognition), taking responsible risks, striving for accuracy, finding humor, questioning and posing problems, thinking interdependently, applying past knowledge to new situations, and remaining open to continuous learning" (Costa, 2008). Outstanding teachers incorporate these sixteen "thinking dispositions" into instructional strategies and unit plans to foster metacognition and creativity. These dispositions are easily found in AASL standards.

It is through respectful collaboration that excellent librarians plan for benchmark assessments, assured experiences, and capstone projects. Planning is intentional, targeted, and responsive. Before designing a lesson, unit, or project the team reflects upon the learning activity. They ask several questions. What do we want our students to know, understand, and be able to do or demonstrate? What 21st-century literacy are we targeting? What is the most current research on the topic? What are the best inform-ational resources to accomplish desired learning outcomes? What technologies will facilitate learning? What strategies or protocols do we want to incorporate? How do we differentiate? How do we assess? How do we know students have achieved under-standing or acquired skills? How do we analyze the evidence? How do we know we are effective? What are our expectations?

Tony Wagner et al., in *Change Leadership: A Practical Guide to Transforming Our Schools*, states, "The New 3R's are rigor, relevance and respectful relationships. . . . Rigor implies holding students responsible for meeting objective, qualitative standards and measuring progress regularly" (Wagner et al., 2006: 38–49).

To ensure the 3Rs, many librarians use UbD (Understanding by Design) to anchor the ISP (information search process) by identifying six facets of understanding: explain, interpret, apply, perspective, empathize, and self-knowledge. The six facets of under-standing parallel the CCSSs, the AASL's *Standards for 21st-century Learner in Action*, and the Partnership for 21st Century Skills (P21).

Excellent school librarians actively construct a learning environment that is safe, respectful, responsive, and 24/7 to promote cognitive, social, and emotional learning. It is an environment that promotes collaborative inquiry, creativity, and productiv-ity. As Carol Ann Tomlinson (2003) states in *Fulfilling the Promise of the Differentiated Classroom*, the "Learning environment is the 'weather' that affects virtually everything that transpires." Intuitive librarians know that how students view them or how welcom-ing and innovative the library environment is effects instruction and student learning. It comes down to interpersonal relationships. Exceptional educators know "their" stu-dents. They are "visible" in their school and at extracurricular activities. Think of it this way: Have you ever seem a picture of a 1960s go-go dancer? Can you visualize it? Yes, unfortunately, she is in a cage, but every eye is upon her, her every move acknowledged. Librarians are like that go-go dancer; they are constantly being judged. So, to shake things up, they know that they have to give a welcoming performance each and every time and invite others to join them on stage.

As Doug Lemov explains in *Teach Like a Champion*, "It's not enough to just stand there; you've got to work the room. If you are teaching actively, make frequent verbal and non-verbal interventions as you circulate. . . . Questioning is data gathering. Check for Understanding requires you to think of the answers to your questions as data" (Lemov, 2010: 86). Ongoing assessment informs a librarian's decision making for inter-vention. Librarians also use mobile devices, such as an iPad, to record observations and task completion, such as homework.

Librarians work the room through engaging, collaborative instruction and assured experience. For example, at one school the librarian coteaches a unit—"Alcohol Debate." The students are placed into groups of three (pro and con) to debate the following issues: The drinking age should be lowered to 18. Alcohol is comparable in destructiveness to other drugs. The legal consumption rate should be .02 in Connecti-cut. Alcohol advertising should be allowed. This unit integrates the CCSS writing, listening, and speaking standards. The librarian scaffolds instruction through a course platform, Moodle.

Per the requirement of the content teachers, students need to research and find five resources (three articles from databases, one book, and one website) that support their position for the debate. They must incorporate this research in their opening statements, in their conclusions, in the questions they ask the opposing side, and in a bibliography. Students are also required by their teachers to evaluate the website resource using a website evaluation worksheet or the library's online CRAAP test (currency, relevance, authority, accuracy, purpose) and submit it. Students are given a debate rubric and a research rubric at the beginning of the project

The librarian gives a brief introduction on advanced search strategies on *Opposing Viewpoints* and *e-Library Science* (with Lexile scores and grade level). She models the CRAAP test using a government website, www.drugabuse.gov, and www.chooserespons ibility.org/legal_age_21, and shows students where it is located on the library's homepage.

The librarian designs a variety of learning pathways (tutorials) to empower students toward independence and self-reliance. Students become "active learners" through interactive learning, such as the online CRAAP test and the use of EasyBib to take notes and generate a bibliography.

Communication is essential to reducing anxiety, building trust, clarifying expectations, and providing a "safety net" for struggling learners. Moodle allows students to contact a librarian 24/7 through the forum. Students can also contact a librarian through e-mail, Facebook, Twitter, school phone, cell phone, and in-person.

Students select, evaluate, and synthesize appropriate resources to defend their position for the debate. They apply the CRAAP test to check for currency, relevance, authority, accuracy, and purpose for their selected website. The librarian conferences with students on how to select appropriate keywords and execute an advance search. During this project, students learn to "use interaction with and feedback from teachers, librarians, and peers to guide own inquiry process . . . and to collaborate with others to broaden and deepen understanding" (AASL, *Standards for the 21st-Century Learner in Action*, 2009).

Students read critically, taking notes on EasyBib or the Cornell note-taking template. Team members get together during class time to discuss what they found. The team collaboratively writes an opening and closing statement that includes information from their resources and crafts questions to ask the opposing team. All documentation—opening statement, questions, closing statement, bibliographies, attached copies of their resources—is given to the teacher for assessment. The librarian assesses students on the bibliography and using the CRAAP test.

Students debate the topic. Each student who is not debating is given a scoring sheet to do a peer-to-peer evaluation and assessment of the debate. They score the team on presentation skills, opening and closing statements, resources sited and who won the debate. The librarian attends the debate and also assesses each team using the scoring sheet. These sheets are handed in for the teacher to tally the results.

Students fill out an anonymous survey (questionnaire) on K–12 Insight (Zarca) on instructional quality and effectiveness. The most recent survey indicated that the majority of students thought that this project was engaging and improved their understanding of the ISP, speaking and listening skills, and health-related issues concerning alcohol.

Such a collaborative project "ensures that each step in the teaching and learning process was designed to guide students toward high level of competence with the knowledge, understanding, and skills" (Tomlinson, 2003: 61) to obtain the 21st-century literacies to compete in global environment.

As Helen Keller once said, "Alone, we can do so little; together, we can do so much." Learning in the coming decades of the 21st century is collaborative. School librarians play a crucial role in this collaboration through innovation, integration of engaging emerging technologies, and implementation of sound instructional practices.

# Chapter 10

# *Assessment*

Accountability, evidence-based practice, and scientifically based research indubitably affect learning outcomes and are essential to the success of a school library program. Learning outcomes should be clearly articulated, achievable, and assessable.

Ross J. Todd (2002), in *School Librarian as Teachers: Learning Outcomes and Evidence-Based Practices* states, "Accountability . . . is a commitment to growth through examining progress and practice. It brings alignment, innovation, collaboration, introspection, and effectiveness. Sustainable development through accountability requires a move from rhetoric to evidence, from 'tell me' framework to a 'show me' framework and from a process framework to an outcomes framework."

Evidence-based practice is crucial to a 21st-century library program. This is a paradigm shift from evidence about services (20th century) to evidence of learning (21st century).

Assessments: formative (diagnostic) and summative (performance) provide data for differentiation, evidence of instructional effectiveness (accountability), and a baseline for decision making (instructional planning).

Thomas A. Angelo (1999) said it best in *Doing Assessment as If Learning Matters Most*: "[T]eachers must set and maintain realistically high, personally meaningful expectations and goals. . . . [W]e need research-based guidelines for effective assessment practice that will increase the odds of achieving more productive instruction and more effective learning."

The alignment of curriculum to standards ensures rigor, relevance, and accountability-realization of goals. Standards provide a guideline for meaningful expectations for learning.

The American Association of School Librarians crosswalk to the Common Core State Standards (CCSSs) delineates 21st-century skills and dispositions for formative and summative assessments (www.ala.org/aasl/standards-guidelines/crosswalk). It is a blueprint for the articulation, assessment, and achievement of planned learning outcomes.

The alignment of the appropriate quantitative (pretest, posttest, rubrics, surveys, questionnaires, checklists, search results, student response system results, and bibliographies) and qualitative (observations, reflection, journaling, reading, non-linguistic representations, and verbatim surveys) assessments to national standards ensures the acquisition of 21st-century skills.

A collaborative and reflective school environment: culture, climate, and conditions require the application of Tyler's *Rationale* (1949) to practice: What are the appropriate learning objectives we are trying to achieve? What content or learning experiences will we use to achieve them? How will we organize the content or learning experiences to achieve them? How will we evaluate the effectiveness of the learning experience? An explanation is online in *Educational Evaluation: Classic Works of Ralph W. Tyler* (Tyler et al., 1989).

Collaboratively librarians examine what students know, understand, and are able to do as a result of purposefully planned learning activities. They integrate a multidimensional approach for "assessment of learning" (summative) and "assessment for learning" (formative) to measure 21st-century literacies as described by *Partnership for 21st Century Skills* (www.p21.org/our-work/p21-framework). (Please see chart on page 101.)

Susan Brookhart (2010), in *How to Assess Higher-Order Thinking Skills in Your Classroom* writes, "Your instruction and assessment should match your intended learning target in both content (what the students learn) and cognitive complexity (what the student is able to do with the learning)."

As part of professional learning communities (PLCs), school librarians systematically review assessment data with colleagues to enhance instruction, assess mastery, and check for teaching effectiveness. They understand that assessment is a "participatory and interactive process" (Indiana University School of Medicine, 2007).

To this end, they use Understanding by Design (UbD), the "backward design" framework developed by Grant Wiggins and Jay McTighe (2005). This outcomes approach to curriculum planning clearly helps to articulate targeted learning goals. "The backward planning achieved in determining the enduring understandings of learning is invaluable in developing the units of study. The UbD tools also help us plan the assessments . . ." (Fisher and Frey, 2008: 114).

Ongoing assessment empowers students to take control of their own learning, self-correct through "timely and informative feedback," and apply new knowledge. In *Inside the Black Box: Raising Standards through Classroom Assessment*, authors Paul Black and Dylan Wiliam (1998) state, "When anyone is trying to learn, feedback about the effort has three elements: recognition of the desired goal, evidence about present position, and some understanding of a way to close the gap between the two. All three must be understood to some degree by anyone before he or she can take action to improve learning."

Timely, personal, and constructive feedback can be given through conferencing, on-the-spot interaction, documents evaluation, and digital technologies. This gives librarians the ability to timely share assessment data with students for revision of performance-based task(s).

For example, during the performance-based project, students are personally responsible for designing a website and uploading evidence of their learning to it: self-reflections, a wellness plan, spreadsheet, a nonlinguistic representation, food labels, an annotated bibliography, and goals. They shared their websites with their teacher, librarian, and technology integration teacher for assessment.

The librarian routinely reviews the uploaded annotated biography page on students' websites to give timely feedback to a student so that he or she can make revisions. For example, the student below did not understand the elements of an annotation and failed to add one of the citations. The librarian added a comment about this. Because of this timely feedback, the student contacted the librarian, who was able to provide one-to-one instruction on the elements of annotation.

> You need to add bibliographic information for the United States Department of Agriculture's website (www.choosemyplate.gov). Also, please re-read "What is an annotated bibliography?" or see a librarian.

This constructive feedback allowed this student to take charge of his own learning and moves him toward independence.

"Conferring is an example of an independent learning task in which individual students meet the teacher or another adult to discuss progress, ask questions, obtain feedback, and plan next steps for independent assignments" (Fisher and Frey, 2008: 103). Conferring allows a librarian to differentiate "content, process, and product" (Tomlinson, 1999). During this same assured experience, a librarian meets with a student who has an individual educational plan (IEP). He is unable to write an annotation. This librarian uses direct questioning to assess understanding.

Three types of assessment are important to improve learning outcomes: self, peer, and teacher. Of the three, the most important is self-assessment. Learning how to self-assess is a vital 21st-century skill. Reflection is a catalyst for self-assessment. John Dewey wrote, "We do not learn from experience . . . we learn from reflecting on experience." Students reflect on learning through research, journaling, threaded discussions, surveys, CRAAP (currency, relevance, authority, accuracy, and purpose) testing, blogging, art, role-playing, and videography-vlogging.

Susan M. Brookhart (2010), in *How to Assess Higher-Order Thinking Skills in Your Classroom*, asserts that "[s]tudents self-assessment requires high-order thinking. . . . They need to understand various aspects of their own work (analysis), evaluate these aspects against criteria (evaluation), and figure out what the next step should be (creating a plan). . . . Self-assessment skills, like any academic skills, should be taught."

Coteachers teach self-evaluation skills through performance-based assessment. For example, architecture students are asked to design a building for personal use. They are given free range in designing the building but need to use research- based evidence to support their design. They are asked to reflect upon and answer the essential question: What makes a good building?

First, students need to think about what makes a good building from their own point of view, then architecturally. It is through this self-reflection aspect of the project that creativity is stimulated. Students need to reflect on what they already know and to assess what they need to know to design the building. The librarian models reflection using *I wonder*, a questioning strategy. I wonder what Louis Sullivan meant by "form follows function"? I think he must have meant such-and-such, but to prove this, I will have to do research. I wonder whether there is a Louis Sullivan homepage on the Internet."

A rubric is a great reflection and self-assessment tool. It provides students with criteria for mastery, clarifies the understanding of high-quality work, and provides students with means for self-assessment. The librarian suggests using a creativity rubric from *How to Create and Use Rubrics for Formative Assessment and Grading*, by Susan Brookhart, for this project.

"Authentic assessments, e.g., rubrics, journals, and portfolios provide ongoing feedback or evidence, to information users through self and peer-to-peer evaluation . . . as well as teacher-learner interactions" (Gordon, "Raising Active Voices in School Libraries": 36). Another key element of assessment is peer-to-peer evaluation. It increase student engagement and responsibility for learning and fosters social interaction and collaboration. For example, at one school during an assured experience, a student is asked to assess the resource(s) selection of a classmate. Does the resource reflect the student's keywords and answer his or her research question? Is this the best possible resource on this topic? Students are given an evaluation tool (rubric) to evaluate selection. They are also provided with guiding questions to assess the quality of the selection for CRAAP. This student-centered learning activity allows a student to formulate a judgment of reliability, validity, and excellence based on a given parameters.

A librarian suggests using the *New York Times*, *The Learning Network*, and *Mulling on Molly: Investigating the Dangers of a Club Drug*, by Jennifer Cutraro and Katherine Schulten, to integrate reading comprehension strategies, the CCSSs, and Subtext (www.subtext.com), a free collaborative reading APP/website. Subtext allows students to simultaneously read the same book, article, or webpage. Students are able to analyze text together, comment on the reading, highlight, discuss, look up the definition of a word, question, annotate, as well as find and layer web (Google) content as evidence of learning. Subtext is a powerful assessment and feedback tool. It allows for real-time monitoring of reading comprehension, timely and constructive feedback, and evaluation of evidence of learning embedded by a student.

e-Assessment provides data for instructional modification. For example, a librarian introduces the students to the CRAAP test. Students are then asked to find, select,

| 2.1. Does the information (content) relate to your topic or answer your question? | 2.2. Is the information (content) suitable for the intended audience? | 2.3. Is the information presented at an appropriate level? | 2.4. Would this information be an appropriate source for a research paper? | Point subtotal for "Relevance" |
|---|---|---|---|---|
| | 3 | 3 | 3 | 9 |
| 4 | 4 | 5 | 5 | 18 |
| 4 | 2 | 4 | 5 | 15 |
| 5 | 5 | 5 | 5 | 20 |
| 5 | 5 | 5 | 4 | 19 |
| 4 | 5 | 5 | 4 | 18 |
| 5 | 5 | 5 | 5 | 20 |
| 3 | 3 | 5 | 2 | 13 |
| 5 | 5 | 5 | 4 | 19 |

and evaluate a resource from the Internet and one from a database. They are asked to compare and contrast the information and to complete an online CRAAP test for one Internet resource. The librarian reviews the submitted CRAAP tests. (Please see chart on page 83.) She finds that students on average gave 12.5 points out of a possible 15 points for currency, 17.5 out of a possible 20 for relevance, 14 out of possible 20 points for authority, 21 out of a possible 25 points for accuracy, and 17 out of 20 points for purpose. The librarian chooses a random sample of selected websites to personally evaluate and compare her evaluations to student's evaluation of these websites.

This librarian realizes that future direct and self-directed instruction needs to be done on the topic because students were still judging websites by appearance and not content.

To scaffold learning, the librarian finds a questionable website for the students to review. During the next class meeting, the librarian briefly introduces CRAAP testing again. She then asks the students to go onto the Moodle and click on the website (questionable) provided on the research topic, examine the site, and fill out a hard copy of the CRAAP test. The librarian rated this website a 39 out of a possible 100. After they are finished, students are asked to turn to the student next to them and defend their rating for each of the 5 components. The librarian and teacher listen to and observe the interaction. The librarian then asks for a show of hands of the students who had rated the website within each range (90–100 points, 80–89 points, etc.). On average, the students rated the website in the 80–89 percent range. The librarian then asks the students to watch a tutorial of her rating the website (with evidence from the website why it was rated so low). Students are asked to reflect on it. The librarian asks students to share new insights on the process.

At the end of the project, the librarian reviews the choice of Internet resources included on the students' bibliographies. The librarian assesses and grades the annotated bibliographies. There is a vast improvement on Internet selection. More than 77 percent of students choose excellent Internet resources, and 18 percent choose very good to good resources. The librarian presents her findings to the PLC online (shared Google Doc) and during a debrief meeting. (See "My Personal Wellness" debrief chart on the following page.)

"Data and evidence are key educational tools as school librarians work to educate stakeholders about school's library's role in preparing students to live and learn in the 21st century" (AASL, "School Library Program Health and Wellness Toolkit: Advocacy").

Another example of the effective use of assessment data is tracking students' performance from a ninth-grade assured experience with the tenth-grade statewide Connecticut Academic Performance Test (CAPT). During this portion of the state-wide test, students are asked to read and respond to three nonfiction texts. By analyzing the reading assessment data from the ninth assured experience and comparing it to the performance on tenth-grade statewide test, the librarian revises instructional strategies and learning activities to further inculcate needed skills required to improve reading comprehension. Make no mistake—this was not teaching for the test, because this portion of the reading test aligned perfectly with the ISP component of the project. Because of this in-depth analysis of student reading assessment data, each year the students improve on the research, with reading and annotated bibliographies showing a corresponding improvement on the states test.

## My Personal Wellness (MPW) Debrief June 2013

| What Went Well | What Could Have Gone Better |
|---|---|
| • Alignment of MPW to NCHS Core Values, Beliefs and Expectations<br><br>• Use of the new school wide rubric **Healthy Living / Choices** (intellectual, productivity, physical, ethical and personal goal setting) by library for assessment<br>https://sites.google.com/a/ncps-k12.org/nchsneasc13/home/rubrics/healthy-living<br><br>• Use of school-wide research rubric—Research<br><br>• Use of annotated bibliography rubric<br><br>• Connection to Common Core State Standards (CCSS)<br>http://www.sde.ct.gov/sde/cwp/view.asp?a=2618&q=322592<br><br>• Students input of food and physical activity into ChooseMyPlate.<br><br>• Keyword and Research Question document to analyze results from ChooseMyPlate—real world connection to health concern (nutrition or physical fitness)<br><br>• Use of keywords and research question to do research on health concern<br><br>• Researching ProQuest database using advanced searching techniques—Boolean operators<br><br>• Self & Peer-to-Peer evaluation<br><br>• 95% very good or above on CRAAP | • FITT data<br><br>• ChooseMyPlate—where to locate login<br><br>• How to expand a screen (bar and X)<br><br>• Snippets/Screenshots—did not capture top of Daily Food Groups-cups & oz.<br><br>• Having all snippets/screenshots in health folder.<br><br>• Submitting, saving as PDF, etc. for Keyword & Research Question<br><br>• It would be useful to have one session to introduce tech tips for the entire project.<br><br>• Screenshots from lessons 16-17: 1. Nutrients report: 3 screenshots for readability (not one single snip) 2. Check screenshots for each kid as exit slip 3. Upload screenshots to webpages and not to Google drive<br><br>• *and* on EasyBib for italicizing title of newspaper article and database<br><br>• Sharing page to annotated bibliography. |

In-depth analysis of practice and data can lead to a greater focus on a single area for improvement or action research. It is a systematic approach to test theories, techniques, and best practices by selecting an area of focus.

This librarian uses "action research" to test and assess her theory on the use of interactive checklists to improve self-monitoring skills and task completion. Prior to this, the librarian would monitor task completion through Moodle Reports. The student would be contacted for support. As you can see from this graphic, Moodle analytics are an important assessment tool. (Please see chart at the top of page 86.)

To encourage self-direction and management, the librarian integrates a lesson checklist to ensure task completion. At the end of each class session, the student checks off completion information and submits the information through the Moodle. These interactive checklists give students the opportunity to self-assess, redirect, and keep on task.

| Task 2 | Health teacher | Health section # | Task 1 | Task 2 | Task 4 | Task 5 |
|---|---|---|---|---|---|---|
| Watch "Citing" Power Point at the bottom of the page all the way through | | 1 | Complete the annotation activity document, save it to your U drive, and print it. You will hand this in today | Write your ProQuest Platinum newspaper article annotation | Register for a NoodleBib account | Create project in NoodleBib |
| Watch "Citing" Power Point at the bottom of the page all the way through | | 1 | | | Register for a NoodleBib account | Create project in NoodleBib |
| Watch "Citing" Power Point at the bottom of the page all the way through | | 1 | Complete the annotation activity document, save it to your U drive, and print it. You will hand this in today | Write your ProQuest Platinum newspaper article annotation | Register for a NoodleBib account | Create project in NoodleBib |

Teacher's observations, comments, and e-mails provide librarians with invaluable assessment information on their own practice. For example one teacher wrote the following:

I'm reading the final journal entries for the calculus projects—here's a great comment: "As with any project that involves research, I found the resources that the library provides, especially with databases, extremely helpful in finding the information that we needed to understand what we were meant to teach. This probably was a little too helpful at times, as it would take us so little effort to find what we needed and therefore got all the research done pretty quickly."

Doug Lemov (2010), in *Teach Like a Champion*, states, "In school, the medium is the message: to succeed, students must take their knowledge and express it in a variety of clear and effective formats to fit the demands of the situation and of society. . . . It's not just what students say that matters but how they communicate it. To succeed, students must take their knowledge and express it in the language of opportunity." The above student used an online journal to reflect on learning.

At one high school, librarians use pretests and posttests on library information skills to inform decisions. The librarian reviews the pretest results. Some questions on the pretest provide the librarian with valuable insight on a student's misconceptions.

For example, when students are asked whether they can distinguish the difference between a summary and annotation, 10 percent answer no. But when the librarian compares the students self-assessment with questions on the pretest related to elements of an evaluative annotation as defined by Wesleyan University Library (http://libguides.wesleyan.edu/annotbib) such as accuracy (comparison), authority (author) and currency, she notes that 25 percent do not understand the concept of accuracy, only 61 percent answered the question on authority correctly, and 53 percent answered the question on currency correctly. Because of this analysis of the pretest responses, this librarian identifies individual student in the class who did not get these questions correct so that she can confer with them. She also tracks activities on the Moodle to make sure they have viewed tutorials and completed all tasks on annotations.

**Summary v. Annotation (pre):**

| Can you distinguish the difference between a summary and an annotation? | Yes | (1.00) | 218/335 | (65%) 65% |
|---|---|---|---|---|
| | No | (0.00) | 33/335 | (10%) |
| | Not sure | (0.00) | 78/335 | (23%) |

| | | | | | | | |
|---|---|---|---|---|---|---|---|
| **Accuracy (pre):** How can you tell if a resource is accurate? | I can't if I don't know anything about the subject | (0.00) | 36/336 | (11%) 73% | 0.445 | 0.71 | .036 |
| | You can usually infer this from the resource title | (0.00) | 18/336 | (5%) | | | |
| | The subject and keywords assigned to this resource can help determine accuracy | (0.00) | 29/336 | (9%) | | | |
| | Detail, outside sources, experts, statistics, and visual aides can all help to measure accuracy | (1.00) | 245/336 | (73%) | | | |
| **Authority (pre):** How can you evaluate the authority of a resource? | From the title, or the publication's circulation | (0.00) | 62/336 | (18%) 61% | 0.488 | 0.68 | 0.35 |
| | From the author's byline, background, or the publication's editorial policy | (1.00) | 205/336 | (61%) | | | |
| | From the subjects or keywords assigned to this (these) resources | (0.00) | 55/336 | (16%) | | | |

| | From the length of the article | (0.00) | 7/336 | (2%) | | | |
|---|---|---|---|---|---|---|---|
| **Currency (pre):** How can you determine whether a resource is current enough for your research purposes? | By comparing the date of publication to the currency of the subject | (1.00) | 178/336 | (53%) 53% | 0.500 | 0.59 | .023 |
| | By comparing the date of publication to the currency of the title | (0.00) | 38/336 | (11%) | | | |
| | By comparing the date of publication to the currency of the author | (0.00) | 29/336 | (9%) | | | |
| | By comparing the date of publication to the currency of the publication | (0.00) | 86/336 | (26%) | | | |

Outcomes-oriented school librarians incorporate assessment as learning, for learning, and of learning. Assessment *as* learning develops metacognition and a culture of reflection. Assessment *for* learning is a diagnostic tool to check for understanding and to modify instructional strategies. Assessment *of* learning evaluates mastery against standards in a real-world context.

At one school, the librarian and technology integration teacher uses Turnitin, an academic plagiarism detector tool, to facilitate personal reflection and to scaffold self-assessment of "fair use." Students are asked to submit rough drafts of their research papers into Turnitin. After examining the checking originality highlighted areas and match overviews, a student is able to visually see how much of his or her content may not be original. Turnitin is used as a learning tool and a formative assessment.

The use of web-based technologies is invaluable to a library program. According to the U.S. Department of Education (2010), in *National Educational Technology Plan*, "Just as technology is at the core of virtually every aspect of our daily lives and work, we must leverage it to provide . . . assessments that measure student achievement in more complete, authentic, and meaningful ways. Technology-based learning and assessment are pivotal to student learning and to generating data that can be used to continuously improve the education system at all levels . . . [I]t collects much more detailed information about how students are learning than manual methods. As students work, it can capture their inputs and collect evidence of their problem-solving sequences, knowledge, and strategy use, as reflected by the information each student selects or inputs . . .

[D]ata streams captured by an online learning system can provide the information needed to make judgments about student competencies [and growth]. These data-based judgments about individual students could be aggregated to generate judgments about classes, schools, districts, and states."

"Connection" is the true classroom and learning begins with responsive connections. Person-to-person is the most powerful! Students have multiple ways (online and offline) to communicate with teachers to clarify or question or to demonstrate understanding. In other words, an educator has multiple ways to assess student understanding and provide timely feedback.

The following is a real-world, connected, multifaceted, collaborative assured experience that illustrates how high expectations, the gradual release of responsibility, and checking for understanding through guided instruction, instructional scaffolding, and formative and summative assessments improve learning outcomes (Fisher and Frey, 2008).

During this research-based project, a student independently input personal nutrition and physical fitness information into www.choosemyplate.gov (formerly www.mypyramidtracker.gov) assesses the results against national standards, compiles a list of keywords from this data, creates a research question, designs an advanced research strategy to find authoritative information, reads critically, takes notes, writes annotations, composes a bibliography, designs a website to communicate enduring understandings, reflects, sets S.M.A.R.T. (specific, measurable, attainable, realistic, and timely) goals, writes a summary, gives a presentation, and answers the essential question: How do I live a healthy and balanced life? (This project is currently archived in the AASL Lesson Plan database.) The coteachers (health teachers, technology integration teachers, and librarians) craft a rubric for this project to assess task completion as well as to give students a guideline for excellence.

By integrating the "big idea," essential questions, literacies, concepts, skills, and curricular outcomes from the state's *Healthy and Balanced Living* framework, the librarians are able to assess a student's "ability to access valid health information, products, and services . . . skills of information analysis, organization, comparison, synthesis and evaluation to health issues provides a foundation for individuals to move toward becoming health-literate and responsible, productive citizens" (Connecticut Department of Education, 2006). This document complements the AASL standards, as well as the CCSSs.

- Comprehend, evaluate, and critique complex informational and literary text.
- Use technology and digital media strategically and capably to communicate effectively and work collaboratively.
- Research to build and present knowledge.
- Gather, synthesize, or cite complex informational evidence.
- Use the technology including the Internet to produce and publish.
- Use the writing process, media and visual literacy, and technology skills to create products that express new understandings.
- Apply new knowledge to create, to solve a problem, or to answer a question.

This project has evolved throughout the years. The following are highlights of some of the assessment strategies, assessment tools, data analysis, and learning outcomes results.

The first attempt toward technology integration came with the use of the School-Center webpage, designed by the school's STEM librarian. This website allowed students 24/7 access to project resources.

This was subsequently replaced by the online course platform Moodle. Each member of the PLC added instructional materials to the Moodle. This online course platform engaged students in the learning process, fostered independent learning, modeled the experience of an online (college) course, and built a culture of learning anywhere and anytime. It also gave students 24/7 access to teachers, librarians, and technology integrations teachers via the forum.

Coteachers were able to collect individual and group learning data, provide timely feedback to students, and modify instruction seamlessly. Teachers were guides in the learning process. As Fisher and Frey (2008) note in *Better Learning through Structured Teaching*, "Guided instruction is, in part, about establishing high expectations and providing the support for students to reach those expectations . . ."

The PLC also incorporated smartboard technology and Zarca (K–12 Insight) surveys to enhance student engagement and to collect anonymous student learning data. Student exit surveys were an effective assessment tool. Library instruction became student-centered through a variety of scaffolded learning activities and tutorials, including an online bibliography evaluation checklist.

The U.S. Department of Education Office of Educational Technology (2010), in *Transforming American Education: Learning Powered by Technology*, states, "An essential component of the 21st century learning model is a comprehensive infrastructure for learning that provides every student, . . . with the resources they need when and where they are needed . . . . An infrastructure for learning unleashes new ways of capturing and sharing knowledge . . ."

The Moodle provides the infrastructure to "capture" or assess individual and group student progress. Because of this ability, librarians, teachers, and technology integration teachers are able to scaffold learning through, checklist, learning guides and tutorials. For example, because of the analysis of assessment data from the online bibliographic checklist, the STEM librarian suggests integrating a bibliography evaluation form.

---

### Bibliography evaluation form

Use this form to check your own Works Cited list (bibliography).
* Required

1. Student name * the document bears your first name and last name, teacher's name, class period and date in the upper right-hand corner

   - ☐  yes
   - ☐  no

---

*(Continued)*

2. Works Cited or Bibliography * the word(s) "Works Cited" or "Bibliography" is centered in the middle of the page, below the student information and above the citation list

   - ○  yes
   - ○  no

3. Did you use an online bibliographic generator such as EasyBib of NoodleTools?

   - ☐  yes
   - ☐  no

4. If so, did you make sure to add **all** bibliographic information not automatically uploaded onto the online bibliographic generator such as author's name or corporate author's name (organization, association, college, company, or institution), title, or date of publication?

   - ☐  yes
   - ☐  no

5. Alphabetical * the document is arranged alphabetically according to the first word in the citation (unless that word is "the", "an", or "a", in which case it should be alphabetized according to the second word).

   - ☐  yes
   - ☐  no

6. Double-spaced * All parts of the document that follow its title are double-spaced.

   - ☐  yes
   - ☐  no

Overall research score for this Works Cited list (bibliography) * 1 point = does not include credible, valid, authoritative, verifiable, relevant and/or timely resources; does not demonstrate that any ICT resources were consulted. 2 points = includes at least 1 credible, valid, authoritative, verifiable, relevant and timely ICT resources; 3 points = includes 2 credible, valid, authoritative, verifiable, relevant and timely ICT resources; includes database resources and other ICT resources; 4 points = includes a wide range of credible, valid, authoritative, verifiable, relevant, and timely resources; includes a balance of database resources, books/ eBooks, Internet, and other ICT materials; at least 3 ICT resources were evidently consulted.

| | 1 | 2 | 3 | 4 | |
|---|---|---|---|---|---|
| Student (self- assessment) | | | | | |
| unsatisfactory | ○ | ○ | ○ | ○ | excellent |
| Librarian's assessment | 1 | 2 | 3 | 4 | |
| unsatisfactory | ○ | ○ | ○ | ○ | excellent |

(Continued)

The Overall page layout score for this Works Cited list (bibliography) * 1 = One "yes" answer on questions 1-6; 2 = Two or three "yes" answers on questions 1-6; 3 = Four of six "yes" answers on questions 1-6; 4 = Five or six "yes" answers on questions 1-6

Student (self- assessment)      1      2      3      4
unsatisfactory                         O      O      O      O    excellent
Librarian's assessment         1      2      3      4
unsatisfactory                         O      O      O      O    excellent

A research checklist can be downloaded by students to scaffold learning around the ISP and to give students a self-monitoring guide. Students can hand in completed forms to a librarian, or submit them online, for review.

**Research Checklist**

**Name:**

**Date:**                              **Teacher:**                         **Section:**

| Check | | 1. Task Definition (*What are you looking for?*) |
|---|---|---|
| | a. | Identify the information needed to complete the task. |
| | b. | Define what you already know, and what you need to know about your topic |
| | c. | Develop your essential question(s) |
| | | **2. Information Seeking Strategies** (*How/Where are you going to find it?*) |
| | a. | Brainstorm about potential resources and how/where to find them (www.nchslibrary.info – print and electronic sources, public library, interviews, podcasts, audio-visuals, etc.) |
| | b. | Identify keywords related to the essential questions. |
| | | **3. Location & Access** (*How/Where within the source are you going to access it?*) |
| | a. | Use www.nchslibrary.info to find books, magazines, audio-visuals, etc. |
| | b. | Use research strategies (quotes, Boolean operaters, truncation and delimiters) |
| | c. | Locate information within a resource by using keywords, indexes, table of contents, and control F or command F. |
| | d. | Use appropriate online databases, online card catalogs and search engines to locate materials |
| | | **4. Use of Information** (*How will you evaluate and use what you have found?*) |
| | a. | Use a variety of resources (electronic, print, audio-visuals, etc.) Use both primary and secondary sources. |
| | b. | Evaluate quality of resources for accuracy, authority, credibility, currency, scope, and relevance to essential questions. |
| | c. | Properly cite all resources using the *NCHS Bibliography Manual*. |

| | | 5. **Synthesis** (*How will you put everything together and present it?*) |
|---|---|---|
| | a. | Organize information from a variety of resources. |
| | b. | Develop a thesis statement that answers the Essential Question(s). |
| | c. | Effectively present the information. |
| | | 6. **Evaluation & Assessment** (*How well did you do?*) |
| | a. | Rubric—the product |
| | b. | Rubric—how the 6 steps were completed |

*Designed by Michelle Luhtala and Christina T. Russo*

Originally, students designed a Microsoft Publisher pamphlet as evidence of learning. But printing and folding it, and the drain on the school's paper supply, was overwhelming.

It was through direct observation, conferencing with students, assessment of students' work, and the results from the K–12 Insight (Zarca) survey that the team decided that it was time to make a change from Publisher to the online publishing/designing a website on Google Sites.

As stated in Rick Allen's (2010) *Education Update* article "Dawn of the New Literacies," Dr. Leu states, "The Internet and other information and communication technologies bring about new ways of doing literacy tasks that require new social practices, skills, strategies, dispositions, and literacies."

The librarians designed a diagnostic pretest and posttest to "modify content, process or product . . . . [Because] students vary in readiness, interest, and learning style . . . [and the] learner will understand important ideas and use important skills more thoroughly as a result" (Tomlinson, 1999: 11).

In addition to the pretest and posttest, numerous other pieces of evidence are assessed by librarians during the information search process (ISP) portion of the project: a student's written self-reflection on his or her website, keyword and research document, essential questions and thesis statement document, annotation activity document, selection of resources (articles), article summary, self- and peer-to-peer evaluation and assessment, checklists, annotated bibliography, and wellness plan posted to website (e.g., http:// ipdeliversuccess.wikispaces.com; http://ipdeliversuccess.wikispaces.com/high_school).

Each year during this project, the STEM librarian assesses 209 arbitrary students using a rubric and defined criteria to ensure accuracy of data and analysis. She assesses multiple learning activities in reading, writing, and ISP.

The STEM librarian meets with the special education (SPED) teacher to examine the project and develop modifications for students with individual education plans (IEPs). The UbD template and the assignment are adjusted to reflect changes in project expectations.

The humanities technology integration teacher and the STEM librarian review all SPED students' websites for completion and assessment data in technology and annotated bibliography to make sure all students are successful during the project. (Please see chart on pages 94 and 95.)

| | Setup | Home | 6D | Fitness | Nutrition | Labels | Goals | Ann Bib (max pts 4) | Checklist | Docs not shared/6 | Blank pages/8 | Pages ok/8 |
|---|---|---|---|---|---|---|---|---|---|---|---|---|
| 9 | ok | ok | -graphic is missing one D -worksheet inserted but not completed | ok | ok | -images ok -worksheet inserted but not completed | -goals written -worksheet incomplete | 2 | -all green down to library session but not accurate since there are missing items -library session checklist has not been completed | | | 3 |
| 9 | -URL incorrect -nav bar out of or | -Photo does not meet -reflection inserted | -graphic ok -essay inserted but without form so not sure if complete | -inserted chart but can't get to boys data to see if complete -chart missing | blank | -image inserted -worksheet missing from page | -written and posted -worksheet missing so all questions may not have been addressed | 2 | -not shared | 1 + 1 missing | 1 | |
| 9 | Will take Health this summer | | | | | | | | | | | |
| 9 | NO LINK IN Diiecto FOUND WITH SITE -nav bar out of or | ok (words don't wrap) | ok | ok | ok | -images inserted -worksheet missing | ok | 3.75 | -inserted but not addressed | 1 missing | | 6 |
| 9 | ok (one typo) | ok (words don't wrap) | ok | -graphics ok -worksheet inserted but not shared | ok | ok | ok | 3.75 / not shared | -inserted but not shared | 3 | | 5 |

| | Setup | Home | 6D | Fitness | Nutrition | Labels | Goals | Ann Bib (max pts 4) | Checklist | Docs not shared/6 | Blank pages/8 | Pages ok/8 |
|---|---|---|---|---|---|---|---|---|---|---|---|---|
| 9 | —— will take health this summer. | | | | | | | | | | | |
| 9 | ok | ok | -graphic ok -worksheet not shared | -chart ok -worksheet not shared | ok | ok | ok | 0 / not shared | complete – all green – but incorrect since docs aren't shared | 3 | | 4 |
| 9 | ok | photo missing | ok | -graphics ok -worksheet not shared | ok | -graphics ok -worksheet missing | ok | 1 / not shared | ok but inaccurate since docs aren't shared | 2 + 1 missing | | 3 |
| 9 | ok | ok | ok | -graphic ok -worksheet inserted but incomplete | ok | -graphics -worksheet inserted but not completed | ok | 3 / not shared | ok but too much red that remains incomplete | 3 | | 4 |
| 9 | ok | ok | ok | ok | ok | ok | ok | 0 | ok | | | |
| 9 | not in directory layout ok | no wrap | ok | chart missing all else ok | ok | ok | ok | 3.5 / not shared | inserted but incomplete | 1 | | 4 |
| 9 | ok | ok | ok | ok | ok | ok | ok | 3.75 / not posted to website | ok but incorrect re bib | | | 6 |

The STEM librarian analysis of the question and verbatim portions of the anonymous K–12 Insight (Zarca) survey is insightful: 87 percent of students surveyed thought the project would result in a balanced and healthy life for them. The following are student-constructed responses (verbatim) to the prompt "How has this health project changed your outlook on nutrition and fitness?" Student 1: "Overall, I think that this project was very helpful to my health. First, I now know, because of the research I have done for this project, that I need to lower my sodium intake. If I don't, I could be faced with serious health problems in the near future. Also, I have noticed (because of this project) that my physical activity score was a 100/100. I was very pleased with and know now that I have a good amount of exercise every day, and plan to keep that up even after this project." Student 2: "The project was a good idea but because i am already fairly healthy i am not going to follow it." These verbatim responses are a gold mine of data. They allow for a deep analysis of a student's personal feelings about learning and instructional effectiveness.

Three key components of this project are communicating effectively, reading complex grade-level text for information, and writing an annotated bibliography. All are elements of the CCSSs. An analysis of the data from the state's *Reading for Information* from 2006–2010 shows a strong correlation between the improvement in the information literacy skills from the health project (research, the reading of the health article[s], evaluation, analysis, synthesize, and writing the annotated bibliography) and the improvement by students on the state test in reading. Again, accountability assures relevance.

In addition to the hardcopy version of the *Keyword and Research Question* document, an online version is integrated in the project. Students now have a choice of format. The online version gave health teachers, technology integration teachers, and librarians vital assessment data. (Please see chart on page 97.) This data could be manipulated to give targeted assessment data, enabling coteachers to target teaching around key concepts and individual needs and also giving the librarian information for grouping for the peer-to-peer assessment on resource evaluation.

The STEM librarian creates a CCSS crosswalk to guide implementation. (Please see chart on pages 98 and 99.)

| Fats | Proteins | Carbs | Cholesterol | Fiber | Calcium | Potassium | Iron | Vitamin B | Protein keyword | Grains keyword | Vegetables keyword |
|---|---|---|---|---|---|---|---|---|---|---|---|
| 5g | Under | OK | OK | OK | Under | Under | Under | OK | OK | Off | Yes |
| 5g | Under | OK | OK | OK | Under | Under | Under | OK | OK | Off | Yes |
| 9g | OK | OK | OK | Under | Under | Under | OK | OK | Under | Off | Yes |
| 6g | OK | OK | OK | Under | Under | Under | Under | Under | Under | Yes | Yes |
| 4g | Over | Under | Over | Under | Under | Under | OK | OK | Under | Off | Yes |
| 6g | Over | OK | OK | Over | Over | Over | Over | Over | Over | Off | Off |
| 5g | Under | OK | Over | Other | Over | OK | OK | Over | OK | Off | Off |
| 8g | OK | OK | OK | OK | Under | Under | Under | Under | Under | Off | Off |
| 3g | Select | Select | Select | Select | Select | Select | Select | Select | Select | Off | Off |
| 18g | Over | Under | OK | Under | Under | Under | Under | OK | OK | Off | Off |
| 5g | OK | OK | Over | OK | OK | OK | OK | OK | Under | Off | Off |
| 6g | Select | Select | Select | Select | Select | Select | Select | Select | Select | Off | Off |
| 12g | OK | OK | OK | Under | Under | Under | Under | Under | Under | Off | Off |
| 28g | OK | OK | OK | Under | OK | Under | OK | Under | Under | Off | Off |
| 17g | OK | OK | OK | Under | Under | Under | OK | Under | Under | Off | Yes |
| 2g | OK | OK | OK | Under | Under | Under | Under | Under | Under | Off | Off |
| 3g | Select | Select | Select | Select | Select | Select | Select | Select | Select | Off | Off |
| 7g | Over | OK | Over | Under | OK | OK | OK | OK | OK | Off | Yes |
| 4g | OK | OK | OK | Under | Under | Under | OK | OK | Under | Off | Off |
| 5g | OK | OK | OK | Under | Under | Under | OK | OK | Under | Off | Off |
| 8g | OK | OK | OK | Under | Under | Under | Under | Under | Under | Off | Off |
| 8g | OK | OK | OK | Under | Under | Under | Under | Under | Under | Off | Off |
| 8g | OK | OK | OK | Under | Under | Under | Under | Under | Under | Off | Off |
| 14g | OK | OK | OK | Under | Under | Under | OK | OK | Under | Off | Yes |
| 6g | OK | OK | Over | Under | Under | Under | Under | OK | Under | Off | Yes |
| 14g | OK | OK | OK | Under | Under | Under | OK | OK | Under | Off | Yes |

*My personal Wellness: 9th grade health and ICT*

| Healthy & Balanced Living Curriculum Framework | Curricular Outcome | Essential Questions | Learning Opportunities | Core Values, Beliefs & Expectations | Common Core State Standards |
|---|---|---|---|---|---|
| Standard 2: Accessing Health Information. | Students Will Understand That (SWAT) access to valid health information, products and services to enhances health, SWUT literacy can take many different forms, SWUT that information needs to be qualitatively evaluated and validated before it is cited or applied, SWUT literacy involves decoding, processing and synthesizing multiple froms of information, in multiple formats, SWUT access valid health information, products and services enhances health, SWUT learning involves metacognition: self-reflection and evaluation of one's ideas, process, and product, SWUT knowledge can be | How Do I live a healthy and balanced Life? What do I need to know to make healthy choices? Why is inquiry important to healthy choices? Why use ICT resouces? Why Create SMART Goals? | Lessons (Moodle): 18-Analysis and interpretation of personal nutrition and physical fitness data from www.choose-mymplate.gov. development of keywords and research question for advanced research strategy and library pretest; Lesson 19 Use of keywords and research question to find current, valid, and relevant health information on a database to answer research question, read and self-evaluation of information text found: Lesson 20, Self & Peer-to-Peer evaluation of informational text, and cite resouces using an online | 1.1 apply analytical and creative thinking to identify and solve problems across discipline 1.2 reflect thoughtfully on their learning 1.3 communicate effectively 1.4 demonstrate an understanding of healthy life choices 2.1 Work responsibly and productively in both independent and collaborative environments 2.2 respect one another 3.1 contribute positively to the culture of NCHS and the larger community | CC.9-10.W.8 Gather relevant information from multiple authorative print and digital sources, using advanced searches effectively, assess the usefulness of each source in answering the research question; integrate information into the text selectively to maintain the flow of ideas, avoiding plagiarism and following a standard format for citation. CC.9-10.SL.2 Integrate multiple sources of information presented in diverse madia or formats (e.g., visually, quantitatively, orally) evaluating the credibility and accuracy of each source. CC.9-10.W.7 Conduct short as well as more sustained research projects to answer a question (including a self-generated question) or solve a problem; narrow or broaden the inquiry when appropriate; synthesize multiple soures on the subjects, demonstrating understanding of the subject under investigation. CC.9-10.R.L.1 Cite strong and thorough textual evidence to support analysis of what the text says explicitly as well as inferences drawn from the CC 9-10.L.3.a Write and edit work so that it conforms to the guidelines in a style manual (e.g., MLA Handbook, Turablan's Manual for Writters) appropriate for the discipline and writing type CC 9-10.R.I.6 Determine an author's point of view or purpose in a text and analyze how an author uses rhetoric to advance that point of view or purpose CC.9-10.W.2 Write informative explanatory texts to examine and convey complex ideas, concepts, and information clearly and accurately throgh the effective selection, organization, and analysis of content. CC.9-10.W.2.d Use precise language and domain-specific vocabulary to manage the complexity of the topic. CC.9-10.W.4 Produce clear and coherent writing in which the development, organization, and style are appropriate to task, purpose, and audience. (Grade-specific expectations for writing types are defined in standards 1–3 above.) CC.9-10.SL.5 Make strategic use of digital media (e.g., textual, graphical, audio, visual, and interactive elements) in presentations to enhance understanding of findings, reasoning, and evidence and to add interest CC.9-10.W.6 Use technology, including the internet, to produce, publish, and update indivi- |

| | | |
|---|---|---|
| organized and reorganized to create new knowledge, SWUT 21st century literacy is dependent on the acquisition, application and transfer of evolving ICT understandings in multiple, dynamic contexts, SWUT inventive thinking is about making connections. | bibliographic generation tool; Lesson 21-Write an evaluative annotated biblio-graphy, and upload annotated bibliography onto Google website, and take library posttest. | dual or shared writing products, taking advantage of technology's capacity to link to other information and to display information flexibly and dynamically. CC 9-10.SL.1 |
| | | Initiate and participate effectively in a range of collaborative discussions (one-on-one, in groups, and teacher-led) with diverse partners on grades 9–10 topics, texts, and issues, building on others' ideas and expressing their own clearly and persuasively. CC.9-10.SL.1.a |
| | | Come to discussions prepared, having read and researched material under study, explicitly draw on that preparation by referring to evidence from texts and other research on the topic or issue to stimulate a thoughtful, well-reasoned exchange of ideas. |
| | | CCSS ELA-Literacy. RST 9-10.7 Translate quantitative or technical information expressed in words in a text into visual form (e.g., a table or chart) and translate informatin expressed visually or mathematically (e.g., in an equation) into words. |
| | | CCSS ELA-Literacy. RST.9-10.8 Assess the extent to which the reassoning and evidence in a text support the author's claim or a recommendation for solving a scientific or technical problemCCSS.Math.Content.HSS-D.A.1 Represent data with plots on the real number line (dot plots, histograms, and box plots). |
| | | CCSS.Math.Content.HSS-ID.A.2 Use statistics appropriate to the shape of the data distribution to compare center (median, mean) and spread (interquartile range, standard deviation) of two or more differnt data sets |
| | | CCSS.Math.Content.HSS-ID.A.1 Represent data with plots on the real number line (dot plots, histograms, and box plots). |
| | | CCSS.Math.Content.HSS-ID.A.2 Use statistics appropriate to the shape of the data destribution to compare center (median, mean) and spread (interquartile range, standard deviation) of two or more differnt data sets |
| | | CCSS.Math.Content HSS-ID.C.9 |
| | | Distinguish between correlation and causation |

To help evaluate ninth-graders' knowledge of evaluation of resources and other library skills, the ICT team decides to give the TRAILS: Kent State University Libraries' *TRAILS: Tool for Real-time Assessment of Information Literacy Skills* (www.trails-9.org). The average score for evaluating resources and information correctly is only 57 percent for all ninth-graders. The STEM librarian creates online tutorials to integrate key elements of this assessment into this project. This data is taking into consideration when planning the learning activities for the coming year collaborative project, such as CRAAP testing. The pretest and posttest for the project showed a remarkable 13 percent improvement in website evaluation skills. (See the following graphics.)

| Q21. Which of the following is NOT reliable when evaluating a web page? | | | |
|---|---|---|---|
| Responses | Count | % | Percentage of total respondents |
| Domain extension (.org, .gov, .net, .com) | 18 | 6.08% | |
| Currency (last updated) | 29 | 9.80% | |
| Author information (individual, group) | 33 | 11.15% | |
| Appearance of the site | 216 | 72.97% | |
| Total Responses | 296 | | 20%   40%   60%   80%   100% |

| Q15. Which of the following is NOT reliable when evaluating a web page? | | | |
|---|---|---|---|
| Exclude 'Did not Answer' | | | |
| Responses | Count | % | Percentage of total respondents |
| Domain extension (.org, .gov, .net, .com) | 22 | 7.31% | |
| Currency (last updated) | 13 | 4.32% | |
| Author information (individual, group) | 7 | 2.33% | |
| Appearance of the site | 259 | 86.05% | |
| (Did not answer) | 0 | 0% | |
| Total Responses | 301 | | 20%   40%   60%   80%   100% |

Black et al. (2001), in *Working Inside the Black Box: Assessment for Learning in the Classroom* say, "Assessment for learning is any assessment for which the first priority in its design and practice is to serve the purpose of promoting students' learning."

Excellent librarians know that a coherent and rigorous standards-based curriculum, the integration of emerging technologies, a blended learning environment, a culture that believes that each student can achieve if challenged appropriately, an interdisciplinary approach, a focus on learning outcomes through ongoing assessment and feedback, data analysis, and a willingness to innovate and change result in gains in student learning outcomes and library relevancy.

Assessments

| Health Teachers | Tech Integration Teachers | Librarians |
|---|---|---|
| Self-reflections | Moodle use/video tutorial use | Information and Research Skills- Pre and Post-tests |
| Self-assessment | Website creation/layout | Moodle views/tutorial use |
| choosemyplate.gov: data | choosemyplate.gov: how tos | choosemyplate.gov: interpretation of personal data |
| Food labels interpretation | charts and graphs: create/insert | Self-reflection (journaling) |
| Website | Google docs: copy/share/insert | ISP (research) and Keyword & Research Question Activity Document |
| 6 Dimensions of Wellness responses | Images & Screenshots: Create/Insert/Modify | Annotation Activity Document |
| FITT chart: data and essay | Google drawing tools | Critical Reading |
| Nutrition graph: interpretation | Navigation bar editing | Self & Peer-to-Peer Evaluation |
| Wellness plan: goals essay | Sharing protocols | Annotated bibliography |
| Rubric/Checklists | Exit survey: data | Exit survey: data |

Assessment is a multistep process, like experiencing a fine wine. You need to select the right vintage, use the correct glass, swirl it to gauge its color and consistency, smell its bouquet, slowly taste it, and finally savor it a sip at a time to fully enjoy it. It sometimes takes multiple years and multiple assessments to get it right, as the chart above indicates, but when you do, learning outcomes increase.

## Chapter 11

# Professional Learning Communities

A professional learning community (PLC) is a "systematic process in which teachers work together to analyze and improve their classroom practice. Teachers work in teams, engaging in an ongoing cycle of questions that promote deep team learning. This process, in turn, leads to higher levels of student achievement" (DuFour, 2004). It is a means for ongoing, embedded professional learning to take place in research-based instruction, strategies, protocols, interventions, assessments tools (online and offline), curriculum design and content, standards integration, equity, classroom management, teaching effectiveness, and best practices.

A PLC builds upon interpersonal relationships and collective responsibility to ensure a positive school environment: climate, culture and conditions. It cultivates leadership, empowers change, enables creativity, builds capacity, promotes collective learning and thinking, supports experimentation and action research, encourages reflection, and strengthens a shared vision for excellence. In essence, it is transformative.

It is usually school-based (grade-level, subject area, or scope/focus), but in the case of ICT professionals (librarians and technology integration teachers), it can also be district-based, state-based, and national-based, depending on the focus of learning. "Current research suggests that the effects of PLCs are optimized when they exist not in isolation but as part of overlapping, interconnected communities of practice. Members of such "overlapping" communities are both formally and informally bound together by what they do, by what they have learned through their mutual engagement in the work, and through the work they have produced" (Annenberg Institute for School Reform, n.d.).

In *Making the Most of Profession Learning Communities*, Hughes-Hassell, Brasfield, and Dupree (2012) identify "eight potential roles for school librarians as a member of PLCs: (1) information specialist; (2) staff developer; (3) teacher and collaborator; (4) critical friend; (5) leader; (6) researcher; (7) learner; and (8) student advocate." These correlate with and support the seven components of successful PLCs identified in *Factors That Promote Progression in Schools Functioning as Professional Learning Community*: (1) the school's vision, (2) the physical and human conditions that encourage teachers to cooperate, learn, and share together, (3) the cooperative culture of the school, (4) the manifestation of leadership from both teachers and principals, (5) the dissemination of expertise and shared learning, (6) the topics addressed based on concerns related to student learning, and (7) decision making based on accurate data (Leclerc et al., 2010).

The multiple roles of a librarian and functions of a successful PLC complement each other, ensuring a positive collaborative learning experience.

Maybe the following scenario will illustrate how one high school librarian uses the adoption and integration of the Common Core State Standards (CCSSs) as a member of several different PLCs (professional learning/development [PD] team, curriculum leadership council [CLC], information, communication, and technologies [ICT] team [school-based], information, communication, and technologies team [district-based], reading team, health/ICT, problem-based learning [PBL]: Natural and Man-made Disasters and Sci-fi, and assessment team) to promote vision, collaboration, school culture, decision-making, professional learning, and, most important, student learning.

As a longstanding member of the professional learning/development team, this librarian is a district curriculum leader. It is her responsibility to know what is coming down the pike. In this case, it was the CCSSs. Because this district has a train-the-trainer model, this librarian attends CCSS workshops; views webinars, such as the ASCD's *Creating Communities of Support for Implementing the Common Core State Standards and Literacy Standards Common Core: Assessment Shifts*, PD team discussions and planning sessions; and reads *Pathways to the Common Core: Accelerating Achievement*, a district CLC-required text. At the same time, she immerses herself in research, beginning with the CCSS website (www.corestandards.org ) and American Association of School Librarians (AASL) CCSS crosswalk (www.ala.org/aasl/standards-guidelines/crosswalk). She reads numerous professional journal articles and books, such as *Reading Comprehension at the Core of the Library Program, The Transliterate Learner,* and *Text Complexity: School Librarians Have a Role,* to ensure understanding of CCSS on libraries, teaching, and learning.

To get her head around this national initiative and ensure understanding, she decides to apply her new knowledge to the existing districtwide ICT competencies and benchmarks document. After inserting the appropriate CCSS English language arts (ELA) and math standards next to the targeted competency or benchmark for 9–12, the librarian decides to extent this process to include the high school's 21st-century core values, beliefs, and expectation (vision statement), as well as the current state standards. She designs her own crosswalk. She shares this Google document with the deputy superintendent of schools as well as with the PD team leader, director of ICT, school principal, and department chair of the library.

The deputy superintendent of schools asks this librarian to share this document with the CLC, the English teachers working on summer curriculum writing for the integration of the CCSSs, and other ICT members. Not only does the librarian share this document, but she also provides the various PLCs with an annotated bibliography of key resources, also making them aware of the CCSS APP, and ASCD webinars.

After working on this document, this librarian notes that the 9–12 ICT competencies and benchmarks are outdated and need rewriting to better correlate with CCSSs, learning theory, "habits of mind," and emerging technologies structures and applications to answer the question *What do students need to know, understand and be able to do to be successful at college and for a 21st-century career?* She e-mails the director of ICT and asks that this be put on the next ICT PLC agenda. Just like Sandra Hughes-Hassell,

Amanda Brasfield, and Debbie Dupree (2012) suggest in *Making the Most of Professional Learning Communities*, this librarian asks to be on the agenda. This librarian shares her concerns at the next districtwide ICT PLC.

After a careful review of this document by the ICT PLC, it is decided to request summer curriculum writing funding to revise the document for K–12. The librarian offers to write the summer curriculum proposal for the team.

This librarian takes a lead role in the revision of the document. She acts as the team's facilitator and project manager. She sends out an *Agenda for Learning* to the participants for the first meeting. "The agenda for learning encourages shared leadership for ongoing professional learning . . . defines process, outcomes, facilitator, and time allocation for each segment of a PD session or a meeting" (NCPS, 2009–2014).

This K–12 PLC meets several times during the summer in person and virtually to discuss the learning and teaching applications of the CCSSs. The librarian sets up meeting times and a shared Google doc.

This PLC closely reviews CCSS ELA and math standards for direct correlations with current ICT standards and 21st-century district learning goals. Because of this close reading and examination of CCSS, the team decides that the current iteration of the 9–12 ICT competencies and benchmark must be totally revamped to reflect CCSS language and changes in ICT teaching practices, but that the K–8 competencies need only to be brought up to date to include CCSS. This librarian sets up a spreadsheet on Google Drive. The spreadsheet is designed as a crosswalk with competencies/benchmarks in one column and corresponding CCSS standards in another. The K–8 librarians and technology integration teachers input the K–8 competencies to the spreadsheet and identify the appropriate CCSSs. The high school librarian begins to write the 9–12 competencies/benchmarks to compliment CCSS. She reviews the K–8 work to ensure alignment. By the end of the summer, this learning team has a working document to share with the entire ICT professional learning community and the district.

This librarian writes the district's required summary of the curriculum work, creates a Wordle to explain CCSS, and submits all documentation to the deputy superintendent of schools, the school principal, the director of ICT, and the library department chair. She also adds the documents to the district shared drive so that all district certified and noncertified staff have access to it. This document is later used by the school's assessment PLC for accreditation purposes.

As a member of the district's ICT professional learning community, this librarian fulfills multiples roles as outlined in the Hughes-Hassell 2012 *Knowledge Quest* article: information specialist, staff developer, leader, researcher, critical friend, and learner.

As a member of the high school reading team, a cross-disciplinary and town library PLC, this school librarian offers to research and present information on reading strategies, text complexity, and complex nonfiction and literary texts to support the CCSSs. Fortunately, as a representative of the district learning/professional development team and ICT PLC, she had already done extensive research and reading on the CCSSs and had created an annotated bibliography of excellent resources: websites, webinars, articles, and books. This librarian revises her annotated bibliography and begins to prepare for her presentation to the reading PLC team.

On close examination of the CCSS website, she spots "Appendix A: Research Supporting Key Elements of the Standards" and "Appendix B: Text Exemplars and Sample Performance Tasks." These CCSS appendices address text complexity and provide a list of complex texts in English, social studies, science, and technical subjects. She does a close reading of these appendices; identifies key concepts, important definitions, and relatable content, graphics, and examples to be included in the presentation.

To ensure that the school library has copies of the complex texts listed in Appendix B, this librarian requests that a collection review be done. This ensures that the library collection is aligned with the CCSS and identifies which complex informational and literary texts from CCSS Appendix B the library owns. After reviewing the list of complex texts not in the library collection, this librarian selects curriculum relevant complex texts from the list to be added to the collection development (purchase order) list.

As the resource liaison for the Professional Learning/Development Team, this librarian sends out an e-mail to the district's certified and noncertified staff with the CCSS link, link to appendixes A and B, and information regarding complex texts, and visual images of books on CCSS in the professional collection.

In preparation for the Reading PLC presentation, the librarian creates a Google presentation. She includes a variety of information in different formats, including information from Appendix A, a science exemplar from Appendix B (teachers get leery at the same old social studies or English applications), examples from science and math databases with Lexile search capabilities (Lexile measurements are important tool for text complexity and leveled reading), and the library's online catalog.

In addition to this information from the CCSS website, the CCSS appendixes, databases, and a science text exemplar, the librarian uses examples from several websites in her reading team presentation:

- www.loc.gov/teachers
- www.sde.ct.gov/sde/cwp/view.asp?a=2618&q=322592
- http://learning.blogs.nytimes.com/2011/06/14/the-times-and-the-common-core-standards-reading-strategies-for-informational-text
- www.corestandards.org

As a follow-up to the presentation, this librarian sends a link to a video from the Teaching Channel, *Simplifying Text Complexity: The Way We Layer Text Impacts Complexity*, by Sarah Brown Wessling (https://www.teachingchannel.org/videos/simplifying-text-complexity) and links to the CCSS *Tookit for Evaluating Alignment of Instructional and Assessment Materials to the Common Core State Standards* (www.ccsso.org/Documents/2013/Toolkit%20for%20Evaluating%20Alignment%20of%20Instructional%20and%20Assessment%20Materials.pdf) and Teaching Channel's *Simplifying Text Complexity* (https://www.teachingchannel.org/videos/simplifying-text-complexity).

After the Google presentation is given to the reading team, the science department chair, a member of the reading PLC, requests permission to share it with the district's

CLC. Google presentations allows the librarian to insert appropriate video to scaffold the presentation.

For the reading PLC, this librarian again performs a variety of roles as defined by Sandra Hughes-Hassell, Amanda Brasfield, and Debbie Dupree in their 2012 *Knowledge Quest* article: information specialist, staff developer, leader, researcher, critical friend, and learner. This librarian promotes national, state, and district learning goals, as well as the CCSS.

The reading PLC team leader is also an active member of the problem-based learning PLC; as such she encourages members of the reading team to form their own PBL professional learning community. This librarian joins a science teacher, English teacher, and a career and technology education (CTE) teacher to form PBL–PLC. All but the librarian are nontenure teachers. This PBL focus is Natural and Man-made Disasters and Science-fiction. The librarian does research on problem-based learning and shares it with her group and with the Reading Team, including articles and Internet content sourced from the *Interdisciplinary Journal of Problem-based Learning*, *Edutopia*, and Stanford University:

- http://docs.lib.purdue.edu/ijpbl/
- http://ldt.stanford.edu/~jeepark/jeepark+portfolio/PBL/whatis.htm
- www.edutopia.org/project-based-learning

Because this is a cross-disciplinary group, the PLC needs to find not only a common meeting time, but also a meeting place. The librarian offers the south conference room in the library. She also offers to be the recorder and fascinator. To expedite the process, this librarian creates an UbD (Understanding by Design) curriculum map on Google Drive and shares it with the group.

To be successful as a PLC and advance student learning through problem-based learning and assessment, the group agrees to a standard-based approach. All members of the PLC add her discipline's specific standards (next-generation science, standards for technological literacy, National Council of English Teachers standards, and AASL standards) to the curriculum outline document. The librarian offers to review all the disciplinary standards on the outline to make sure all aspects of the project are covered, including additional standards to fill any gaps between standards to match the learning objectives. Then she transfer them to the UbD.

In addition to the AASL standards, the librarian offers to identify and record the CCSSs, as well as other Connecticut standards onto the district's UbD (Understanding by Design) template. The CCSSs provide a unifying framework for student learning. With this information in hand, the librarian begins to create enduring understandings and essential questions and input them to the UbD form.

At the next meeting, the Natural Disaster PLC discusses these enduring understandings and essential questions; establishes a timeline for completion of the project; sets up interdisciplinary communication discussion groups, aligns the English, science, and CTE assignments; and discusses potential authentic audience possibilities for student presentations. The librarian offers to reserve the multipurpose room for the student presentations, which she has done for PL/PD days. She also sends an Edutopia article by Suzie Boss, "Focus on Audience for Better PBL Results," on authentic audience, to the team (www.edutopia.org/blog/focus-on-audience-for-better-pbl-results-suzie-boss).

Because of the authentic audience aspect of PBL and the needs to review student data and update the UbD, the Natural Disasters PLC decides to request summer curriculum writing work for this PBL project. This librarian offers to write the proposal to the assistant superintendent of schools.

In the meantime, the science teacher and librarian meet to discuss coteaching opportunities for the project: advance research, ethical use of information, images and data, CRAAP (currency, relevance, authority, accuracy and purpose) testing, note-taking, Subtext (a reading comprehension app/web tool), and online bibliography tools.

The librarian guides the Earth science students through advanced research skills; visual, digital, and literacy skills; and evaluation skills (CRAAP testing: currency, relevance, authority, accuracy, and purpose), as well as use of Subtext, note taking (online and Cornell), and bibliography creation (EasyBib and NoodleBib). She sets up a Moodle block to disseminate information, creates online tutorials for self-directed learning, and conferences with students. She uses various avenues of communication—forum (Moodle), school e-mail, library's Facebook page—for teachers to communicate with learners.

In addition to the information search process (ISP), this librarian also conducts in-person and virtual book talks on natural and man-made disasters and science fiction.

The health/ICT PLC is a well-established team (health teachers, technology integration teacher and librarian) that works in tandem on three different assured experiences: My Personal Wellness (MPW; ninth grade), Substance Abuse (10th grade), and Alcohol Debate (11th grade). For MPW, the librarian is the team coordinator. The PLC meets often before, during, and after this rigorous and robust semester-long collaborative assured experience to improve learning and health. They meet formally and informally, including virtually.

To structure the discussion around learning and future planning, this librarian shares a four-quadrant form with the other members of the PLC: What Went Well, What Could Have Gone Better, Organizational Needs, and Future Implications. Members of the PLC fill out this form throughout the semester as issues arise or ideas emerge. They meet formally at the end of each semester to discuss issues listed on this form. Each member of the PLC uses a different color. A graphic of this chart appears in the chapter on assessment, page 85.

This four-quadrant form is a powerful planning tool for the health PLC, because it helps inform decisions. It is an asynchronous document (anywhere, anytime) through which team members can relate successes, concerns, and ideas to the whole team without the structure of a formal meeting. It helps move the PLC forward.

In addition to the four-quadrant form, this librarian uses a goal setting protocol to organize the work. A goal setting protocol "is designed to help groups set agenda the beginning of the school year or at their last meeting of the previous year. It will allow the PLC to develop an overall picture of what they hope to accomplish over the course of the year and provide a shared sense of ownership for future meetings" (Hughes-Hassell et al., 2012).

This is another example of how this PLC operates. At the AASL conference *Rising to the Challenge*, held in Hartford, Connecticut, in November 2013, this team copresented at *Instructional Partnerships That Deliver Success: Meeting the Leadership Challenge*. During the discussion on reading, the lead presenter, Judi Moreillon, highlights information on reading strategies from her book *Coteaching Reading Comprehension Strategies in Secondary School Libraries*. The team immediately seizes on this information and decides then and there to include these reading strategies in the next year's MPW. This librarian purchased the book at the ALA store at the conference to expedite the integration of this information into the project. As a member of the reading PLC, this librarian knows that the integration of these reading strategies go hand in hand with CCSS. This librarian adds this to the four-quadrant form, under Future Implications, to ensure future discussion and implementation of the strategies during the research and reading component of MPW.

This librarian reads *Coteaching Reading Comprehension Strategies in Secondary School Libraries*. She suggests that the team begin with *Reading Comprehension Strategy 3: Questioning* for several reasons: To use the Cross-Discipline and Discipline-Specific Question Matrixes, because the lesson plan provides an excellent wellness and health example and connection, because the team has used other questioning strategies and protocols to promote not only reading but creativity, and because this librarian has already attended a district workshop on questioning by consultant Todd White.

During a discussion for another health assured experience, the Alcohol Debate (11th grade), the teachers decided they need an additional debate topic (existing topic statements were as follows: All advertising for alcohol products should be banned; The legal age should be lowered to 18 years of age; The legal limit for driving under the influence should be lowered to .02 in Connecticut).

This librarian researches various other related topics to ensure student success in finding information. She e-mails members of the team a couple of suggestions: Texting causes more driving accidents than alcohol; Alcohol is as addictive as heroin. After a discussion, the PCL decides to expand the second debate topic suggested by the librarian. The fourth topic for research and debate becomes the following: Alcohol is comparable to other drugs in addictiveness and destructiveness. In addition to modeling CRAAP testing and good questioning and debate techniques, this librarian revises the Moodle, tutorials, and learning materials to include this new debate topic, to update information on the older topics, and to integrate the CCSSs through a variety of verbal and nonverbal techniques and learning strategies, such as *Stop, Look, Listen, Think, Respond, Self-talk/Think Aloud*, and *Guided Imagery*. This librarian uses the Self-talk/Think Aloud strategy when she demonstrates the CRAAP test using *Choose Responsible: Balance, Maturity, and Common Sense* (www.chooseresponsibility.org/home).

This librarian assesses student learning by looking at student work (including documentation and bibliography), attending debates, and scoring debates using the debate rubric. This librarian also uses a mobile device during the debate to record assessment information on ISP—the use of appropriate resources (CRAAP testing) and suggested resources, such as the Centers for Disease Control and Prevention (CDC) and the National Institute of Drug Abuse.

A PLC can be school-, district-, or professionally-based. The exchange of professional knowledge and expertise is not limited by building or geography. Professional organizations are a different type of PLC. The exchange of theory, strategies, and methods are important at all levels of professional learning.

The annotated bibliography and accompanying research presented to the reading team and CLC are updated and refined by the librarian to be presented at a Tech Forum round table, New York, and also at a joint librarians and technology educators CASL/CECA (Connecticut Association of School Librarians/Connecticut Educators Computers Association (conference in Connecticut).

Because of her work on the CCSSs for professional development and for the reading and ICT PLCs and her presentations at the CASL-CECA conference and the Tech Forum, this librarian is also asked to provide a statement for EdWeb about the integration of the CCSSs and the role of the librarian in the integration process.

As Richard DuFour states, "The professional learning community model flows from the assumption that the core mission of formal education is not simply to ensure that students are taught but to ensure that they learn. This simple shift—from a focus on teaching to a focus on learning—has profound implications for schools" (DuFour, 2004).

# Part VI
# Network

# Chapter 12

# Establishing a Professional Learning Network

In 2004, Richard DuFour wrote in ASCD's online journal *Educational Leadership*, "The professional learning community model flows from the assumption that the core mission of formal education is not simply to ensure that students are taught but to ensure that they learn." In the article, he puts forth three big ideas:

1. Ensure that students learn.
2. Promote a culture of collaboration.
3. Focus on results.

Establishing a professional learning community (PLC) within your school means grouping educators who share the same vision and mission to work together for student success. Teachers at the elementary and middle school levels have long worked in teaching teams with members meeting daily during common prep time to share practice and collaborate to plan integrated units of study. Teaming has traditionally been less frequent in high schools where teachers are often grouped departmentally.

New teacher evaluation programs have advanced the concept of PLCs as the new collaborative model K–12 in the belief that common practice, common assessment, and shared philosophies will have marked effects on student learning. The success of a PLC is dependent on consistently scheduled dialog, openness to new ideas, and honest examination of student learning results to inform next steps.

Much has changed since 2004, when Richard DuFour wrote about PLCs. Back then, the communities he referred to were generally school- or district-based. Today, the culture of collaboration DuFour wrote about has greatly expanded implications, with school-based learning communities merging into vast professional learning networks (PLNs). Made up of educators from around the world, today's PLN members gather online to share content, resources, reflections, and opportunities. Many of these globally minded teachers are searching for like-minded educators and classrooms to join an initiative or conversation. Teachers looking to get started will find a myriad of options in blogs, social networks and online learning platforms. Whatever the topic, there is always much to be learned from educators and students in other cultures.

# PLNs in Social Networks

It's never been easier to get involved in a professional learning network. Many of today's social networking apps feature educators' accounts to link teachers with similar interests. Social studies teachers working on African studies can publish a request on various social networks for teachers in Africa who would like to collaborate. Biology teachers with students conducting local water quality studies can join with others around the world to see how their water supplies compare. And world language teachers can make connections that let their students communicate with others in the target culture.

Although millions of educators and students are searching for matches, many times teachers don't know how to get started. Librarians can help by compiling a list of online options and helping them establish viable contacts. There's no need for teachers to begin with a project in mind. There are hundreds of proposals already posted and waiting for collaborators.

Online learning platforms like Moodle, ePals, and Edmodo share a vision and goal to create worldwide networks of teachers all working to benefit student learning and to establish mutual respect among people of all nations. Accordingly, they make it easy to find classrooms all over the world that want to link their students to others for dialogue exchange and shared learning. Services such as Skype, Google+, and WizIQ let classrooms from any connected point on the globe talk face-to-face. Google+ also features Communities where special interest groups can connect. Many of these are focused on education.

Online professional communities such as LinkedIn and EdWeb can connect teachers from all points on the globe. LinkedIn, with its more than 200 million members, lets educators connect with professionals in the field. What better way to find experts who will interact with your students? LinkedIn also features special interest groups that will appeal to teachers from kindergarten through higher ed in all subject areas. EdWeb.net is an online community of 75,000 educators where you can find 800 special interest groups, free webinars that take place almost daily, live chats, and blogs that let members read up on what's new in education. Diigo, the social bookmarking site, sponsors educational groups such as Diigo in Education, with its more than 43,000 members. Diigo also sponsors a PLN called Google for Education, as well as smaller networks for teachers of math, science, and others.

Twitter offers a unique learning network of educators that can be accessed through hashtag searches. Search Twitter for #edchat to find a surprising professional learning experience. Each Tuesday at noon Eastern Standard Time (EST), and again at 7:00 p.m. EST, #edchat hosts a live tweeted chat. Chat topics are voted on by community members every Sunday and Monday at #twtpoll, with the top choice featured during the evening chat and the second-place choice featured at noon. If you're wondering how a robust chat can happen at 140 characters per tweet, check it out next Tuesday! #edchat is the brainchild of Tom Whitby (@tomwhitby), who also created the Educator's PLN and two LinkedIn groups, Technology-Using Professors and Twitter-Using Educators; Steven Anderson (#web20blogger), who blogs at the Web 2.0 Connected

Classroom (http://blog.web20classroom.org); and Shell Terrell (@shellterrell), whose Teacher Reboot Camp blog connects classes globally through social media.

In Edutopia's Teacher Leadership blog, How to Use Twitter to Grow Your PLN (George Lucas 2012) lists hashtags and scheduled chats for kindergarten teachers (#kinderchat), science (#scichat), music (#musedchat), ELL (#ellchat), new and pre-service (#ntchat), art (#artsed), and world language (#langchat) teachers, among others. Searching for hashtags is like entering keyword searches into a search engine. Make one up and see what you find. Typically, one will lead to many others, and soon you'll be tweeting with hundreds of others who share your passion.

Networking online affords a platform where teachers can ask questions and count on lots of answers. It's also an opportune way to involve your students in global learning with students from near and far. Teachers at the Center for Global Studies in Norwalk, Connecticut, network with educators in Arabic-speaking countries, China, and Japan to create meaningful authentic experiences for students on three continents. They—and groups like them—are always looking for ways to broaden cultural understanding through student experiences and connections.

PLN opportunities for educators are plentiful. Start your search anywhere on the web and follow links, tweets, and blogs to expand your network of likeminded educators. Then take the next step: Make a global connection for your students and watch how it can change their perspectives, their goals, and their lives.

# Part VII
# Search

# Chapter 13

# Google Search

*Google's mission is to organize the world's information and make it universally accessible and useful.*

Google Scholar, Library Support, 2014

In *Teaching the Digital Generation*, Ian Jukes writes that in this digital age, "the need for high school libraries with printed materials will diminish significantly. . . . Librarians must become digital research experts rather than just archivists" (Kelly, 2009: 40).

That's a difficult message to deliver to librarians, but just as our century-old model of education doesn't make sense to 21st-century kids, neither does our century-old model of school libraries where kids armed with note cards sit with books and periodicals to research and write reports and essays. Using the Google search engine in the library can revolutionize the way kids work and learn. But most of our students—and teachers—fail to benefit from the real power of Google search. In this chapter, we'll explore new ways to better searches.

The World Wide Web enables today's connected libraries to offer unprecedented access to infinite worldwide resources. Students can search in web-based search engines such as Google or Yahoo, or in licensed databases such as ABC-CLIO. The librarian can help students understand the difference and learn the most efficient way to use each. Whereas a single search on a web-based search engine like Google, Yahoo!, or Bing can yield millions of results, licensed databases yield far fewer, with options that have been authenticated by a staff of editors to yield scholarly resources. When required to use academically focused library databases, students report finding primary source documents, papers in professional journals, and work from experts in the field that add value to their work. Yet, despite constant reminders that the focus of a web-based search engine is not academic, students of all ages will tell you that they prefer to "google it," and that, when left to their own resources, they almost always start with a Google search. Why? Because even when armed with a clear understanding of the attributes of databases, they argue that formulating queries is nonintuitive, making this work time consuming, confusing, and frustrating. Furthermore, for younger students or those who read below their grade level, primary sources or expert testimony in a given field can often be sophisticated and difficult to understand. Google, they tell us, with its quick and easy format, might not guarantee expert and primary sources, but it will give them enough to get by with.

As for the more than a million results, students find this irrelevant—their practice is to hastily gather information on articles found on the first and second screen, with little thought to origin or veracity.

High schools and even universities are struggling with today's kneejerk tendency to "google it." Many have concluded that if you can't fight it, you need to find a way to join it! Fortunately, Google has worked to find reliable ways to deliver a more academic search to students. Today, Google Search is much more than the basic search engine that was created in 1997, now featuring numerous specialized search engines that have been developed to help searches yield viable research-based results.

Who doesn't love Google search? There's no faster way to check the spelling of a word, to learn how to plant and prune the new bush you just received as a gift, or to find the exact altitude of Machu Picchu. Hardly a day goes by that we don't google something. Quick, easy searches make Google everyone's best friend, but when search becomes research, Google can be frustrating and misleading, with the user struggling to find the exact combination of keywords that will yield the right stuff. Type "imperialism" into Google, and in 0.21 seconds, the screen will give you 53,800,000 results. Three years ago, there were only 14,600,000 results. With information on the web growing exponentially, how can a student hope to locate worthwhile resources? In this Google search for "imperialism," the first links are to Wikipedia and several dictionary sites that define the word. These are followed by sites like Imperialism 101 and other encyclopedic types of web pages. At the bottom of the screen, Google features **In-depth Articles** from publications like the *New York Times* and the *Guardian*, followed by suggested related searches. Google's second screen offers definitions, synonyms, organizations, a few more articles from publications, and a webquest. Although links found on the third screen are the most worthy thus far, most students will never get that far, having spent all their time taken notes on the definition, the encyclopedic version of imperialism, and information gleaned from those university sites that aren't password-protected. These students will not yet have found a single primary source or expert paper on the topic.

Google's **Search Tools** option lets the user set date parameters, eliminate already visited pages, or set the reading level. In the case of our Imperialism search, Google defaults to an Intermediate reading level, where 85 percent of results can be found. Changing the level to advanced will display only 13 percent of the most advanced results, with 3 percent categorized as basic reading level. Asking students in middle and high school to select advanced reading level will help them find more worthwhile resources in the first few screens. Asking them to skip the first and second screens is also a good bet for locating more worthwhile information. The basic Google Search menu offers links to images, videos, books, and news that match your search, but aside from images, students rarely check out any of those options. In most cases, they will tell you that they never really noticed them. Showing students all the options will help them conduct more worthwhile searches.

Google search helps students by predicting options for keywords as they type. Entering the first few letters of a word will trigger a dropdown menu of suggested searches. Type "imp" and Google will suggest "imperialism, imperialism definition, imperialism in africa, in china, in ww1, in india, imperialism examples" (Google Search, 2014), and so forth. As the student continues to enter letters, the predictions will shift. Students often disregard Google predictions, thus missing options that they might not otherwise have considered.

Google never fails to return more results than one person could ever read, and certainly enough for students to call research. But Google search offers no authentication of resources. Who wrote it? Who published it? Is there a bias? If so, what's the counterpoint? Does this article represent the latest data? Is the point of view held by experts in the field? Although you can find valid resources on Google, each link needs to be authenticated by the user to be sure of the information. Students who don't bother with that important step often find themselves quoting from a report posted by a fourth-grader or a fiction writer! You can help students get the most out of Google search by taking them to the "Google Guide" at www.googleguide.com. Created by Nancy Blachman and Jerry Peek (2013), there are guides created for novices, experts, and teens. The novice site defines search terms to help kids get started.

## Google Advanced Search

Under the cog icon in the upper right corner of Google search, users will find **Advanced Search**. Here, Google offers even more ways to help narrow a search by using a series of prompts. Formulating keyword searches is made easier by options such as "Find web pages that have: all these words, this exact wording or phrase, one or more of these words." or by using a series of Boolean symbols (+, –, *). Advanced search permits the user to ask for a specific file format, or to search only for pages in a certain language or published in a certain region. Requesting that pages be filtered by last update date will yield the latest findings. Limiting your search to a single domain such as .gov or .edu can give users a better chance for authoritative, timely, and accurate resources. Working with students on copyright law and fair use is always critical to successful completion and publication of a project. Advanced search can assist by permitting the user to set the filter to search for web pages that define various levels of usage rights: "not filtered by license; free to use or share; free to use, share or modify; free to use, share or modify commercially" (Google Advanced Search, 2014).

Google makes setting advance search parameters effortless. But educators will have to start each session with a reminder to students to do so. After the habit has been established, teachers will see better results from Google searches. Help them to understand the ramifications of advanced searches by showing them an example like the following one:

Let's revisit the imperialism search that returned more than 53 million web pages. Repeating the process in Advanced Search, we were able to limit the search to "Imperialism + South America but not Peru," returning 699,000 results. Further refining to include those resources rated at an advanced level filtered pages down to 66,400. Further refining the search to look for web pages written in Spanish took the count down to 399 pages. Changing the usage rights to "free to use, share or modify" left us with five results in Spanish (four were Wikipedia). Changing the language to English gives us 890 selections.

A little-known tool in the Google search arsenal is the backward search. Teaching website evaluation strategies is key to successful research, and backward searches return a list of all websites that link to a given web page. This type of search can be of greatest value when authority and bias are in question. Results of a backward search give the user a quick view of the types of sources and organizations that value the work on the original website. Many readers will already be familiar with Alan November's work on authenticating websites. He points to www.martinlutherking.org as an example of a web page that draws kids in by misrepresenting the subject, Dr. King, then exposing them to a racist and hateful message (November 2012). Google enables the users to use a link command to conduct a backward search. In this case, entering *link:martinlutherking.org* into the browser reveals links to white supremacist and hate organizations, hate-watch organizations, and college courses designed to teach website evaluation. Additionally, teach students to add a Whois search. Whois database searches reveal the names of domain owners. (Type Whois into Google to find numerous Whois search engines.) In this case, the Whois search revealed that the MLK site is a propaganda site built and owned by a hate organization, although to a casual observer and a naive student, it looks totally legitimate. Research conducted here would be replete with false statements about Dr. King's life and legacy.

Kids will need explicit instructions to learn advanced search techniques and constant reminders to make them a habit. They'll soon realize that the extra minutes they spend tweaking the search settings before they begin their work will let them work faster and smarter.

## Google Search around the World

For students of world languages or for those in ESL/ELL programs, Google offers three opportunities. Under the Google cog (upper right), users can go to **Advanced Search** and narrow their search to pages in one of 46 languages. Task bars and menus will remain in English. A more robust option is to select **Languages** under the cog to set Google to display entirely in one of nearly 200 languages. This lets students see taskbar and menu options in the selected language. The third option takes you directly to that country's Google search engine, which will return searches specific to that culture. Searching within another country's resources is advantageous, eliminating the need to change language preferences, avoiding poorly translated documents, and giving the student a broader and more authentic search in the target language. To access searches from other countries, users can simply change google.com to google + the country code. For example, Google.cm takes you to Cameroon's search engine, Google.fr takes users to France, and Google.es to Spain. Searching for imperialismo in Google.es will give students nearly 2 million Spanish language results. The search engine for Spain offers all four of Spain's languages: Spanish, Catalan, Galego, and Euskara. Searches in Google search for India lets users select from any of the 14 different languages of that country. World language students will find more authentic pages within the target language search engine. Access to target language news feeds will let kids compare international reactions to and reporting of world events to that provided by U.S. news outlets. ESL or ELL students can keep pace with classmates as they work and research in their native language to support work rendered difficult by the language barrier.

## Google Image Search

Although Google doesn't readily post statistics, Wikipedia tells us that as of 2010, Google image search had more than 10 billion indexed images, with a billion views per day ("Google Images," 2014). This easy-to-use search engine includes search tools to filter by image size, color, and type (face, photo, clip art, line drawing, or animated). The **Show Sizes** view includes the image resolution beneath each image to help determine if whether original image will work for your particular project without pixelating or blurring. Categories can be further refined by using the Advanced Search options accessible through the familiar Google cog. Most useful when students are engaged in image search is to ask them to click on **Usage Rights** in the Search Toolbar to request a specific level of licensing. For most work, students should search for images labeled for reuse with modification. Students still need to attribute the image to its owner but can freely use it in its original form or modify it for use in their online publication.

Students searching in Google images without preselecting usage rights should click through to the website where the image originates. Scrolling to the bottom of the screen, they should look for a Privacy, Copyright, or Permissions link that will guide how they should attribute the work. In the event that the copyright states that all rights are reserved, students can locate the Contact Me link and write to ask for permission to reuse the resource. See the chapters on Plagiarism and Copyright for more details.

## Google Reverse Image Search

It's a good idea to introduce Google reverse image search to students. In the Google Images search bar, the camera icon lets the user upload an image. Google will use that image to search for images that are the same or have similar attributes. It will also pull in text descriptions—that is, metadata and/or captions. If you're out and about, Google reverse image search is a useful way to find out what you're looking at. Just snap a photo and upload it. If you're a professional photographer or graphic artists who requires a fee for reuse, it's the go-to way to find instances of copyright infringement, since the search will lead them back to web pages that are illegally posting.

## Google Public Data Explorer

The Google Public Data Explorer is designed to help the user deal with large data sets through manipulation, visualization, and animated timelines. According to Google, "You don't have to be a data expert to navigate between different views, make your own comparisons, and share your findings" ("Google Public Data Explorer," 2014).

Students and teachers will be fascinated by the movable charts and maps in Google's Public Data Explorer. Draggable timelines animate change over a period of time. These animated visualizations help students understand changes that happened during a specific time frame and allow them to select multiple variables to yield visual comparisons. Charts and maps generated with Google Public Data Explorer are easily inserted or embedded into presentations or web pages as dynamic links that update automatically each time Google's data is updated. Because Public Data Explorer draws its statistical information from reliable sources such as the U.S. Census Bureau and the World Bank, regular updates are consistent, making this an authoritative source for research, especially in social studies, economics, and statistics.

Google Public Data Explorer features a chart that can track the population of the United States or of any individual or group of states between the years 1968 and the present. The data was downloaded from the U.S. Census Bureau and includes a "last updated" date. The user can select the states to be viewed and compared and choose from a variety of graphing types: bar, line, map chart, or bubble chart of the United States. By dragging the bar on the timeline, you can see the population of each selected state increase or diminish over several decades. This chart also allows the selection of variables, such as age group or sex. A play button will animate the chart over time (Google Public Data "Population in the U.S.," 2014).

Each public data chart works a bit differently, but each is fascinating to manipulate and offers a visual time capsule to students and teachers. Other options include a chart on flu trends that can display data by country or by specific U.S. state, or a worldwide infant mortality rate chart for data between 1960 and 2009. Students can switch variables; select countries, states, or regions; or change chart colors, type, or scale. It's easy to view one country's data or to add more layers to compare and contrast numerous data sets. Teachers and students working with these charts always express surprise at what the data reveals ("Google Public Data Explorer," 2014).

Additionally, note that Google Spreadsheet offers a "motion chart" that will add a similar kind of animation to any chart or graph. To use it, simply select the range of cells, click on the **Google Charts Wizard**, and let Google do the rest.

## Google Scholar and Google Library Links

Google search is so ubiquitous that students from kindergarten through higher education generally favor it over licensed databases, where formulating a reliable query can be cumbersome and complex. Librarians, seeking ways to drive their students toward primary source documents and scholarly works in the library's licensed holdings, find themselves battling the "I want it now, and I want it fast!" mentality. Google has a solution that has proven successful. Google Scholar Library Links uses Google Scholar as a portal to link students to underutilized library databases. And Google Scholar, with its familiar Google interface, is easy to use. Here's how it works:

"Google Scholar helps you find relevant work across the world of scholarly research . . . drawn from academic publishers, professional societies, online repositories, universities and other websites." And Google Scholar selects documents the same way as licensed databases, basing acceptance on full text, author, publisher, and "how often and how recently it has been linked to other scholarly work." Although many searches in Scholar will, indeed, bring you to a full-text document, other search results will point you to the database that holds the article, requiring a user name and password for access. In this way, Google Scholar can increase traffic to library databases, where students will always find full text and fully authenticated results ("Google Library Scholar Support," 2014).

The Google Library Links program, like Google Scholar, is free and has been successfully implemented by major universities like MIT, Emory, and Northwestern, (Google Scholar Library Support, 2014). Jeff Garrett, former associate Northwestern University librarian, explained in a 2007 article how Northwestern University's library used Google Scholar's Library Links to maximize users' access to its licensed materials (Garrett, 2007).

The Google Library Links program connects a library's licensed holdings to Google Scholar (Google Scholar Library Support, 2014). Northwestern (NU) joined the program in 2005, adding a Google Scholar button to the library's home page and launching a plan to educate students and staff about it. Garrett wrote that the library promoted the program to benefit from Google's popularity "to get people to capitalize on the high-quality information we're paying for" (Garrett, 2007). Northwestern University, whose goal was to realize a 20 percent increase in the first year, was thrilled at the 78 percent increase in requests for articles coming from Google Scholar users.

Garrett's report dates back to 2007. In May 2011, we spoke with Geoff Morse (2011), then reference and instruction librarian at NU, to get an update. Morse echoed Garrett's sentiments of several years earlier and added that instruction on using Live Links is now delivered during freshman seminar. He explained that to enable Live Links, NU had given Google permission to crawl the NU SFX server weekly for updates, always maintaining access to current database resources. Although Google is not licensed to deliver content from every database, those able to be included had seen a marked increase in traffic. He explained that the entire Library Links program is electronic and uses the ISSN number for identification. This does not include books, so the library collection is not linked in. As students search on Google Scholar, they see results marked **Find it at NU**, allowing students to click through to the full text article in one of NU's licensed databases. Geoff agrees that Google Scholar Library Links has been successful in driving database use and, although a school's IT staff will have to set up this same thing at your school, Google is happy to work with you to achieve that. Garrett, in his 2007 article, summed it up by writing: "Users want ease of access. We want comprehensive coverage . . . . Google Scholar can do both."

## Google Library Search

As previously mentioned, Google Scholar Library Link does not link to a library's book collection. But Google offers Library Search, through which the library's collection can be listed in the Online Computer Library Center's (OCLC) Open WorldCat. In this case, users searching for a book will find a Library Search link to the Open World-Cat database, where they will see a list of local libraries that have the book they are requesting.

Google Scholar Library Link and Google Scholar Library Search have successfully increased usage of databases and book collections in major universities around the country. Perhaps they will work for your students as well.

# Google Books

One of Google's missions is to make the world's books accessible online. To date, numerous libraries have granted permission to Google to scan their entire collections to add to the Google Books catalog. Despite legal battles over copyright issues, Google continues to add print resources to its library. (On November 13, 2013, Google won a decisive decision that allowed it to continue scanning books. An appeal is expected.) In August 2010, Google announced its goal to scan all known existing books (129,864,880) by the end of the decade, encompassing more than 4 billion digital pages and 2 trillion words. By April 2013, Google had scanned more than 30 million (Wikipedia, "Google Books").

Are your students using books in their research? Are they finding what they're looking for? Locating just the right information in books is sometimes like looking for a needle in a haystack. Content that doesn't appear in the index will routinely go undiscovered. Because book-based research can be time-consuming and frustrating, students turn to search engines and databases. Google Books offers a solution that many haven't yet discovered. Its multifaceted search engine allows the user to not only search for books and other print media, but also fully search the complete text of each publication for content. Google search engines make it easy to find nonindexed details of every piece of writing. And book indexes are hyperlinked to quickly jump to the search term within the book's text.

Google Books gives users numerous options for access. Out-of-copyright texts and those in the public domain are available in downloadable PDF versions. Books still protected by copyright are sometimes fully available, but more often can only be previewed. In some cases, the user can pay to download them. If you prefer to buy the book, Google offers a list of sellers. The Google Play store now offers some titles as eBooks. Would you like to add your writings to the Google Books collection? Authors can apply to Google to make that happen.

Visitors to Google Books will find thousands of rare books, historical books, historical documents, pamphlets, theatre programs, journals, diaries, lithographs, prints, old books in poor condition that can no longer be circulated, uncut books that date back several centuries, as well as entire university collections, including those of American universities, such as the University of Michigan and Harvard, and of universities from around the world, such as Oxford University in the UK and Keio University in Japan. Well-known libraries such as Spain's National Library of Catalonia and the New York Public Library have also partnered with Google to digitize the world's books. Google Books protects volumes from natural disasters, such as hurricanes, floods, and fire, and allow us to examine historical volumes without leaving our desk and without danger of damage to delicate and relevant works. Google's specially engineered scanners also guarantee no damage to books and documents being added to the library ("Google Books History" 2014). Google Books now enables search for content in magazines.

Google Books continues to add to its program to allow the individual to access and interact with books and print media in different and more personalized ways. These tools are often experimental and thus are not always available:

**About This Book** links readers to relevant related resources to enrich the experience. This typically includes book reviews and ratings, related books, selected pages and references from scholarly works, and maps. A word cloud displays common words and phrases found in the text. Bibliographic metadata and information about the author can also be found. Readers are also invited to add a review. A QR code gives users mobile access the same information.

**Popular Passages** will often trace the passage or quote back to its first publication date. Users will also find links to the various sources that requote it.

**Advanced Search** lets the reader search by author, title, publisher, subject or publication date, as well as by ISBN or ISSN. It's also possible to track a single passage or quote by entering it into the "search for exact phrase" box. A search can be further defined by selecting or eliminating the categories of books, magazines, or eBooks.

**My Library** gives readers the opportunity to assemble a personal book collection where they can review and rate selections, then share their library with others. eBooks can be read on mobile devices using the Google Play Books app. Some offer an audio or video option. You can even upload your own PDF or ePub files to read. Google Play Books lets you add notes and highlight, translate, or define a word or, in some cases, when the word selected is a place, tapping on it may reveal an information card or a map with a description and information about that place. Tap on the map to view it in Google Maps or Google Earth (Google Play Books, 2014).

Have you ever been mentioned in a book? Type your name into the Google Books Search engine. Even if your name didn't make it into the index of that book, Google will find you and tell you the page number where you appear; in many cases, you will be able to read the text right on the screen. Have you written and published a piece of writing? Google may be able to find it and tell you what libraries include it in their collections.

Google Books, with its user-friendly Google search interface, gives librarians the means to reacquaint students with the vast body of work that over the past centuries has appeared on the printed page. It can be quickly accessed by clicking on Books on the main Google search screen.

# Google News

While today's online news makes it simple to gather information from news outlets around the world, the process of finding just the right information on each of these can be time-consuming. Google News can help by aggregating and organizing news stories worldwide. (To search in Google News, click on News in the Google Search menu.) The home page brings the user to the day's featured stories, some with real-time coverage. The user can begin by selecting their nation's edition. Filters allow the reader to receive top picks from around the world, from their nation, or from news local to them. It's fascinating to switch to another country's edition of Google News, where students can see how top stories that dominate the news are treated from country to country. Whether students speak other languages or are monolingual, take them there to compare "front pages"—each featured article is accompanied by a photo that will allow students to compare what they see affording an excellent lesson in visual literacy.

Google News readers can select the content that interests them the most. Categories include Business, Science, Technology, Entertainment, Sports, and Health, along with a Spotlight feature. Readers can also type in additional topics of their choice. Many stories can be expanded to read more details, see real-time coverage, and click through to related articles. Encourage your students to click through to the entire article, where they can become part of the news story by posting comments online. And chances are you'll find comments that reflect a higher degree of critical thinking when kids know the world will read them.

Google news aggregators select and rank articles by using computers that evaluate how often and on what sites a story appears online as well as by "certain characteristics of news content such as freshness, location, relevance and diversity. As a result, stories are sorted without regard to political viewpoint or ideology," allowing the reader to select "from a wide variety of perspectives on any given story" (Google, 2013). Without human bias at work behind the scenes, users can be assured that they will find expressions of all viewpoints and perspectives among search results. Should the user want to read news reported from a certain perspective, he or she can adjust the sources from which their homepage draws its news, selecting from news outlets around the world.

Students tend to believe what they see and read in the media. Google News offers teachers an excellent opportunity to help students learn to filter the media in order to develop an awareness of all categories of bias: cultural, social, religious, race, political, and media. By gathering reports of any one story from various publishers both in the United States and abroad, Google News readers can experience the event or issue from various perspectives and viewpoints all on one screen. When the World Trade Center was attacked on September 11, 2001, students were asked to search the Internet for headline news around the country and the world. International reactions as seen in these publications helped students realize that we don't all think alike or react to a given situation in the same way. It was a fascinating and eye-opening lesson in nationalistic bias. World language teachers were able to have students read accounts from around the world in their target language. Google News can aggregate that information quickly and easily bringing it to the classroom on a single computer screen.

**Google Trends** tracks searches on top stories, and links to more information on each. Users can also find dynamic charts that compare searches on two or more topics from 2004 to the present. For example, students preparing to apply to colleges could enter the names of several schools (e.g., Harvard, Yale, Princeton) to see which is getting the most search traffic today or over the past decade. **Google Zeitgeist**, accessible from Trends, lets readers see the top searches from the previous year.

## Conclusion

Although library databases are unrivaled in the access they grant to primary sources and expert writings, students still want to google! This close look at Google's specialized search engines might convince you to give them a try. Each one is unique in how it searches, generating efficient and reliable results through strictly defined parameters. Ian Jukes reminds us in *Teaching the Digital Generation* that digital tools that provide kids with a "sensory-rich world full of color, sound, graphics and video" make "learning about the world dynamic, relevant, and fun" (Kelly, McCain, and Jukes, 2009: 15, 13). Google's specialized search engines will help minimize frustration while engaging your students in more robust research.

# Chapter 14

# *Literacy*

Literacy in the second decade of the 21st century is a complex issue due to the functionality of HTML5 and the dawn of Web 3.0 (extended web, Web3D, semantic web). Emerging technologies have created a sea change, as witnessed in interactive books, social readers, on-demand resources, as well as web-based products and apps.

What does it mean to be literate in the second decade of the 21st century? It means being armed with an array of complex literacy skills necessary to navigate, interpret, and understand complex text and images, as well as the "extended web." These include, but are not limited to

- "Location-awareness"
- Nonlinear, hypertextual navigation
- Data mining for integration
- Customization for application
- Metadata management (data about data or information about information)
- Augmented reality (mediated reality) recognition
- Knowledge representation discernment
- Curation aptitude
- Metacomprehension (asking questions before, during, and after) reading
- "Filter bubbles" (algorithm gatekeepers of information) recognition
- Transliteracy competency
- Deep reading of complex text
- Crowdsourcing

Read/write/web (selection, evaluation, interpretation, synthesis, presentation) is just the tip of the iceberg. Literacy, as Tony Wagner points out in *The Global Achievement Gap*, is a matter of "navigating complex [forms of digital content and] information" and being your own "reference librarian" (Wagner, 2008: 179). There are numerous learning and instructional strategies that librarians employ to instill the qualities of a reference librarian: online notebooks, role-playing, word/tag clouds, questioning experts, essential questions, reciprocal peer questioning, brainstorming, content curation, interactive scavenger hunts, annotated bibliographies, debate, interactive reading activities, and modeling. These strategies teach students to reflect, self-direct, and actively question.

Librarians are technologically savvy navigators of complex information formats. They possess habits of mind—the dispositions necessary to successfully understand

and navigate multifaceted digital content: persistency, accuracy, flexible thinking, and adaptability. They are skilled reference librarians who communicate with clarity and question with intent. They know how to "teach in the interrogative."

The real art of a productive reference interview is insightful questioning. The construction of "[d]eep questions drive our thought underneath the surface of things; force us to deal with complexity. Questions of purpose force us to define our task. Questions of information force us to look at our sources of information as well as at the quality of our information. Questions of interpretation force us to examine how we are organizing or giving meaning to information and to consider alternative ways of giving meaning. Questions of assumption force us to examine what we are taking for granted. Questions of implication force us to follow out where our thinking is going. Questions of point of view force us to examine our point of view and to consider other relevant points of view. Questions of relevance force us to discriminate what does and what does not bear on a question. Questions of accuracy force us to evaluate and test for truth and correctness. Questions of precision force us to give details and be specific. Questions of consistency force us to examine our thinking for contradictions. Questions of logic force us to consider how we are putting the whole of our thought together, to make sure that it all adds up and makes sense within a reasonable system of some kind" (Foundation for Critical Thinking, 2009).

How to question effectively can be taught through modeling, online learning activities, constructive feedback, using social media, during face-to-face and virtual book chats, during reference interviews, questioning strategies during instruction, and while interacting during extracurricular activities.

Word/tag cloud scaffolds information literacy by visually capturing important words—the words that appear most frequently in a document. They visually capture the essence of poems, book passages, articles, Facebook posts, blog posts, essays, diary excerpts, speeches, legal documents, primary sources, creative writing, and so on. And they develop a variety of literacy skills:

- Keyword recognition
- word identification and vocabulary
- Sequencing
- Inference and context
- Purpose
- Predication
- Point of view
- Scanning
- Analysis
- Summary and comprehension
- Mapping

Tag clouds are customized, interactive word clouds. Customization allows words to be designed into a variety of shapes and themes and to hyperlink to Google or to a specified source, such as a dictionary. This allows a learner to scroll (hover) over a word and link to more information. At one school, the librarian creates tag clouds and has students find the appropriate hyperlinks to add. Students need to assess, decide, and do. First, each student must assess the word in context; question whether it is necessary to add additional information to clarify meaning; locate, select, and evaluate information about it; and suggest what links or information should be added to it. To further foster critical thinking, students are asked to create their own word/tag clouds on suggested topics. Students are responsible for selecting an appropriate passage on this topic, designing and inserting hyperlinks. Students share their tag clouds with the class.

Word/tag clouds may also be used as a creative writing assignment. Students are asked to select an image and write about it. A word/tag cloud is created from the writing, and the word/tag cloud is then projected. Working in teams of four or five, students analyze and evaluate it, predicting what the image is. Each team reports its prediction. The student who created the word/tag cloud then reads what he or she wrote. The teams are asked to confirm or change their prediction. The image is then revealed.

Word/tag clouds can also be a curation tool to help students with decision making and keyword searching. A student prints a copy of a website and creates a word cloud from it. He or she analyzes the keywords in the cloud for relevancy for inclusion in a digital collection. He or she can also use the keywords to further research a topic to develop a digital collection.

Reference librarians excel at developing information sets and collections. They cull timely and accurate resources for patrons using appropriate selection tools. They are, in essence, information curators. "Content curation" is an instructional strategy to instill the skills of a reference librarian. It embeds multiple literacies or "new literacies" as outlined by New Literacies Research Lab at the University of Connecticut:

- Comprehension monitoring /self-questioning
- Visual–spatial thinking
- Knowledge-based research

Students are asked to become "content curators." They find, group, organize, and share the best and most relevant digital content on a topic. They become researchers and content experts. Students are given a research rubric to guide them and define what is "expert." Each learner shares his or her findings online in an open forum. Other students post comments, suggestions, or ask clarifying questions. Through this process students learn effective questioning, as well as reasoning and assessment skills.

There are five basic models of content curation: aggregation, distillation, elevation, mashup, and chronology. Aggregation is curating the most relevant information on a topic. Distillation is curating the most important information in its simplest format. Elevation is curating information by trends or posts. Mashup integrates elements from various web resources to create a unique site.

Another effective learning strategy to integrate how to be your own reference librarian is role-playing. Students play the part of a reference librarian. They reenact the reference query. Doing so taps into multiple literacies and intelligences and helps learners develop critical thinking skills, empathy, and "habits of mind."

After the process has been explained and goals defined, the librarian asks for a volunteer and models the reference process. Students are then divided into groups of four: investigator (reference librarian), questioner (patron), observer (teacher), and videographer. Students get to choose their own roles. Each group is given a problem to be solved or an open-ended question to be answered. These are developed collaboratively by the teacher and librarian. For example: Is relativity relevant? Each group enacts the reference process. The reference inquiry process is recorded by the videographer for self-assessment and feedback purposes. The questioner poses the question or problem. The investigator asks clarifying questions. The questioner answers the clarifying questions. Together, they devise a search strategy with appropriate keywords/subject. They conduct the research together using valid information, communication and technologies ICT resources. If this does not produce an answer that satisfies the questioner, the process is repeated. The observer is given a rubric and an observation checklist to assess the process. The videographer records the reference interview. The school librarian and the collaborating teacher move from group to group facilitating the process, if necessary. Students then watch the videos and reflect on the activity through librarian/teacher prepared essential questions. What skills are necessary to find an answer or resolve a problem? What is a good question? Each students fills in a debrief form or online questionnaire. Role playing works at all levels. It is a great learning tool. Students not only re-enact the reference process, but also are able to view the action later. This really brings home what it means to be a reference librarian.

An online "interactive notebook" is also an excellent engagement tool to inculcate reference skills: persistency, questioning, metacognition, and communication. A learner downloads a virtual notebook and then divides a page into right side and left. The right side is for information and facts: It is on this side a learner inputs and organizes new knowledge—class notes, lab work, visuals, data, and research. He or she then rereads the content on the right side critically, identifying keywords and ideas. Keyword strategies, such as visualization (mental picture) or the 3M keyword method (must, might, mustn't), are integrated into the lesson.

Next, the learner analyzes, evaluates, and synthesizes the content to formulate a coherent response. On the left side of the notebook page, the learner inputs his or her response to this new knowledge. Deep questioning is critical to formulating a coherent response. As coteachers, school librarian models self-generating question strategies in various ways to guide the response process. One way is through the Revised Bloom's Self-Questioning Taxonomy. The response (left side) is an excellent formative or summative assessment tool for 21st-century literacy. "It is through the process of actively interrogating the content through provocative questions that students deepen their understanding" (Wiggins and McTighe, 2005: 106).

Using an interactive scavenger hunt as a literacy tool engages learners through a variety of senses: visual, audio, and tactile. Students use handheld devices to download or connect to clues: video clips, audio recordings, QR codes, and links. Using the clues, students weave their way around the library's physical and online collections to answer the questions or to solve the problem.

Another method used by school librarians to integrate and model questioning skills is the posing and posting essential questions: face-to-face, online, during instruction, in the library, and on the library's homepage. Students learn to formulate a variety of questions types: divergent, evaluative, clarifying, probing, and reflective. One school librarian includes essential questions on the course platform she uses. (See the graphic below for an example of the use of essential questions on an online course platform.)

"Cognitive monitoring" further extends questioning skills. Checklists in the form of guided questions are another way to help a learner to self-monitor and develop literacy skills, such as metacomprehension (Koechlin and Zwaan, 2007). Online task checklists promote the gradual release of responsibility for learning and time management. Learners learn to set and prioritize goals and are accountable for results (Partnership for 21st Century Skills, 2010).

### NCHS - 21st Century Learning Expectations:

- **1.1** apply analytical and creative thinking to identify and solve problems across disciplines
- **1.2** reflect thoughtfully on their learning
- **1.3** communicate effectively
- **1.4** demonstrate an understanding of healthy life choices
- **2.1** work responsibly and productively in both independent and collaborative environments, Information literacy-to evaluate information critically and competently
- **2.2** respect one another
- **3.1** contribute positively to the culture of NCHS and the larger community

**Understanding:** *A 21st century learner must be adept at determining currency, relevancy, authority, accuracy, and purpose of information.*

**Essential Questions: How do I live a healthy and balanced life? What do I need to know, understand and do to make good health choices?**

**Objectives: Create an essential question on one of the health related components below. Using your essential question as a guide find, select, and evaluate health resources on your selected component.**

- **cardiovascular/cardiorespiratory endurance**
- **flexibility**
- **muscular endurance**
- **muscular strength**

Transliteracy is a learner's ability to read, write, and network across a range of platforms using a variety of tools and media. It is contingent on a learner's ability to skim, scan, scroll, and switch. As information specialists, librarians apply transliteracy skills daily. They use a variety of informational tools on multiple platforms. Librarians naturally scan text for keywords to answer a reference query. At one school, the librarian inculcates scanning, as well as CRAAP testing (currency, relevance, authority, accuracy, purpose) using a social reading app and web tool—Subtext. The librarian downloads an article from Wikipedia, a popular resource with students. Subtext allows the librarian/teacher to highlight a word, phrase, or sentence that he or she wants the student to pay particular attention to. This helps develop effective scanning for information. Under the activities or assignment feature of Subtext, this librarian is able to use Common Core Assignment templates for any book or article to assign learning tasks using assignment icons such as *Highlight & Tag* and *Show Me What You Know,* and give explicit directions: Find and read the information on primary circulation in the article. Find additional information on Google on the topic. Compare and contrast the new information (find similarities and difference) with the information found in the original article. Add new information (image, link, video) to the article on Subtext. The librarian uses the discussion component of Subtext to add comments or a question about the addition information.

Transliteracy depends not only on technical aptitude, but also on online reading skills and strategies. Hsieh and Dwyer (2009), in *Educational Technology and Society: The Instructional Effect of Online Reading Strategies and Learning Styles on Student Achievement*, state, "Online reading strategies incorporate three reading strategies in an online environment: re-reading strategy, keyword strategy, and question and answer strategy." As coteachers, librarians model and integrate all three online reading strategies.

Social networks are an excellent means to engage students and to promote online reading skills. For example, one East Coast school uses Facebook as an integral part of the junior research paper. It is used as an instructional tool for ISP and an assessment tool for keywords, questioning skills, creativity, and high-order thinking. As part of a closed group, each student posts his or her topic to research. Other members of the group post comments and search suggestion or strategies. For example, for research on peer pressure, a librarian posts include "try the psychology collection [database]" and "you might use 'peer acceptance' instead of peer pressure." Each member of the community becomes accountable for learning outcomes and "build relationships with others to pose and solve problems collaboratively. . . . Manage, analyze and synthesize multiple streams of simultaneous information. . . . Design and share information for global communities to meet a variety of purposes. . . . Create, critique, analyze, and evaluate multi-media texts" (NCTE, 2008).

School librarians empower students with information fluency skills and strategies to query validity of multimodal text. Information fluency is an essential skill to 21st-century literacy. Jukes, McCain, and Crockett (2010), in *Understanding the Digital Generation: Teaching and Learning in the New Digital Landscape*, define information fluency as the ability to take a critical stance after the critically evaluation of a digital resource for accuracy, authority, and relevance. CRAAP testing (currency, relevance, authority, accuracy, and purpose) is one way that school librarians introduce information fluency. Other ways to achieve this are through an evaluative annotation bibliography process and reviews. Flexibility or information exchange knowhow is vital to information fluency and literacy competency. Information exchange is the mutually beneficial systematic electronic passing of information or data among one another. It is efficient, effective, equitable sharing of information. Excellent school librarians embed "information exchange" theory into cybersafety, identity management, and literacy instruction.

"User task analysis" assessments provide librarians with data to assess flexibility and fluency. For example, a school librarian uses the Subtext app/premium (a premium account gives you access to CCSSs templates, allows you to track progress, access other educators in the Subtext community, and allows for text to speech; Subtext is also web-based at www.subtext.com) to integrate the Common Core State Standards (CCSSs). She uses the CCSS templates to choose the appropriate grade level, text type, reading range, and standard. Subtext allows this librarian to track students' progress and evidence of learning.

Innovative school librarians exploit emerging technologies to augment the application of Marzano's research-based strategies for acquisition of 21st-century literacies: identifying similarities and differences (classifying), summarizing and note taking, reinforcing effort and providing recognition, nonlinguistic representation, cooperative learning, setting objectives and providing feedback, and generating and testing hypotheses, as well as cues, questions, and advance organizers. They integrate Venn diagrams, KWL, and online graphic organizers such as Gliffy-flowcharts, Webspiration-outlining, and SpiderScribe-brainstorming to clarify thought, formulate a search strategy, and to identify key concepts and keywords.

The integrating keyword strategies for research, keyword strategies for reading, and the interpretation of visual cues into literacy instruction are important in a digital world. Online reading and offline reading differ. Students do not read online or process information in the traditional left-to-right sequence. They scan, skim, and scroll.

The application of online reading strategies are essential to successfully navigating nonlinear text—hypertext. According to Hsin-Yuan Chen, "Hypertext structure is another focal issue in online reading comprehension. . . . The hypertext structure helps the reader understand the organizational pattern and establish a mental process for finding the information from the text" (Chen, 2009).

The capacity to access, evaluate, analysis, synthesize, interpret, predict, question, process, visualize, manage, manipulate, apply, create and communicate information, data, and media in various formats is fundamental to literacy in a digital environment. This is evident in a study by Eszter Hargittai, Lindsay Fullerton, Ericka Menchen-Trevino, and Kristin Yates (2010), "When using a search engine, many students clicked on the first search result. Over a quarter of respondents mentioned that they chose a web site because the search engine had returned that site as the first result, suggesting considerable trust in these services. In some cases, the respondent regarded the search engine as the relevant entity for which to evaluate trustworthiness, rather than the web site that contained the information." Because of this, librarians teach "conceptual unity" and keyword strategies to students as a 21st-century skill.

To be literate in cyberspace, today's students need to possess the following skills: critical thinking, creativity, problem solving, self-direction, questioning, and reflection. To be literate tomorrow, students will also need to be investigative, responsive, and penetrating. Librarians afford students with decision-making competency to assess the multidimensional literacies of computer-generated "realities."

The web is in constant flux. Currently, the Internet is participatory, social, content-driven (informational), hyperlinked, user-centered, keyword-interfaced (shallow natural language), augmented, and mobile. The emerging web is personalized/customized, virtual, semantic, data-linked (cloud-based data), service-driven, natural language–interfaced (question-based), and portable. It is not about links, but about how data is structured, standardized (ontologies), and systematized.

Students need the knowhow to navigate in a nonlinear, metadata "think" web. They do so through inquiry. Questioning is central to inquiry—especially information inquiry.

According to the Association of College and Research Libraries, "Information literacy is a survival skill in the Information Age. Instead of drowning in the abundance of information that floods their lives, information literate people know how to find, evaluate, and use information effectively to solve a particular problem or make a decision . . ." (ALA, 1989). It is imperative that students learn higher-order thinking skills and habits of mind to navigate an evolving web, an environment that requires multiple literacies/transliteracy, and that school librarians, as information specialists, guide and mentor them in this process.

The CCSSs outline 21st-century literacy (reading, writing, speaking, listening, language), providing a "staircase" of complexity, integration of higher-order thinking skills and academic growth. Inquiry and text complexity are at the core of the CCSSs. Text complexity is defined as qualitative evaluation, quantitative evaluation, and task considerations with an emphasis on reading informational text. These standards are really about obtaining knowledge by researching, reading text, analyzing text, and creating text. Literacy in the coming decade is a complex skill, but fortunately for our students, excellent librarians can surf and navigate with the best of them.

# Chapter 15

# Visual Literacy

*If students aren't taught the language of sound and images, shouldn't they be considered as illiterate as if they left college without being able to read or write?*

George Lucas (Daly, 2004)

In the course of writing this book, I wrote to several people requesting permission to include them. Most of them were teachers who wrote back to accept. Their e-mails were congenial, often offering further information on the topic and asking questions about the book. But one of my e-mails went to a teenager named Jack Andraka. Jack came to my attention while watching a television news magazine that reported that in 2012, at age 15, he had developed a test to detect pancreatic, ovarian, and lung cancer. Driven by the death of a close family friend to pancreatic cancer and determined to search for a better detection system, Jack began his research on Google and Wikipedia (he couldn't afford scientific or medical documents on his five dollar weekly allowance) (Axelrod, 2013). I asked Jack's permission to include him in the chapter on Access and the Filtering Debate to demonstrate the merits of open access for high school students. Why then am I including this story in a chapter on visual literacy? When I wrote to Jack for permission to include his story in my book, he sent back an answer that surprised me. He simply wrote, "Sure! Do you want a photo?" I laughed out loud when I read it. Of course, I wanted a photo although, I told him, the editor might not include it in the final printing. But not a single educator had thought to ask me that question. Jack's generation is far more visual than we ever were and in six short words, he proved it!

These days we are bombarded with visuals. It's never been easier to document an event, large or small, with everyone snapping photos, recording videos, and posting them to Instagram or Facebook. People of all ages pull smartphones from pockets to share photos of best friends, last night's concert, a grandchild, the new house, and the ever-popular selfie! While it is true that we see hundreds or even thousands of visuals each day—images, photos, designs, drawings, videos, diagrams, maps, to name a few—it is also true that with a few startling exceptions, we rarely take the time to really look at them. Learning to interpret visuals as well as knowing how to select just the right one to support exact meaning can be challenging and time consuming. Including the study of visual literacy in a K–12 curriculum will serve to make students aware of and think critically about the visual world around them. The Association of College and Research Libraries (ACRL) gives us the following definition of visual literacy:

> Visual literacy is a set of abilities that enables an individual to effectively find, interpret, evaluate, use, and create images and visual media. Visual literacy skills equip a learner to understand and analyze the contextual, cultural, ethical, aesthetic, intellectual, and technical components involved in the production and use of visual materials. A visually literate individual is both a critical consumer of visual media and a competent contributor to a body of shared knowledge and culture. (Hattwig 2011)

ACRL goes on to provide these guidelines:

"A visually literate individual is able to:

- Determine the nature and extent of the visual materials needed
- Find and access needed images and visual media effectively and efficiently
- Interpret and analyze the meanings of images and visual media
- Evaluate images and their sources
- Use images and visual media effectively
- Design and create meaningful images and visual media
- Understand many of the ethical, legal, social, and economic issues surrounding the creation and use of images and visual media, and access and use visual materials ethically"

These ACRL guidelines were written for higher education, but they can be easily simplified, modified, and scaffolded to be accessible to students K–12.

Teachers themselves sometimes fail to grasp the impact of teaching visual literacy to students. Despite the fact that they ask students to communicate research results with presentation slides or video, teachers tend to focus predominantly on the written or spoken word, paying little attention to the student's image selection. What's more, project visuals are often relegated to a minor role in the project rubric as if acknowledging them as no more than a decorative afterthought. In response, students tend to include visuals for their appeal rather than for their relevance to the content, seemingly unaware that more thoughtful choices would serve to strengthen their presentation and deepen audience understanding. Teachers can raise awareness by instructing students in visual literacy and making it a part of every lesson and project rubric.

Once students grasp the concept that visuals matter, educators need to remind them to attribute their sources just as they do for articles, books, and blogs. While we scrutinize project bibliographies for consistency, we tend to overlook the fact that students (and teachers) routinely "harvest" visuals at will, downloading, copying/pasting, and embedding them into blogs, websites or presentation slides with no thought to copyright. After all, we reason, the "borrowed" image is just a design element to make the product more appealing! But when we are unequivocal about our belief that we need to teach visual literacy, we can profoundly impact student awareness as they learn to use images to support, enhance, and clarify the meaning of the work. Once the selection becomes a conscious process, it will make more sense to them to cite the source or creator.

The Partnership for 21st Century Skills (P21) identifies media and visual literacies as critical for preparing students to thrive in their future studies, life, and work. They also acknowledge that teachers who are unfamiliar with how today's visually oriented generation lives are less apt to advance their students' understanding of visual literacy. P21 urges the following for schools in their professional development programs:

> When appropriate, take advantage of 21st century tools, such as real world, rich media examples, video clips, interactive exercises, simulations based on historical or real-time data sources, acoustically- and visually-rich primary sources and digital repositories, to support 21st century skills.
>
> Given that a main objective of building students' 21st century skills is to prepare them to communicate across multiple media as well as manipulate and make sense of complex data sources, it is important that teachers are aware of such resources and feel comfortable about incorporating them into their curricula. (Professional Development, 2007)

Teachers who learn to work with visuals will be more likely to transfer this learning and these skills back to the classroom.

Once we accept the premise that visual literacy should be an essential part of a well-rounded 21st-century education, we need to determine how to define and teach it. There are increasing numbers of lesson plans on the Internet to help teachers get started. One of these, called "Picture This," asks students to view and interpret historical and present-day primary source images. This site from The Oakland Museum of California defines visual literacy as "the ability to understand communications composed of visual images as well as being able to use visual imagery to communicate to others." The museum believes that "students become visually literate by the practice of visual encoding (expressing their thoughts and ideas in visual form) and visual decoding (translating and understanding the meaning of visual imagery) (Picture This, 2014).

Librarians are in a position to help teachers and students move to a position of better understanding and clearer appreciation of the visuals all around them. One way to do this is to create an assured experience that will reach every student. In one high school, departments were asked to adopt one or more 21st-century skills. The social studies department claimed responsibility for visual literacy, agreeing to make it a goal for all teachers and students. Technology integration teachers visited each class to ask kids to brainstorm a definition of visual literacy and to identify as many kinds of visuals as they could think of. They then showed each class a series of carefully selected photos, asking them to think critically about them, to interpret them, to decide if they believed them, to speculate as to the circumstances, to detect bias or prejudice in the work, and to imagine what might have come before or after the moment the photo was captured. Having raised awareness and introduced the term "visual literacy" to every freshman, the lesson was immediately reinforced with an assignment to create three slides on a given topic, paying close attention to the selection of visuals and being able to justify their choices. Creating, posting, and sharing the slides in the cloud let teachers and peers offer feedback on how well the chosen images in each slide set painted a clear picture of the assigned topic. It's crucial when teaching this skill to give kids the time to practice and understand it.

When this kind of lesson takes place early in the school year and touches every student, teachers across the curriculum can reap the benefit, sometimes asking kids to interpret a visual and other times asking them to find or create one to support their work. It's important to consistently remind students that a well-chosen visual can add dimension to a thought, can change opinions on a topic, and can cut through the complexity and confusion that often comes when the explanation is only in words. The right visual can elucidate, inspire, create wonder, arouse curiosity, and bring clarity. By contrast, one that is poorly or hastily selected can cause confusion, misleading the viewer or creating a disconnect between the image and the topic.

## Questions to Ask When Teaching Visual Literacy

Mario Mattei, president and cofounder of Visual Peacemakers, an organization dedicated to "peacemaking and breaking down stereotypes by displaying the beauty of cultures around the world" (visualpeacemakers.org) wrote *10 How To's for Visual Peacemaking*, suggesting questions to help people understand the "connective experiences between the viewer and the image" (Mattei, 2011). These can be easily adapted to help teachers and students determine the value of an image. The following are inspired by and adapted from his words:

- What do I want the images to say?
- What impact should the images have on the reader or audience member?
- Does the image I have chosen lead to a better understanding of my premise, hypothesis, conclusion or topic, or is it misleading or misrepresentational? Does it create misconceptions?
- Is the image the most powerful representation I can find?
- Is the image relevant and timely?
- Is it authentic or has it been altered to falsely represent an event that never happened?
- What does the image reveal about the topic, the person, the time period?
- Does the image reveal a bias, a stereotype or a point of view? If so, is it what you are trying achieve or are you trying to sway judgment?
- Do you need to balance it with another image or find an image that is more neutral?
- What emotion are you trying to elicit from viewers? Does it correspond to the tone of your writing or is it different to the point that it is confusing?
- Does the image you chose support and strengthen your thesis or statement?
- Does it connect the viewer to your text or distance him? What connections do you want him to make?
- What conclusions should your images help him to draw?
- How convincing are your selections? How powerful?
- What elements are you trying to highlight?
- Do your images broaden or narrow the viewer's mindset and understanding?

David Galalis, photographer, wrote on his Flickr site that he is "Always seeking greater engagement with reality" through his camera (Galalis, 2014). In an e-mail he wrote, "A photograph is always a judgment on reality and thus, it always implicitly reflects the values of the person making the judgment." Students who are taught to understand this will acknowledge that their chosen or created visuals have the power to speak as loudly and clearly as their words, sometimes negating the need for words.

## Where Should Students Go to Find the Best Images?

Librarians can point students to the numerous online repositories of public domain images. Some of the finest can be found at the National Photographic and Historical Archives and the American Memories collections at the Library of Congress National Digital Library. Wikimedia Commons holds more than 20 million media files that are free to use, with millions more carrying Creative Commons licensing from Flickr. On The Commons on Flickr, users can now find thousands of images uploaded from places around the world, including the National Archives, the Smithsonian, the British Library, the National Library of Sweden, the Royal Australian Historical Society, and many more. The public is invited to contribute tags, comments, notes, and other identifying information to the photographs found there. Check out Public Domain Images for more options. Wikipedia's Public Domain Image Resources lists a complete set of links to historically relevant photos that are available for student and teacher use.

The following are links to the sites mentioned above:

National Photographic and Historical Archives:
http://www.archives.gov/
http://digitalvaults.org/

Library of Congress National Digital Library:
http://memory.loc.gov/ammem/dli2/html/list.html

Brooklyn Public Library's Brooklyn Collection of Photography:
www.brooklynpubliclibrary.org/brooklyncollection/photo-collections.jsp

Wikimedia Commons:
http://commons.wikimedia.org/wiki/Main_Page

The Commons on Flickr:
www.flickr.com/commons

National Archives at Flickr:
www.flickr.com/usnationalarchives/

Public Domain Images (PD Images):
www.pdimages.com

Wikipedia's Public Domain Image Resources:
http://en.wikipedia.org/wiki/Wikipedia:Public_domain_image_resources

John Szarkowski, director of the photography department at the New York Museum of Modern Art from 1962 to 1991, has been much quoted when he said, "The image survives the subject and becomes the remembered reality" (Gangwer, 2009). That will only be true of those who think deeply about their chosen image. It's incumbent upon us to help our students choose well. A simple question that is easily understood by all age groups might help kids to understand. Ask them to ask themselves: "If a picture is worth a thousand words, which thousand do you want to paint with your choice of image?"

# Part VIII

# Create

# Chapter 16

## Creativity and Curiosity

Wow! Gosh! Yikes! Really? These are just some of the reactions to the following headlines: Is Your Job Among the 47% That Robots Could Steal? Is Your Job About to Be Outsourced by a Computer? According to Oxford Study: 47% of U.S. Jobs Could Be Done by Machines. These headlines describe the groundbreaking research of Frey and Osborne (2013), *The Future of Employment: How Susceptible Are Jobs to Computerization?*

Frey and Osborne's study examines the various aspects of computerization and automation on the U.S. labor market: robotics, artificial intelligence (AI), big data, computational statistics, smart algorithms, task model, brain emulation, telekinesis/mind-moving technology, sensory technology, and smart/mobile technology. According to this landmark analysis, emerging technologies have a significant effect on the American labor force—i.e., human capital—education, training, and skills that people need to bring to their jobs.

The good news is that it also affirms that the probability for computerization and automation is lower for occupations that require "originality, knowledge of human heuristics, and the development of novel ideas and artifacts" (Frey and Osborne, 2013).

Yes, creativity, creativity, creativity! It is the essential aptitude for the coming decades of the 21st century. The other good news is that it is a process that can be taught, as evident in Bloom's Revised Taxonomy (multitiered thinking classification) and Bloom's Digital Taxonomy.

In Bloom's Revised Taxonomy, Lorin Anderson identifies the progression of higher-order-thinking processes from remembering, understanding, applying, analyzing, and evaluating to creating. Creativity is the highest-order thinking process: designing, constructing, planning, producing, inventing, devising, composing, formulating, developing, making, publishing, programming, videocasting, filming, blogging, animating, remixing, combining, and customizing, as well as synthesizing. Take a closer look at these words. They all have something in common: They are about doing. There is an element of cognitive agility, flexibility, and resourcefulness in the action they achieve.

This is supported by O*NET (Occupational Informational Network), the U.S. Department of Labor's occupational analysis of workplace "skill sets: values, styles, abilities, interests, knowledge, skills, and work values. According to O*NET, 'thinking creatively' includes developing, designing, or creating new applications, ideas, relationships, systems, or products, including artistic contributions" (O*NET, n.d.).

Bloom's thinking classification is a continuum: All prior levels of thinking—remembering, understanding, applying, analyzing, evaluating—must be attained before creative thinking can occur. In addition to this, there are four critical thinking "interrelated elements" that need to be explicitly and simultaneously developed (Global Learning Centre):

- Inquiring: identifying, exploring, and clarifying information (questioning, processing, transferring)
- Generating and developing ideas and possibilities (imagining, seeking, visualizing)
- Reflecting on thinking, actions, and processes (metacognition)
- Analyzing, evaluating, and synthesizing information (applying and drawing conclusions)

To progress from remembering to creativity takes a cognitive leap on the part of a learner, as well as a robust, standards-based curriculum that provides the framework for him or her to take the leap. One such framework is the American Association of School Librarians' (AASL's) *Standards for the 21st-Century Learner in Action* (2009). It is easy to see how these standards complement the sequences of steps established in Bloom's Revised Taxonomy and Bloom's Digital Taxonomy and how they support the critical thinking interrelated elements.

To teach for creativity, it is important to understand the creative process. J.P. Guilford, in *Characteristics of Creativity* (1973), analyzes the steps of the creative process: "preparation (skills, techniques, and information), concentrated effort (finding a solution or suitable form), withdrawal from the problem, insight or illumination, and verification, evaluation and elaboration." He describes this as divergent (synthetic) thinking: fluency, flexibility, originality, and elaboration.

In addition to all this, the creative process also involves reflection, brainstorming, questioning, analysis, synthesizes, communication, and cognitive agility. Does this process sound familiar? It should—it is what librarians do best. It is fundamental to information (library) science, especially to the information search process (ISP). One need only look at the AASL crosswalk to the Common Core State Standards (CCSSs) to make the connection.

Po Bronson and Ashley Merryman (2010) substantiate this in "The Creativity Crisis and the *Daily Beast*" when they state that "creativity isn't about freedom from concrete facts. Rather, fact-finding and deep research is vital stages in the creative process . . . ." Deep research! This is part and parcel of library science—information, digital, media, and technology literacy. "Deep research" gives a learner the foundation to conceptualize connections or patterns to formulate or develop an original solution—in other words, to be creative.

Teaching for creativity and innovation is rudimentary to achieving the new learning paradigm of self-directed learning, such as flipping the classroom or library. A flipped classroom is a blended learning approach that inverts the instructional cycle. Students are introduced to new content knowledge through online tutorials and reading materials outside the traditional class time, usually for homework. And class time is used for one-to-one interactive instruction and problem solving. Learners develop "habits of mind" that encourages wondering, questioning, self-directed investigation, and analysis of complex content and text, as well as combinational and critical thinking. Maybe the following scenario will shed some light on this concept.

A science teacher and a librarian design a collaborative project on the solar system. They map the curriculum using UbD (Understanding by Design), a backward design methodology. UbD is a planning and assessment tool that includes enduring understandings and essential questions to integrate Bloom's Revised Taxonomy, Bloom's Digital Taxonomy, the AASL's *Standards for the 21st-Century Learner in Action*, the CCSSs, and the Next Generation Science Standards (NGSSs). The ultimate objectives for this collaborative project are creativity—the highest level of thinking and college and 21st-century career readiness.

It is important to these research-based professionals to consult current scholarly works to ensure that the learning objectives of this project are met. What does the current literature say about creativity and the 21st-century workforce?

Erik Brynjolfsson and Andrew McAfee, of MIT's Center for Digital Business, in *The Second Machine Age: Work, Progress, and Prosperity in a Time of Brilliant Technologies* (2014), state that there are three convergence trends in technological progress that will influence employment and the economy: computational power (memory and storage), digital information (big data), and the combinational nature of innovation (digital innovation). At the heart of this digital revolution is the combinational nature of innovation. It is through connecting and combining ideas that a new paradigm of creativity occurs. Steve Jobs said it best in a 1996 *Wired* interview, "Creativity is just connecting things. When you ask creative people how they did something. . . . It seemed obvious to them. . . . That's because they were able to connect experiences they've had and synthesize new things" (Wolf, 1996).

This project asks students to combine and connect in order to come to an original solution-to create an alien. The enduring understandings for this collaborative project ensure that students will understand that

- Creativity is essential to scientific understanding, discovery, and advancement
- Creativity is a process that can be learned
- Scientific inquiry requires questioning, evidence, and the use of "deep research"
- Scientific literacy is awareness, understanding, application, and improvement upon scientific facts, concepts, and theories
- Literacy can take many different forms
- Literacy involves decoding, processing, and synthesizing multiple forms of information in multiple formats

The essential questions students will be able to answer at the end of the project include

- What is creativity?
- Why does creative thinking involve "deep research"?
- What does it mean to be literate in the 21st century?
- How do I locate, select, evaluate, and synthesize information?
- How does Earth differ from other known planets?
- Why might life forms on other planets be different from us?

In order to achieve their objectives, these coteachers decide to use an interactive learning module—Moodle (an open-source learning management system)—to engage students in self-regulated learning and creativity. Moodle allows for synchronous and asynchronous learning. Blended learning provides for targeted teaching: whole group, one-to-one, peer-to-peer, and student-to-expert. Computer-based instruction provides for differentiation, scaffolding, engaging, interactive learning, assessment, timely feedback and communication, group dynamics, as well as the gradual release of responsibility (RTI—response to intervention). Technology-enhanced learning provides a platform for self-paced and self-directed (regulated) learning, learning that fosters self-observation, self-evaluation, self-reactions, and self-reflection.

The science teacher and librarian act as guides in the learning process. Guided learning moves the process from task origin to task completion-creativity. They leverage emerging technologies to fuel creativity from the traditional artistic level where students create non-linguistic representations using online drawing tools to illustrate ideas and concepts to a more theoretical approach to creativity developed by Torrance (fluency, flexibility, originality, and elaboration) wherein students reflect, evaluate, synthesize, organize, and create based on "deep research" and task completion.

To engage students, address a variety of learning styles, bolster independence (flip learning), self-regulation, and creativity, the librarian and science teacher

- Blend creative problem solving (CPS) and the incubation model of teaching to so that students can achieve the highest level of thinking—creativity
- Produce a variety of online tutorials on advanced researching skills and strategies, information, digital and visual literacy, CRAAP testing (currency, relevance, authority, accuracy, purpose), physics, scientific theory, and the Solar System
- Incorporate a variety of technologies/media: Pinterest, Google search and related features, VoiceThread, RSS, podcasting, forums, live chat, Facebook, Apps, EasyBib, NoodleTool, Moodle
- Design supplementary learning materials to scaffold learning: checklists, graphic organizers, note taking templates, critical reading templates
- Employ an array of learning strategies for close reading, deep research, and self-regulation: reciprocal teaching, what if, KWL, Think–Ink–Pair–Share, brainstorming, I wonder, comparison matrix, connect two, questioning the text, identifying similarities and differences (compare and contrast), summarizing, writing connection, forum
- Integrate a variety of resources with multiple entrance points: websites, library homepage (databases, Internet, card catalog, Moodle, social media), town library, state resources, field experts
- Pose open-ended questions and Bloom's stem questions

In class, the science teacher provides learners with an overview of the assignment, the targeted 21st-century learning expectations, and key concepts. The librarian gives a very brief introduction to the Moodle block, the research and creativity rubrics, how to access and evaluate current, valid online and offline informational resources on the planets, note taking, summarizing, and online bibliographic generators (EasyBib or NoodleTools).

Because good questioning skills lead to problem resolution and innovation, the science teacher and librarian model these skills in person and online. The coteachers advance creativity and combinational thinking through online and offline questioning strategies such as no opt-out, Think–Ink–Pair–Share, questioning board/wall, socratic questioning, question/check/connect, question stems, I wonder, CRAAP testing, and question–answer relationships (QAR).

They decide to integrate question stems based on Bloom's Revised Taxonomy to guide students toward creative thinking. These questions stems (evaluation and create stems) include

- How else would you find . . . ?
- If you had access to all resources, how would you deal with . . . ?
- Can you design a . . . to . . . ?
- Judge the value of. . . . What do you think about . . . ?
- What data was used to reach the conclusion?
- What evidence can you find?
- What will happen if . . . ?
- How many ways can you think of to . . . ?
- What way would you design . . . ?
- What could be combined to improve . . . ?

These higher-order thinking stem questions demonstrate the interrelation between creativity and deep research. For example, the librarian poses the following questions: Can you design an advance search strategy to answer your research question? How else would you find information on your topic? What keywords could be combined to improve your results? Judge the value of your sources? What do you think about them?

In addition to these stem questions, this collaborative project inculcates questions of purpose, information, interpretation, assumptions, implications, point of view, relevance, accuracy, precision, consistency, and logic. Questioning allows students to combine known knowledge with new knowledge to draw conclusions and find original solutions.

Thinking is of no use unless it goes somewhere, and again, the questions we ask determine where our thinking goes.

Deep questions drive our thought underneath the surface of things; force us to deal with complexity. Questions of purpose force us to define our task. Questions of information force us to look at our sources of information as well as at the quality of our information.

Questions of interpretation force us to examine how we are organizing or giving meaning to information. Questions of assumption force us to examine what we are taking for granted. Questions of implication force us to follow out where our thinking is going. Questions of point of view force us to examine our point of view and to consider other relevant points of view.

Questions of relevance force us to discriminate what does and what does not bear on a question. Questions of accuracy force us to evaluate and test for truth and correctness. Questions of precision force us to give details and be specific. Questions of consistency force us to examine our thinking for contradictions. Questions of logic force us to consider how we are putting the whole of our thought together, to make sure that it all adds up and makes sense within a reasonable system of some kind. (Foundation for Critical Thinking, 2009)

This is how the assignment progresses. After studying a unit on Earth, students are asked to choose another planet within the Solar System to make a more in-depth study of it. If two or more students pick the same planet, they are given the choice to work individually or collaboratively—in fact, collaboration is encouraged. The two-heads-are-better-than-one theory—real life. Students are asked to brainstorm—to recall the information they have already learned about Earth. The science teacher uses the *note check* strategy. Students are given a few minutes to write a summary of the facts they know about Earth. Working with a partner, they read each other their summaries. Then they question each other's statements and finally combine information for one coherent statement of facts.

Using this information (background knowledge) culled from the *note check* activity, students are asked to formulate research questions on their planet; identify keywords and concepts; develop an advanced search strategy to find and select information to answer their research questions using a variety of current, valid offline and online resources, such as NASA (authority); select complex texts; read critically; and evaluate the information judiciously using the CRAAP (currency, relevancy, authority, accuracy, purpose) test available on the library's website.

The librarian models the ISP process in person and designs a variety of blended learning activities for self-directed learning: PowerPoint, video tutorials, keyword and essential question worksheet, graphic organizers, and checklists. All learning materials are added to the Moodle for 24/7 access. The students research their planets using databases, books, eBooks, and web resources.

After their in-depth research is completed, students use the information to identify similarities and differences (Marzano et al., 2001) between their planet and Earth: atmosphere/air, hydrosphere, orbit and rotation, seasons, water source(s), surface structure/landforms, chemical and physical properties/composition, natural resources, magnetic field, climate /weather, length of day, habitability, and distance from the Sun.

To scaffold, identifying similarities and differences, earlier in the project, the coteachers used a *no opt-out* question strategy drawn from Doug Lemov's book *Teach Like a Champion* (2010). This text was a district anchor text for the curriculum leadership council and professional learning/development team. Using *no opt-out* ensures that students understand the physical aspects of Earth so that they can compare and contrast (identifying similarities and differences).

Students are asked to look at their *comparison matrix* to reflect on their findings—to think deeply about the similarities and differences (compare and contrast) and to build upon their thinking (knowledge) to connect and combine. How and why is another planet like Earth? How and why is it different? What patterns can I identify? What conclusions can I draw? How does this all make sense? Students have to combine new and background (old) information to make sense of it all to create a viable alien.

This supports Frey and Osborne's belief that "one process of creating ideas (and similarly for artifacts) involves making unfamiliar combinations of familiar ideas, requiring a rich store of knowledge. The challenge here is to find some reliable means of arriving at combinations that 'make sense'" (Frey and Osborne, 2013). Students are asked to imagine and predict what life would be like on that planet. They are then asked to create an alien that can live on that planet, write a detailed description of how this alien's anatomical features are suited to their chosen planet's environment, draw or use online drawing tools to illustrate what their alien would look like, and present and defend (critical stance) their conclusions and nonlinguistic representations to the class. Their drawings and written descriptions are posted in the classrooms to generate discussion and for students to ascertain patterns and trends. The librarian, an art history major, suggests that they use a teaching strategy developed by Harvard's Project Zero: visual thinking—see, think, and wonder. These coteachers ask the students to look at the aliens: What do you see? What do you think about that? What does it make you wonder? This leads to interpretation and deeper questioning. They ask students to Think–Ink–Pair–Share about what they observe. Students think about what they have just observed and write about what they see, think, and wonder, then share what they have written with another student. Finally, this information is shared with the whole class.

To achieve understanding and to answer the project's essential questions and the students' personal research questions, students are asked to incorporate background knowledge with new knowledge and to seek more information (knowledge) if necessary to answer their essential/research question(s). This is part and parcel with the creative process as described by Guilford, Torrance, Robinson, Sternberg, and Richards, as well as Kuhlthau's model for ISP. In other words, they need to know when more information or data is needed to answer their research question(s) and how to find, select, evaluate, and synthesize that information. The librarian models and guides students in this process using both synchronous and asynchronous learning tools, protocols, and strategies to accomplish this stage in the learning experience.

Students have to question everything. Questioning is at the heart of this assignment. They need to ask themselves the following questions: Why and how does my alien look, move, see, hear, and eat (or get nourishment)? How does my planet's environment affect the senses? What are the physical attributes—skin tone(s), posture, sex, body shape—of my alien? What effects does the planet's environment have on the anatomical features of my alien? What are the anatomical features of my alien (respiratory system, digestive system, reproductive system, muscular system)? How would these systems manifest themselves? Why would they be different than those of Homo sapiens (man)?

Open-ended questions educe critical thinking, problem solving, risk taking, and creativity. They allow for divergent thought and an opportunity to challenge different views. The librarian uses a variety of open-ended questioning strategies, one being the *opening question* strategy. Why is knowledge of Earth important to creating an alien? An opening question gives students the opportunity to connect prior knowledge to new content.

Students question, questions some more, and question again. They imagine, find unique solutions, and create! They build upon facts gathered through deep research, synthesize that information to find an original solution, and communicate that solution in writing, through an imaginative nonlinguistic representation, and through a class presentation. This combines the best of the CCSSs and AASL and NGSS standards.

Another critical aspect of this assignment is assessing (not grading) for creativity. The librarian proposed using Susan M. Brookhart's rubric on four levels of creativity: variety of ideas and context, variety of sources, combining ideas, and communicating something new (Brookhart, 2013).

Students are given this rubric at the beginning of the assignment as an aid for understanding the creative process. It is used as a guidepost for students and not as a grading tool: What does creativity look like?

Looking at this rubric clearly indicates the vital role the school librarian plays in developing and assessing for creativity. Students are assessed by this rubric for the inclusion of a variety of sources: "Created product draws on a wide variety of sources, including different texts, media, resource persons or personal experience" (Brookhart, 2013). This is consistent with the AASL standards (inquire, think critically, gain knowledge) to "demonstrate creativity by using multiple resources and formats" (AASL, 2009).

The librarian assesses students' engagement, information, digital, and visual literacies skills, as well as creativity using Moodle analytics, observations, and project artifacts. During this project, habits of mind and dispositions, such as "flexible thinking" (curiosity), are taught through blended instruction, modeling questioning based on Bloom's Revised Taxonomy, strategies, visual thinking routines (Harvard's Project Zero), and a variety of resources, and by giving students time to think and respond. These habits of mind and dispositions are compatible with creative personality factors—the thirteen checklist creative strengths from the Torrance Tests of Creative Thinking (TTCT): open-minded, emotionally expressive/energetic in action, verbally expressive, humorous, imaginative, unconventional, lively or passionate, perceptive, connective of seemingly irrelevant things, synthesizing, seeing things from a different angle, breaking boundaries, and visualizing internally. Although these factors are not formally tested by TTCT, they are assessed with the creativity rubric and other districtwide rubrics.

This lesson personifies creativity and incorporates many elements of it:

- Incubation (metacognition, brainstorming, self-awareness, insight, reflection)
- Questioning (problem solving, evaluation, assumptions)
- Fluency (generate or explore a large number of ideas or alternative solutions, and total number of meaningful ideas, synthetic ability, lateral thinking, and generative phase)
- Flexibility (possibilities, categories, generating varied ideas, preparation, opposing viewpoints, strategy, mental agility)
- Originality and innovation (unique or unusual ideas or possibilities, problem seeking and solution, inventiveness, application, productivity, practical ability, synthesis)
- Elaboration (innovative or ingenious connections, associations, added details, enhancing preexisting ideas, modifying and expanding, planning, clarity, analytical ability, vertical adaptive thinking, evaluation)
- Visualization (sensory perception, images, imagining, conceptualizing, envisaging, literacy)

Students are engaged in high-order-thinking skills (HOTS): remembering, understanding, applying, analyzing, evaluating, and creating throughout this project, especially during ISP.

Sir Ken Robinson believes that "a big part of being creative is looking for new ways of doing things within whatever activity you're involved in. . . . [It] may begin with a flash of a new idea or with a hunch. It may just start as noodling around with a problem, getting some fresh ideas along the way. It's a process, not a single event, and genuine creative processes involve critical thinking as well as imaginative insights and fresh ideas . . . . So an essential bit of every creative process is evaluation (Azzam, 2009). Evaluation is at the heart of the ALA standards and the ISP.

Given independence to think, the students are inventive and productive. They demonstrate the cognitive ability to make connections, combine, and resolve therefore to be creative. They develop dispositions and habits of mind for creativity. Perhaps the following scenario will illuminate the process further.

During a collaborative sci-fi project, students are challenged to rewrite (create a storyboard) the final game/contest of *Ender's Game*. Students are asked to reread chapter 14 of *Ender's Game* and think deeply about how Ender won the final contest. They are asked to question the why, how, where, when, and what of Ender's final game. This initiates the background phrase of the assignment.

To do this, they need to envision winning the game themselves. They need to connect or combine background information—Ender's and their own need to question. What strategies would they use? What would be their solution? How would they execute it? How would it work? Would they break the rules—cheat like Ender? How would they play the game differently? What would their choice look like?

They are asked to imagine themselves as Ender. How would they feel? What would motivate them? What is their definition of winning? What choices would they make, and why? This exercise causes students to reflect, build on background information, examine answers to questions, requestion, clarify the problem, generate new ideas, find information, and develop a workable solution, generating a plan of action. This learning experience works, because "creative teaching is an open and inspiring approach for encouraging students to explore and innovate in order to develop their ability to create and think" (Lou et al., 2012).

In another case in point, a STEM (science, technology, engineering, and math) librarian introduces a decision tree, a graphical depiction of options and consequences, during a life science class. A decision tree is an excellent evaluation tool to analyze choices and to stimulate questions. It enables a students to visual the probability and possibilities of their decisions and helps resolve uncertainty and predict outcomes. It scaffolds creativity.

Students in this class are asked to reflect upon and answer the one of the following questions: Is it ethical to clone a human being? Are genetic manipulation technologies ethical? The librarian acts as a guide for students during the research process. She integrates research and reading strategies throughout the project using a variety of teaching protocols and online tools. Students research, read critically (contextualizing, questioning, reflecting, summarizing, evaluating, comparing and contrasting texts), make a decision tree listing the positives and negatives and possible solutions or outcomes, and finally come to a decision or make a choice based on their analysis. A decision tree enhances innovation and higher-order thinking. According to the ASCD, it is a 21st-century learning tool that enhances learning and innovation skills, information, media and technology skills, and life and career skills (ASCD, 2011).

School librarians collaborate to design meaningful independent and creative learning opportunities through

- Curriculum design
- Integration of successful models: creative problem solving (CPS), the incubation model of teaching, and the lateral thinking process
- Differentiate instruction
- Research-based techniques and strategies for active learning
- Self-directed learning interventions (gradual release of responsibility model—RTI)
- Connecting with students' passions
- Providing real-world applications
- Designing interactive learning materials and self-guided tutorials

Sir Kenneth Robinson, a leading thinker on creativity, said, "Creativity is as important in education as literacy and we should treat it with the same status" (Robinson, 2008). This is particular true today. Creativity is our students' best hope for a bright future. Librarians are vital in inculcating creativity and the creative process in education.

# Part IX
# Digitize: Publish and Produce

# Chapter 17

# Plagiarism: What Is It? How Can Schools Deal with It?

In January 2002 National Public Radio ran a story that was fueled by plagiarism charges against two nationally renowned historians, Doris Kearns Goodwin and the late Stephen Ambrose (Writing History, 2002). During the two-minute segment, the original text was read by a man and the plagiarized text was simultaneously read by a woman. The ebb and flow between the two was a powerful illustration of the fine line between paraphrasing and plagiarism. Educators take this distinction for granted, but it is genuinely ambiguous for students.

While many students plagiarize for the wrong reasons, almost as many plagiarize because they simply don't know better. We can tell them that if someone quotes, reuses, restates, summarizes, or paraphrases a piece of work without attribution, that is indeed plagiarizing. But some terms like summarizing, paraphrasing, and restating are open to broad interpretation by students. And although they understand that words can't be copied, they often misinterpret the finer details. Whether it be the result of intentional copying or the innocent misinterpretation of what constitutes plagiarism, we continue to search for ways to eliminate the issue. But even educators are often confused by the tangle of copyright laws and the befuddling fair use clause that seems to suggest to students—and to many teachers—that as a member of a school community, you have carte blanche to copy, reuse, and modify almost anything. Plagiarism has always been an issue, but the Internet took it to a new and gargantuan dimension. Today's search engines and databases, coupled with our ability to copy and paste, make it easier than ever before to piece together an "original" piece of writing that is anything but original.

So what can we say to kids to help them understand what they can and cannot reuse in their own writing? Libraries should begin with simplified "kid-speak" guidelines like those posted by plagiarism.org:

All of the following are considered plagiarism:

- Turning in someone else's work as your own
- Copying words or ideas from someone else without giving credit
- Failing to put a quotation in quotation marks
- Giving incorrect information about the source of a quotation
- Changing words but copying the sentence structure of a source without giving credit
- Copying so many words or ideas from a source that it makes up the majority of your work, whether you give credit or not

Plagiarism.org encourages teachers to tell students that "simply acknowledging that certain material has been borrowed, and providing your audience with the information necessary to find that source, is usually enough to prevent plagiarism."

Plagiarism.org invites educators to share these materials with students, asking only that the URL be cited when using their content: www.plagiarism.org/plagiarism-101/what-is-plagiarism/.

At the same time that educators are trying to clarify issues around plagiarism to students, we read articles like Dennis O'Reilly's 2010 "Tools for Rooting Out Web Plagiarism, Copyright Violations." In it, he underscores our 21st-century plagiarism dilemma, letting us know that it's not only kids who don't get it: "Some misguided souls in the Internet publishing world still consider all online material as being in the public domain." He continues: "Unfortunately, this misapprehension is widely shared—and often by high-level executives who should know better." O'Reilly decries a general lack of concern around the issue of copyright, with people in all sectors borrowing, guilt-free, from the Internet and republishing without permission. Considering this lackadaisical attitude among adults, it might seem a daunting task to teach students to avoid plagiarism by understanding and respecting copyright.

In 1996, John M. Barrie of Plagiarism.org and now CEO of iParadigms, LLC, was at the University of California at Berkeley when he recognized that "a significant minority of students were cheating their way to an unfair competitive advantage over their peers." He acknowledged that he was "aiding and abetting by providing hundreds of students with their peers' manuscripts via the class website" and determined to put a stop to it (Barrie, 2008). So he and a group of researchers at the University of California at Berkeley joined forces to create software that would screen undergraduate research papers to identify those that had been recycled. They then enlisted mathematicians, teachers, and computer scientists to form plagiarism.org, "the world's first internet-based plagiarism detection service." Today, Plagiarism.org offers a full range of anti-plagiarism resources for teachers and students. Their Plagiarism 101, Citing Sources, Ask the Expert, and Resources pages, although too complex for young students, can be freely used by teachers to fashion lessons that are more age-appropriate. For older students, Plagiarism.org "grants all reprint and usage requests without the need to obtain any further permission as long as the URL of the original article/information is cited" (Plagiarism.org, 2014). These are excellent teaching materials.

Plagiarism.org recently published the following statistics gleaned from two recent surveys (Plagiarism.org Facts and Stats, 2014): In a survey of 43,000 high school students on the topic of plagiarism, "One out of three high school students admitted that they used the Internet to plagiarize an assignment." A second survey of 24,000 students at 70 high schools found "58 percent admitted to plagiarism and 95 percent said they participated in some form of cheating, whether it was on a test, plagiarism or copying homework."

Of approximately 90,000 college and graduate students surveyed, "40 percent admitted to cheating on written assignments." In a 2010 report on iParadigms.org, almost 85% of college students said cheating was necessary to get ahead.

Cheating by plagiarizing is rampant, and it seems, based on these results, that many students feel that it is justified. But even those trying to do the right thing can unintentionally misstep. Teaching kids project management and resource tracking skills will help cut down on the number of incidences. But complicated as it can be, learning to understand and avoid plagiarism is an essential part of a 21st-century responsible and ethical education. The good news is that there are web tools that can help kids learn to eliminate incidences of plagiarism from their work and help teachers identify them.

## Web Tools for Dealing with Plagiarism

Not so long ago, teachers were excited to discover that search engines had made the task of finding instances of plagiarism easier by letting them enter the suspected language into a search to identify the origin of the quoted text. Initially, teachers were delighted with this new weapon against plagiarism. But the task of entering quotes from handwritten or printed paper documents proved arduous, with often confusing and ambiguous results. And search engines failed to identify passages that had been carefully paraphrased by replacing one word here and there with another. To further thwart teachers' attempts to seek out and confirm plagiarism, search engines were not able to discover that a student's submitted paper had been copied verbatim from an older sibling or a friend. Articles like "How to Find Plagiarism" (Bailey, 2011) offered advice to help weary teachers, admonishing those searching on Google not to search for the title, since plagiarists often change that as an easy way to escape detection. Instead, they recommended searching for a "statistically improbable phrase" of six to twelve words occurring in the body of the work. For those still using web browsers to root out plagiarism, that's pretty good advice. But today's search engines are still not able to uncover and confirm plagiarism with a high degree of accuracy. Their inability to crawl library databases where students are required to work, to track recycled papers, and to search for long strings of text make finding results unreliable. Teachers can require students to publish their work online, but depending on permissions set by the student, their work may still elude search engines. Frustrated, educators began asking for better tools to be able to verify that a piece of writing had been illegally copied in whole or in part. Today, a quick web search for a plagiarism checker will yield more than a million results, with many of these services available free of charge.

## Plagiarism-checking Services

**Copyscape:** If student work is published online, Copyscape allows the user to enter the URL of the original work, then conducts a web search to find duplicate work. CopyScape's paid premium version will yield more results. CopyScape's companion application is Siteliner, a web page analysis tool that searches your site for duplicate content, broken links, and key issues that impact a site's function.

**Grammarly's Plagiarism Checker** compares submitted text to more than 8 billion web pages to detect plagiarism. This checker also doubles as a grammar checker, finding errors in grammar, spelling, and usage. Grammarly will generate citations in MLA, APA, and Chicago styles. This service describes itself as a grammar coach and writing tutor, with the goal of helping students to identify instances of plagiarism in their own writing as they learn to be better writers. Grammarly will check a piece of writing and return results for free, but if you want details about what exactly was found, you have to register and pay.

**Viper:** You'll find Viper at scanmyessay.com (not viper.com). This free service is available only to those using Microsoft Windows. In 2014, Viper claimed over 10 billion resources scanned and accepts submissions of unlimited length. They bill themselves as the free alternative to Twitter.

**Mashable's** "Use These 10 Sites to Detect Plagiarism": http://mashable.com/2012/08/29/plagiarism-online-services (Petronzio, 2012).

**PlagiarismChecker.com** lets users enter phrases from a work. It will scan and check a web page, and set up a Google alert to let you know when your work has been reused.

**CheckforPlagiarism.net** offers its service at a range of subscription prices for students, teachers, and institutions. This service does not store submissions in a database.

These are just a few of the plagiarism services mentioned in top 10 articles. All offer varying degrees of reliability and require varying degrees of work on the part of the user. In all cases, the free services, while convenient, are less robust than their paid counterparts. To achieve the highest degree of accuracy, reliability, and security, schools search for the most robust option. Many select **Turnitin**, a product of iParadigms, LLC, a service that, when used consistently, has been documented to help kids understand copyright laws and learn to be plagiarism-free.

## Turnitin: What Is It, and How Does It Work?

"**Turnitin** is the world leader in educational tools for originality checking and plagiarism prevention" (Turnitin: Our Company, 2014). Schools need to support teachers in their efforts to curb plagiarism by finding a consistent means of identifying it. But it's not all about catching cheaters. If we accept as fact that many times students plagiarize unintentionally due to misconceptions or sloppy research skills, then consistent use of Turnitin can also help teachers build better writers as students learn to recognize plagiarism and understand how to correct it.

In 2011, iParadigms, LLC, and plagiarism.com wondered where students get their plagiarized content and decided to conduct their own research examining student papers submitted between June 2010–March 2011. Their findings were reported in a white paper entitled "Plagiarism and the Web: Myths and Realities" (Basromine, 2011). They repeated the study in 2012, publishing their findings for high school students based on an "analysis of over 44 million content matches from more than 9 million student papers submitted to Turnitin between July 2011 and June 2012" (Turnitin: The Sources in Student Writing, 2012). They found that "students are relying on sources that have weak academic validity," with 50% of matches leading to sites that are academically suspect, including 18 percent from cheat sites and paper mills, shopping sites like Amazon where kids go to read book blurbs and reviews, and social and user-generated content. The study also revealed that the most quoted site remained Wikipedia, accounting for 8 percent of all matches, a 1 percent increase from the previous study. And although plagiarism from social networking sites was down 3 percent, the incidence from paper mills was up 3 percent. To minimize these two sources of plagiarism, iParadigms suggested that teachers require students to use only primary and secondary sources in their research. Working in the school library with a certified librarian will ensure that teachers and students are pointed toward the best database resources.

**Turnitin** is a subscription-based service that can be licensed by a school or district. Each teacher will have access to a Turnitin account, organized by course, where class assignments can be posted. Students also have individual accounts where they submit assignments directly to the service, eliminating the teacher's time-consuming task of copying and pasting questionable content into a search engine. Each student paper submitted to Turnitin is "compared to massive databases of content including billions of webpages, millions of student papers previously submitted to Turnitin and research databases of subscription-based journal articles and periodicals" (Turnitin: Our Company, 2014).

Statistics quoted from the Turnitin website make a compelling argument for the power of this service. As of January 2014, 36 million student papers from 2,800 high schools have been archived. Overall, worldwide and including higher ed, Turnitin databases hold more than 300 million submitted papers, double the 150 million reported in June 2011. They search more than 40 billion current and archived web pages and 130,000 journals, periodicals and books, including many in subscription databases. Turnitin services 10,000+ educational institutions, both K–12 and higher education. In 2014, 20 million students, taught by more than 1 million instructors in 126 countries, depended on Turnitin to generate reliable originality reports in eighteen languages (Turnitin: Our Company, 2014).

Turnitin searches not only for obvious instances of recycling, but also for "the substitution of words or sentences within an already existing work or the cutting and pasting of phrases or entire paragraphs from an outside source into a new document" Students often go to great lengths to disguise plagiarism. Ironically, suggested Plagiarism.org in its 2011 article on plagiarism solutions, the amount of work students put into creative plagiarizing in order to hide the crime is often more time-consuming and burdensome than had the student simply written a nonplagiarized piece (Plagiarism Solutions, 2011).

Once a student submits a piece of writing through Turnitin, it takes, on average, 24 seconds for an **originality report** to be generated, indicating what percentage of the work seems to match an online resource or one located in the Turnitin database. Teachers can elect to use this report as a "gotcha" tool or instead can allow students to read and diagnose their own report, making use of it to edit and resubmit for a new originality assessment. Reading an originality report is easy. At first glance, the student will see his or her similarity index expressed as a percentage. A higher percentage indicates a higher amount of content that is similar to a source located within the scope of the Turnitin search, indicating the possibility of plagiarism. This is followed by a color-coded icon: red indicates that a high percentage of the work is not original, yellow signals a need for attention, and green indicates that the work has a high degree of originality.

Turnitin isn't able to judge the value of the student's citations and does not determine plagiarism, meaning that even correctly attributed quotes will be flagged as potential plagiarism. As a result, each bit of feedback in the originality report must be individually screened and analyzed to determine next steps. By clicking on the similarity index, a new window will open, revealing the original paper on the left and the list of matching sources on the right. Sources and student text are numbered and color-coded to make interpreting the matches straightforward and uncomplicated. Turnitin leaves it up to the reviewer to determine actual originality. If the student examines an item and determines that the quoted text or restated idea is correctly attributed, he or she can disregard it and go on to the next. If attribution was not properly executed, the student must return to the original text to make corrections. After working through the entire originality report and correcting flagged items, the student can resubmit for a new originality report. Documentation on the Turnitin website suggests that students benefit the most from their service when they are permitted to view their own originality reports, take time to edit, and then resubmit. In this way, students can learn by their own example without fear of failing. This is supported by a statement published on the WriteCheck website that speaks volumes about how students learn:

> Educators consistently told us that their students do not have a clear understanding of how to work with source material and that lectures and writing handbooks have very limited impact on their students' comprehension of this topic. For many students, it is not until they can SEE the highlighting of potentially problematic material in their own work that they begin to understand their errors. Such insight and self-editing is crucial to their development as 21st-century writers and thinkers. (WriteCheck FAQ, 2011)

**WriteCheck:** Not all schools allow students to edit based on their originality report. For students working in an environment where resubmission isn't permitted, Turnitin offers WriteCheck, a relatively inexpensive pay-as-you-go option for those who want to use the Turnitin database resources to check their writing for plagiarism and originality before submitting it for a grade. WriteCheck differs from Turnitin in that it doesn't add student papers to its database as it does for students submitting directly to Turnitin (WriteCheck for Students 2014).

Turnitin continues to add enhancements that make it more user-friendly for schools. It has worked with more than 50 of the major online course platforms, including Moodle and Blackboard, to create a plug-in that enables teachers to post Turnitin assignments within the online course structure. Here, students are able to submit work directly to Turnitin without having to leave the course. Submitted work will generate an originality report just as if the student had logged directly onto Turnitin. The student saves time and effort, as does the teacher, who can access papers submitted through Turnitin without leaving the online course. All papers submitted in this way become part of the Turnitin database. Google and Dropbox users can submit work to Turnitin directly from the cloud. A key advantage for world language classes and ESL students is that papers can be submitted and processed in thirty languages.

Turnitin for Educators accounts include an online gradebook called **GradeMark** that gives teachers the ability to add electronic comments as they grade submitted papers electronically. Teachers can also reinforce critical thinking skills by engaging students in Turnitin's peer review. This process, which can be anonymous, can be customized by the teacher, who can add guiding questions. The Turnitin app for the iPad lets teachers grade work and enter feedback anywhere online or offline (when assignments are synced). Interactive rubrics let teachers tap the screen to instantly calculate scores. There is no option at this time for students to submit work through mobile technology.

There are new applications added to Turnitin every year. As of 2014, teachers can upload rubrics from Excel, and originality reports can be generated from PowerPoint slide sets. Check out the Turnitin.com website for updates.

Other Turnitin services include **iThenticate.com** to help researchers, publishers, legal firms, and government institutions verify content originality, confirm proper attribution, and protect intellectual property. College admission officers can benefit from **Turnitin for Admissions** (turnitinadmissions.com) to assess documents submitted by applicants, such as personal statements, admissions and scholarship essays.

Although many plagiarism checking services are free, be aware that when submitting original work to Internet-based services one should carefully read intellectual property rights policies. Turnitin states unequivocally that it neither profits from nor shares student submissions. Papers submitted remain the sole property of the author. Be aware that no-cost or low-cost plagiarism checking services might not offer this protection. In fact, in some cases an online service that claims to offer free plagiarism checking will harvest submissions and resell them to international paper mills. Reading the fine print will help protect intellectual property rights.

Turnitin's extraordinary service isn't free, but the time saved by faculty and the writing support offered to students makes it invaluable in helping students understand what plagiarism is and what they have to do to turn research into original writing.

## Teaching Kids about Plagiarism

Plagiarism has never been so simple to achieve, and yet, with the ever accelerating pace of the Internet, never been more difficult to avoid. Without painstaking attention to detail during the research process, our copy/paste mentality makes it difficult to recall which notes are original and which are lifted from a web page. We must teach our students to be meticulous in their note-taking and resource-gathering, checking and rechecking sources for quotes, paraphrasing and summarizing in order to give proper attribution. Students should learn to search for copyright notices governing a website and read them in order to comply. They should be encouraged to write to the author or publisher to get permission to use materials labeled All Rights Reserved. Students interviewed have reported that taking the time to do so has resulted in gaining access to password-protected biology research at a major university and to All Rights Reserved photography of a former Olympian. Both of these students went on to say that they received affirming responses within twenty-four hours and were delighted to benefit in ways they hadn't expected. Teach kids to click the Contact Me button and to write a straightforward e-mail stating who they are (e.g., a high-school English student) and why they want to use the materials (I'm writing a paper on Mark Twain and am interested in using your quote on Huck Finn . . ."). Students are also reminded to ask how the owner of the property would like it to be attributed. Online content owners are often thrilled and delighted to know that someone is interested in their work and often grant permission. Students should be attentive to conditions set forth in the responses and ready to comply with those who refuse. Whatever the outcome, writing to the owner is an excellent experience that can open the door to valuable professional resources and contacts.

Although many high school students have misconceptions regarding plagiarism and theft of intellectual property, ignorance of copyright and attribution rules does not protect one from prosecution. Engaging in plagiarism is fraudulent behavior and can, in extreme cases, result in fines. It is incumbent upon schools to teach students what they need to know about copyright, fair use, and intellectual property rights to help them stay on the legal side of writing. It's never too early to introduce these concepts to children. At a very young age, most children have been taught to ask before taking something that doesn't belong to them and, in return, to share what is theirs with others. They know that writing their name on their stuff will identify it as theirs and protect it from being stolen. This is a good way to introduce the concept of intellectual property. Each year, the lesson can be reiterated and ratcheted up until, in high school, students have developed a habit of mind and practice that will remain with them forever. Throughout their schooling, every lesson that involves research should include an aspect of new teaching or reiteration on the topic of copyright and attribution. Sites such as Cyberbee .com and CopyrightKids.org can help teachers get started using language that kids will understand. At the high school level, TeachingCopyright.org offers a curriculum with lesson plans, white papers, and legal cases that can guide your students. If you prefer videos, typing "copyright for kids" into YouTube will yield a variety of resources.

# Conclusion

Today's educators, many of whom grew up in an Internet-free world, need to recognize the incongruity of on one hand insisting that kids collaborate and share and on the other penalizing them for doing just that in their writing.

In Turnitin's 2011 White Paper entitled "Plagiarism and the Web: Myths and Realities: An Analytical Study on Where Students Find Unoriginal Content on the Internet" (Basromine, 2011), it shares this thought-provoking statement on the collision between sharing and originality:

> A digital culture that promotes sharing, openness and re-use is colliding with one of the fundamental tenets of education—the ability to develop, organize and express

original thoughts. For many students who have grown up sharing music, retweeting thoughts and downloading free software, the principle of originality in research and writing can seem antiquated. It is important for educators to draw a clear line between what can be reproduced and what must be created. If not, there is a risk that a generation of students will not develop the critical thinking and communication skills necessary for a productive life.

Whether a student is intentionally plagiarizing, or intended and attempted to do the right thing really makes no difference in the dizzying and ever-changing maze of 21st-century copyright law. It is incumbent on our schools to find the best way to keep legal guidelines foremost in students' minds. The answer can be found in services like Turnitin.com.

Students and their teachers often question the details of copyright, intellectual property and fair use laws and guidelines. Let them know that the best resolution is to ask the school librarian, who, when in doubt, can place a call to the Library of Congress Office of Copyright to access the most up-to-date information. This will also serve to demonstrate the complexities of copyright law to students and faculty and remind them that we all need to learn to work with experts. No one person can easily keep up.

Librarians should encourage teachers to work with them to add a copyright segment to any lesson where students are researching, writing, and publishing. Students will benefit from consistent and recurring reminders to be diligent record keepers, to attain permission for use from the source, and to post appropriate attributions. Although correct format matters, most sources on this topic agree that an honest attempt at careful consistent attribution is what matters the most.

# Chapter 18

# *Intellectual Property, Copyright, and Fair Use*

According to former U.S. Supreme Court justice Sandra Day O'Connor, in *Feist Publications, Inc. v. Rural Telephone Service Co.*, 499 US 340, 349 (1991) "The primary objective of copyright is not to reward the labor of authors, but "[t]o promote the Progress of Science and useful Arts. To this end, copyright assures authors the right to their original expression, but encourages others to build freely upon the ideas and information conveyed by a work. This result is neither unfair nor unfortunate. It is the means by which copyright advances the progress of science and art" (United States Supreme Court, 1991). No wonder librarian proponents of free and unfettered access to information for learning whole-heartily support and applaud this transformational fair use ruling.

As information specialists, school librarians acknowledge and apply the American Library Association's code of ethics to "respect intellectual property rights and advocate balance between the interests of information users and rights holders."

An assiduous assessment of current copyright policy safeguards a library's right to protect and provide fair use. Information specialists, as school leaders, access a variety of resources to stay up to date on current intellectual property, fair use, and copyright legislation, court cases, and news from places such as the Library of Congress, U.S. Copyright Office (www.copyright.gov), SULAIR, Copyright and Fair Use, Stanford University Libraries (the Stanford Universities Libraries fair use and copyright website includes information on copyright guidelines, public domain, fair use, requesting, permission statues, current legislation, and relevant copyright charts and tools; http://fairuse.stanford.edu), LibraryLaw.com (www.librarylaw.com), and the American Library Association (www.ala.org/advocacy/copyright). Another way school librarians stay current is through RSS feeds from the Copyright Office (www.loc.gov/rss/copyright/rss.xml), Federal Register (www.loc.gov/rss/copyright/fedreg.xml), and legislative developments from the Library of Congress (http://www.copyright.gov/legislation).

Librarians use the tools provided by Michael Brewer and the Copyright Advisory Subcommittee of the ALA Office for Information Technology Policy—the Public Domain Slider, Section 108 Spinner, Fair Use Evaluator, and Exceptions for Instructors (http://ala.org/advocacy/copyright/crtools)—to share with students, faculty, administrators, staff , and the community information on copyright and intellectual property.

According to the American Library Association (2010), in *Questions and Answers: Access to Electronic Information, Services, and Network: An Interpretation of the Library*

*Bill of Rights,* "Librarians have professional and ethical responsibilities to keep abreast of copyright and fair use rights . . . and infor[m] library users of copyright laws that apply to their use of electronic information. Libraries are an essential part of the national information infrastructure, providing people with access and participation in the electronic arena. They are fundamental to the informed debate demanded by the Constitution and for the provision of access to electronic information resources to those who might otherwise be excluded. Yes, because information is information regardless of format. Library resources in electronic form are increasingly recognized as vital to the provision of information that is the core of the library's role in society."

Students, teachers, administrators, and staff do not want to know what they cannot do. They want to know how they can do it. It is about inclusion, not exclusion. It is through mutual respect that others acknowledge expertise and heed the advice given.

Alvy and Robbins (2010) in *Learning from Lincoln: Leadership Practices for School Success,* write, "School leaders make conscious choices about their capacity to grow by activities in which they choose to engage." Librarians engage in copyright issues in order to maintain the balance of fair use for our patrons. Alvy and Robbins further state, "Research on leadership is clear: personal example is the most powerful human resource available to lead an organization." It is through personal example, modeling, purposefully plan instruction awareness occurs:

- Fair use
- Public domain
- Creative Commons
- Mashup and peer-to-peer technology
- Orphan work
- "Innocent infringement"
- "Work for hire"

Today, students and teachers are not only consumers of copyrighted works, but as 21st-century learners are transformers, producers, and creators of intellectual property. School librarians help them protect their rights of ownership through traditional copyright application or through the Creative Commons process. This is a first-rate fair use learning tool. Students and teachers come to grips with the various aspects of copyright by making decisions on their own works. It is important to ask what do you want others to be able to do with your work. It is through this process that students and teachers understand the other side of the fair use equation—ownership.

School librarians understand that the Copyright Act of 1976 (Title 17, USC) is the foundation of the current copyright law and that "[c]opyright is a form of protection grounded in the U.S. Constitution and granted by law for original works of authorship fixed in a tangible medium of expression. Copyright covers both published and unpublished works. Copyright, a form of intellectual property law protects original works of authorship including literary, dramatic, musical, and artistic works, such as poetry, novels, movies, songs, computer software, and architecture. Copyright does not protect facts, ideas, systems, or methods of operation, although it may protect the way these things are expressed. Under the copyright law, the creator of the original expression is its author. The author is also the owner of copyright unless there is a written agreement by which the author assigns the copyright to another person or entity, such as a publisher. . . . Section 107 of the United States copyright law contains a list of the various purposes for which a copy or reproduction of a particular work may be considered fair use, such as criticism, comment, news reporting, teaching, scholarship, and research" (U.S. Copyright Office, 2009). The application of *Circular 92, Subject Matter and Scope: 107. Limitations on exclusive rights: Fair Use* to practice helps determine

whether the use made of a work in any particular case is a fair use by considering:

1. the purpose and character of the use, including whether such use is of a commercial nature or is for nonprofit educational purposes;
2. the nature of the copyrighted work;
3. the amount and substantiality of the portion used in relation to the copyrighted work as a whole; and
4. the effect of the use upon the potential market for or value of the copyrighted work.

The fact that a work is unpublished shall not itself bar a finding of fair use if such finding is made upon consideration of all the above factors.

All four factors must be considered to determine whether a particular use is fair. Clearly, public schools are nonprofit, and "copying" by teachers, staff, and students for instruction and to advance learning is for educational purposes. Is the purpose transformational or verbatim? If a copy is purely verbatim, fair use can be questionable. Transformational works add value to or "advance the progress of science or the arts." (Parody is an example of a transformational work.)

What is "the nature of the copyrighted work?" This is more ambiguous and therefore causes the most problems. It is also the area that brings about the most copyright lawsuits. Currently, the cost of a copyright lawsuit is about $100,000. According to the Purdue University Copyright Office, the current copyright infringement lawsuit can cost up to $150,000 (Purdue, 2009).

Consumable, unpublished, creative, fictional, artistic works do not lend themselves to fair use, but factual, nonfiction works generally do. This may be because factual, nonfiction works lend themselves to be transformational and also, as explained on the Library of Congress website under Copyright Basics, because "[c]opyright does not protect facts, ideas, systems, or methods of operation, although it may protect the way these things are expressed." According NYU libraries, "in general, published works and factual, nonfiction works are more likely to qualify for fair use" (NYU Libraries, 2014).

The third factor in deciding fair use is "the amount and substantiality of the portion used in relation to the copyrighted work as a whole." The U.S. Congress intentionally left the interpretation of Section 107 broad. Interestingly, its beauty is in its vagueness. This "vagueness" is generally difficult for teachers, students, and administrators to accept. Assigning numbers, percentages, or minutes limits fair use. The U.S. Office of

Copyright states in *Frequently Asked Questions about Copyright: Can I Use Someone Else's Work? Can Someone Else Use Mine? How Much of Someone Else's Work Can I Use without Getting Permission?* that "[u]nder the fair use doctrine of the U.S. copyright statute, it is permissible to use limited portions of a work including quotes, for purposes such as commentary, criticism, news reporting, and scholarly reports. There are no legal rules permitting the use of a specific number of words, a certain number of musical notes, or percentage of a work. Whether a particular use qualifies as fair use depends on all the circumstances. See FL 102, Fair Use, and Circular 21, *Reproductions of Copyrighted Works by Educators and Librarians*." The 1978 Circular 21 offers guidelines with qualifications under the heading *Agreement on Guidelines for Classroom Copying in Non-For-Profit Educational Institutions with Respect to Books and Periodicals and Guidelines with Respect to Music.* Although the Library of Congress's Office of Copyright refers educators and librarians to Circular 21 guidelines, nowhere in the current copyright law is there a list of percentages, numbers of pages, numbers of words, or musical notes.

Even when "copying" a small portion of a work, another consideration to take into account is whether that portion is the essence, the "heart," of the work? A great explanation of this can be found on the Stanford University Libraries' Copyright and Fair Use site, *SULAIR*, using the Rolling Stones' *Satisfaction* to demonstrate this point.

Is "the effect of the use upon the potential market for or value of the copyrighted work?" School systems are vulnerable to lawsuits if they copy consumables, workbooks, worksheets, entire or large portions of books, software, and audiovisuals, because the "author" is denied revenue or financial gain from his or her original work.

All four factors must be considered for fair use. The fair use doctrine is open to interpretation, so well-informed librarians know that there are no steadfast rules. Rigorous analysis of each deciding factor ensures a meaningful balance between the "promotion of art and science," as defined under the U.S. Constitution and rights of "ownership."

Although digitalization has transformed access and use of copyrighted materials, current copyright law still addresses fair use regardless of mode of delivery. It is about the use of content for educational purposes, not how it is obtained or delivered. "The Digital Age presents new challenges to fundamental copyright doctrines that are legal cornerstones of library services. Libraries must be leaders in trying to maintain a balance of power between copyright holders and users . . ." (ALA, "Copyright").

What does "fair use" mean in an electronic academic environment? How do librarians as coteachers ensure that students are able to access, evaluate, analyze, synthesize, transform, and share information, multimedia, and other protected resources for "educational purposes"? The Association of Research Libraries, in *Fair Use in the Electronic Age: Serving the Public Interest* (2010), maintains that "[a]s more information becomes available only in electronic formats, the public's legitimate right to use copyrighted material must be protected. In order for copyright to truly serve its purpose of 'promoting progress,' the public's right of fair use must continue in the electronic era, and these lawful uses of copyrighted works must be allowed without individual transaction fees (or added restrictions): to read, listen to, or view publicly marketed copyrighted material privately, on site or remotely; to experiment with variations of copyrighted material for fair use purposes, while preserving the integrity of the original; that rights of use for nonprofit education apply in face-to-face teaching and in transmittal or broadcast to remote locations where educational institutions of the future must increasingly reach their students."

Understanding and applying the definitions of copyright terms in *Subject Matter and Scope of Copyright* (United States Copyright Office, Circular 92, n.d.) helps alleviate most problems. These definitions provide explanation, clarifications, and meaningful descriptions of current copyright terminology. For example, to understand the term "fair use," it is important to understand what constitutes a "copy." The definition provided by the Library of Congress's Copyright Office is that "copies are material objects, other than phonorecords, in which a work is fixed by any method now known or later developed, and from which the work can be perceived, reproduced, or otherwise communicated, either directly or with the aid of a machine or device. . . . A work consisting of sounds, images, or both, that are being transmitted, is 'fixed' for purposes of this title if a fixation of the work is being made simultaneously with its transmission."

With the advent of digital technologies, online/distance learning became not only possible but desirable. Recent research conducted by the U.S. Department of Education indicates that the integration of online learning is a means to engage students, augment, and scaffold learning, and reduce spending through "mediated instructional activities."

To address "fair use" and "mediated instructional activities," the Congress of the United States has amended the 1976 Copyright Act. There are now provisions under the current statute for distance learning (TEACH Act) and for special need populations that further expands the authorized reproduction of copyrighted works.

Another avenue of fair use to be considered is works in the "public domain." Unfortunately, determining what is in the "public domain" can be daunting. It is now easier to determine whether something is in the public domain by using the digital copyright slider provided by Michael Brewer and the ALA Office for Information Technology Policy.

This tool is made available under the auspices of the Creative Commons Attribution Non-Commercial Share Alike (CC-BY-NC-SA) license and is easily accessed on the Internet. This, again, inculcates not only the concept of public domain, but also those of ownership and fair use. Excellent school librarians model and incorporate current copyright law, as well as the use of Creative Commons as a means to demonstrate fair use of sharing intellectual property and copyright protection. Its six levels of protection easily explain the concept of "fair use:" Creative Commons license is a means by which content creators can share intellectual property, define the level of sharing, and maintain legal ownership (copyright) to the original work. The use of Creative Commons licensure helps students and faculty understand the who, what, why, where, and how of copyright in easy and comprehensible language, especially as they upload to YouTube.

Unfortunately, many people believe that anything in a U.S. archive or on a government (.gov) website is in the public domain. This is not true, but permission is easy to obtain through www.loc.gov/search/?q=permissions&fa=digitized:true.

Other options to obtain copyright permission are the Copyright Clearance Center (CCC), a "global rights broker"; AcqWeb, an international directory of publishers; and the Motion Picture Licensing Corporation (MPLC) for copyright and legal access for films in more than 20 countries, including the United States.

The dissemination of intellectual property, copyright, and fair use information to learners is paramount in a digital learning environment as copyright holders are using automated scanning software to identify infringement violations and academic plagiarism detector tools. Excellent school librarians protect students against unintentional violations with the use of copyright detection tools, such as Turnitin. They use these detection tools as a learning opportunity and not a "gotcha" moment.

School librarians continuously bring ethical and responsible use issues to the forefront, because "the consequences and costs of unethical use of information and communication technology: hacking, spamming, consumer fraud, virus setting, intrusion cutting and pasting-intellectual property theft is staggering for an educational community" (Kelly and Haber, 2005: 71).

As learning leaders, school librarians provide electronic access to current and reliable information on copyright and fair use. To this end, they design and maintain a copyright and fair use link on the library's webpage or on a district or school system's homepage, engage in and provide professional development on copyright issues, continuously review scholarly literature, and participate in online activities: blogs, webinars, and other digital venues. There are numerous resources that can help you stay current: the U.S. Copyright Office (Current Legislation, Reports and Studies, Circulars and Brochures *Newsnet*), the American Library Association (tools, legislation, challenged and emerging issues information), the Library Copyright Alliance (ALA: American Library Association; ARL: Association of Research Libraries; ACRL: Association of College and Research Libraries), the Stanford University Libraries (Copyright and Fair Use [SULAIR]; Copyright Overview: *What's New*, with links to legislation, regulations, articles, blogs, and case summaries), and the Center for Social Media (American University *Code of Best Practices*). Well-informed librarians follow copyright experts, such as Carrie Russell, Ken Crews, Mary Minow, Peter Hirtle, and Michel Brewer. Other resources are Justia.com, Nolo Law for All, LibraryLaw.com, the Copyright Clearance Center (CCC), and the World Intellectual Property Organization (WIPO).

Most experts in the field of intellectual property and copyright law hold with the notion of transference of the rule of law to emerging technologies and new forms of media or content. Therefore, the established fair use of hard copy content applies to digitized content. As stated in the U.S. Copyright Office's *Copyright in General* (United States Copyright Office, n.d.) a "work is under copyright protection the moment it is created and fixed in a tangible form that it is perceptible either directly or with the aid of a machine or device." Ease of access does not supersede copyright law. If the work is in a tangible format, it is protected.

Libraries are at the forefront of the fair use and intellectual property debate. They know that digital borders should not be closed. The Internet should expand educational possibilities. As succulently stated in Carol C. Henderson's "Libraries as Creatures of Copyright: Why Librarians Care about Intellectual Property Law and Policy" (n.d.), "With a good balanced copyright law and intellectual property policy, there is no reason why the digital information environment should not increase the opportunities for creators, publishers, and users. . . ."

# Chapter 19

# *Cybersafety and Digital Citizenship*

The Internet is an invaluable educational resource, a social network, and an entertainment vehicle. It is a platform that expands all possibilities for deep learning. This 24/7 digital backdrop provides a collaborative venue that promotes critical thinking, cognitive information processing, problem-solving, "social cognition," and effective communication skills: writing and reading—all of which are very important 21st-century skills. This electronic medium also provides students with authentic learning experiences that have real-world relevance and application. According to Klopfer et al. (2009: 6), in *Using the Technology of Today in the Classroom Today*, digital technologies augment "the development of new cognitive abilities that translate into the key skills for our transformed world: ability to process information quickly, process information in parallel, explore information in a non-linear fashion, access information through imagery, a familiarity of non-geographically bound networks of communication, and the capacity to experiment with one's surrounding as a form of problem solving."

The challenge for teachers, librarians, administrators, and parents is to educate students in digital literacy, safety, and citizenship. How do students learn to navigate a nonlinear hypermedia environment safely and effectively? Marc Prensky wrote in "H. Sapiens Digital: From Digital Immigrants and Digital Natives to Digital Wisdom" (2009) that "[d]igital wisdom can be, and must be, learned and taught." How do students develop digital wisdom? The answer is simple by using technology for knowledge construction, collaboration, creativity, and productivity.

How do librarians embed meaningful digital content, social media, and emerging technologies to enhance student learning while stemming the fears of parents and the community? The answer simple is scientifically based research and evidence. Samantha Biegler and Danah Boyd (n.d.), of Harvard University's Berkman Center for Internet and Society, in *Risky Behaviors and Online Safety: A 2010 Literature Review*, believe that "research can and should play an important role in shaping policy, education, interventions, parenting, technology, and public discourse. Research helps map ongoing changes and teases out the complex dynamics that are often at play when trying to make sense of societal issues. Research can also be an antidote to fear." Fear plays a major role in the anti–social media movement in schools. Fears must be placated and addressed head-on with evidence of learning, scientific-based research, and forecasting. Facts really do calm fears!

Current research tells us "Being connected on a 24/7 basis will be the norm in 2020 . . . personal and business activities will mingle seamlessly, as the day fragments into a flexible mix of personal and business activities—work, . . . the pervasive popularity and performance of social collaboration technologies and mechanisms, including social networks, voice channels, online groups, blogs, and other electronic messages, the size and diversity of networks of personal relationships will continue to grow. . . . Concerns about privacy and the security of personal data decline as consumers come to perceive the benefits as outweighing the risks and as mechanisms to secure and process personal information become smarter. Growing use of social networking increasingly determines consumption patterns . . . and positive peer reviews become essential to success . . ." (Booz & Company, 2010).

Social networking has unparalleled potential as an instructional and learning tool. Social media allow students to connect to experts, peers, teachers, friends, family, companies, charitable agencies, organizations, and associations for multiple purposes, especially informational ones. "In addition, social network sites provide learners with environments in which they can take more control of their own learning" (Warschauer and Liaw, 2010: 15). Social networks give students autonomy over learning.

At one school, the librarians and technology integration teachers anonymously surveyed students on their use of social media. The data generated from a recent online survey, correlates with national trends. Twenty-three percent of the high school student body responded to the survey. Of those, 90 percent of the students had a personal Facebook page, 23 percent of those checked their page three times a day, 26 percent of the students used it for "nonsocial stuff," and 38 percent used it to communicate with family members. Students responded that they used social networking for information, for school work, and as a communication tool. The following student statements reveal how student view social media in context to learning: "Believe it or not, Facebook can be an extremely helpful educational tool. Using it to connect to friends about academics and homework is always nice to rely on." "It's like having a study group, but over the Internet. I have a Facebook group for every one of my classes, and we ask questions and help each other out online. I sure know it has helped me do well on tests." "I believe that Facebook is a great way to communicate with people that are friends of yours or peers in your classroom and that it helps you interact in many different ways [and is] helpful in many areas as well."

To ensure continuation of unfettered filtering policy and to alleviate parental and community concerns, the librarians and technology integration teachers at this school

- Created online resources on cybersafety (YouTube)
- Added links on cybersafety to the library homepage
- Showcased student and professional work using social media
- Provided professional development on cyberbullying and intellectual property, fair use, and copyright
- Conducted surveys on the use of emerging technologies for instruction and evidence-based practice
- Lobbied government officials
- Addressed the board of education
- Offered workshops for parents and the community

As Klopfer et al. (2009) state in *Using Technology in the Classroom Today: The Instructional Power of Digital Games, Social Networks and Simulations and How Teachers Can Leverage Them*, "Games, simulations, and social networking are already permeating the workplace as productivity and development tools—we may be doing our students a large disservice by not integrating these tools into their education. At the same time, we must acknowledge that there is a reason these tools have been adopted so pervasively in the workforce—these groups are identifying the advantages of these tools and are leveraging them to enhance their work. If they are able to see many of the advantages of these tools in their productivity, what might educators find in student performance?"

The school librarians and technology integration teachers at this school integrated social media for information, visual, and digital literacy

- To model ethical and productive use of social networks
- To collaborate with students, faculty, and staff
- To promote an inquiry-based learning environment
- To announce new instructional tutorials
- To highlight new acquisitions to the collection: books, audiovisuals, and databases
- To publicize new services
- To feature photographs of student events
- To link to YouTube and Vimeo tutorials aligning with curriculum
- As a discussion platform for the library's TAG (teen advisor group)
- To announce upcoming book chats (in person and virtual)
- To feature upcoming events, such as author visits, Teen Read Week, World Read Aloud Day, American Library Association Banned Books Week, or Banned Sites Day
- To link to and promote community events, to highlight ICT online resources
- To reach out to the larger community
- To feature library and technology survey results.
- To post technology help
- To post school announcements

As coteachers, these librarians modeled the use of Twitter for instruction. Twitter is a first-rate current events analysis tool. Students learn real-time informational evaluation. Twitter helps to teach students who, what, when, where, and why. Twitter also forces students to think strategically and concisely.

Facebook and Google+ hangouts are also used. It is a great way for students to collaborate. Students can set up groups to work together on class work, a project, homework, or an assignment. Students understand that positive collaboration and a respectful environment are vital to their success. The use of social media inculcates habits of mind: persistence, empathy, flexibility, questioning and probing, applying past knowledge to new situations, and communicating with clarity.

For example, during an AP calculus research project, students were asked to do research on a mathematician or mathematical theory and to design a presentation using multimedia to teach their peers. One student designed a Facebook page for a famous mathematician. He wrote a profile, created a video, and added images, links, and events. His peers were highly engaged. Some students even friended the mathematician, producing a very timely and relevant avenue for discussion. It also modeled a positive personal profile and online identify (digital footprint). This student took a 21st-century approach to writing biographical information and giving a presentation.

Online identify, cyberbullying, and sexual solicitation are areas of concern for parents and educators. According to the Washington State Attorney General's Office, "64% of teens say that they do things online that they wouldn't want their parents to know about and 1 in 5 children are sexually solicited online (only 25% of those told a parent) . . . and nearly 50% of teens don't know what to do if cyber bullied" (Youth Internet Safety Task Force, 2010). These are starting statistics.

As members of various school professional learning communities (PLCs), school librarians and technology integration teachers play a major role in formulating policy and procedures for cybersafety and ethical use of digital resources, such as acceptable use policies (AUPs).

Librarians and technology integration teachers provide instruction for students and professional development for staff on

- Identity theft
- Facial recognition technology
- Privacy options
- Online footprint and identity
- Netiquette
- Intellectual property, fair use, and copyright
- Personal responsibility on an unfiltered Internet
- Website evaluation

For example, in one school, freshmen engaged in a technology orientation program that addressed these issues through direct instruction, online tutorials, and social networks. Students examined all aspects of the AUP and were made aware of their responsibilities.

Research conducted by Hargittai et al. (2010) illustrates the need for librarians to provide learning activities on web evaluation and advance researching strategies: "[W]hen using a search engine, many students clicked on the first search result. Over a quarter of respondents mentioned that they chose a Web site because the search engine had returned that site as the first result, suggesting considerable trust in these services. In some cases, the respondent regarded the search engine as the relevant entity for which to evaluate trustworthiness, rather than the Web site that contained the information."

For students to be safe and productive on the Internet, they must be "good" consumers and producers of digital content. Advanced technology and literacy skills are imperative in successfully navigating a digital environment wisely and safely. School librarians empowered students to independently evaluate information validity and make wise uses of e-content. Savvy educators know that "by embracing values over filters, we are expressing trust in our children, they will judge wisely when the opportunity for misjudgment presents itself. By stressing values over filters, we send the clearest message to our children: As is true in the real world, you can go anywhere you wish, and it is ultimately up to you to decide what is right and wrong and face the consequences of your judgment" (ALA, *Especially for Young People*).

# Part X
# Innovate and Adapt

# Chapter 20

# New and Emerging Technologies

What could be better for kids than mobile technology with devices that are lightweight and easy to carry around? Compare that to the typical school backpack. The *New York Times* (Parker-Pope, 2009) reported that the average sixth-grader carries around 18.5 pounds, with some packs weighing almost twice that. High school students carry much more. Experts tell us that each child should carry no more than 15–20 percent of his or her body weight to avoid possible permanent back injury.

Today, with the market flooded with mobile devices, students no longer need to face injury from lugging heavy packs. Instead, they can replace heavy textbooks and unruly papers with a tablet or lightweight laptop. Secondary to the weight factor is organizational considerations. Students are forever losing papers in backpacks that are crammed and disorganized. Documents saved on a laptop or, better yet, in the cloud are always able to be located and will go far in eliminating excuses (the dog ate my homework) for being unprepared. Mobile technology is the solution, but what we don't always have is permission or funding to make it happen. Schools that can't purchase a device for each student can look to a model that has become known as "bring your own device" (BYOD) or "bring your own technology" (BYOT). As more and more schools go to this model, more and more kids gain access to computing power through easy to transport, affordable mobile options.

## BYOD

In the 2010 National Education Technology Plan (Scholastic, 2014), the U.S. Department of Education recommended that districts initiate a BYOD plan to help cut costs and increase student engagement. The article goes on to warn that this plan "brings with it a host of security concerns, including data protection and compliance with the Children's Internet Protection Act (CIPA)." The debate over 1:1 computing has ended. There remains little doubt that this is what schools need, but with the cost of education skyrocketing, new hardware is among the first items to be cut from a budget. BYOD offers a seemingly simple solution asking kids to buy and bring their own computing power. The program has some caveats, including a price tag for implementation both from the school and from the families of students who might not have the funds to comply, as well as the above mentioned network security considerations that make educators and network administrators nervous.

Schools frequently reject BYOD for socioeconomic reasons, believing that students in their building can't afford to purchase their own laptop or tablet. Schools will need to offer scholarships or purchase loaners to be sure every child has a device. But what about cell phones? It is an uncommon—almost rare—sight these days to see a teenager or even a younger child without a smartphone. Common Sense Media (New Research 2013) released a report in October 2013 stating that 38 percent of children younger than age 2 are already using smartphones or tablets. In 2011, it was only 10 percent—an amazing increase in two short years. We see it all the time in restaurants these days: children in high chairs happily navigating a smartphone or tablet without the slightest hint of frustration. These kids will be a technological force to reckon with as they grow older. And a school without devices will be unacceptable and unbearable to them. We have to work fast!

According to the PEW Research Internet Project (Madden, 2013), 78 percent of teens own a cell phone, with 74 percent using them to access the Internet at least occasionally. In overall internet use, youth ages 12–17 who are living in lower-income and lower-education households are still somewhat less likely to use the Internet in any capacity—mobile or wired. However, those who fall into lower socioeconomic groups are just as likely as, and in some cases more likely than, those living in higher-income and more highly educated households to use their cell phone as a primary point of access.

Smartphones are in fact powerful computers that can be used in classrooms that otherwise have no computers or tablets. One of the dilemmas is that schools frequently view cell phones as the enemy that robs teachers of valuable teaching time as kids play games or text friends beneath their desks. Some schools confiscate phones at the door each morning, then spend the day wishing they had more technology in the building. But what if phones were required to be on desktops during classes? What if students could use them for research, social learning, and collaboration? What if the camera in each phone could be used to snap photos relevant to studies or to record interviews that can be sent directly to YouTube? And what if students could use their phone as an audience response system or a voting device to help teachers check for understanding during class or to get a response to an online survey? You often hear schools say they can't afford enough devices for all students, but what we're learning from the statistics is that the majority of kids already have their own and the number is increasing rapidly from year to year. We just need to let them use what they have!

BYOD programs seem simple and straightforward, but this plan is still a bit more complicated than one might think, requiring careful planning and pre-work on the part of the district. Although students buy their own technology, once at school, these devices all need wireless Internet access (Wi-Fi). This is done by strategically adding wireless access points (WAPs) around the building. These WAPs are costly and need to be carefully installed to avoid overload and dead zones. Although a single WAP is designed to handle 200+ devices, setting it up to do so will enormously slow your computing power, resulting in frustration for teachers and kids. Organizations such as Cisco will conduct an audit to determine how many access points are needed and where they should be placed to distribute the network load. Wi-Fi audits can be an expensive undertaking but might save money in the long run when access points are installed correctly and abundantly to provide even coverage.

Network security issues are often the sticking point for many districts. Worries over how to protect school data, how to comply with CIPA, and how to control what students are doing online top the list of concerns. Schools will need to do some research, scrutinize their acceptable use policy, and weigh the costs as they plan to let students and teachers bring more devices into the building.

## The BYOD Classroom

Whether it be school-supplied or BYOD, the need for one-to-one computing has become indisputable as schools feel the pressure to find ways to keep teachers, staff, and students up to date with new and emerging technologies. It is incumbent upon us to prepare students to live, work, and thrive in a quickly evolving technological landscape.

With the influx of new devices and the constant shift in current educational technologies comes a need for professional development for faculty and staff. Librarians and technology integration teachers must lead the pack, preparing themselves to assist teachers as they learn to teach technology-rich lessons in a classroom where there are ten or more different devices being used simultaneously. Can a student with a smartphone be able to achieve the same goals as one armed with a laptop? And will the laptop be able to do everything the smartphone can? How can we sync an iPad app with work being done on a computer and vice versa? Assemble all your questions. These will take time, patience, and experimentation to answer.

Multidevice classrooms require organizational strategies. Encourage teachers to take inventory of which student is working with which device, then group students accordingly. Perhaps one task will work best if each group consists of one laptop, one tablet, and one smartphone. Or perhaps groups of kids with similar devices can work on different aspects of the same project. Be sure to involve the students in the discussion. They like taking the lead and sharing their thoughts and expertise. Ask them for ideas. They often have quick solutions to what seems to the teacher to be an overwhelming dilemma. Gather suggestions for apps from them and let the kids test them to find the best solutions. The staggering number of new apps that do it better and faster can leave teachers bewildered. There are apps that let students work in an environment that mimics a computer screen and many more that work together with the online program. In the case of Google, for instance, users can download a full suite of Google Mobile Apps. These include Google Search, Google Maps, Google Drive, Chrome, YouTube, Google Play, Blogger, and Google Earth, among others. Some work better than others and some require a bit of training, but it's rare these days to use a PC or Mac application that doesn't advertise a mobile counterpart. It seems certain that BYOD with new and emerging technologies can create an exciting classroom landscape that keeps kids engaged and learning.

# Chapter 21

# *Access and the Filtering Debate*

What does your district do about access to information? What should they do?

When the State of Connecticut imposed a strict new filter in September 2008, our librarian, our director of technology and I (the technology integrator) requested a hearing with the State Commission on Educational Technology to appeal for the return of individual district control. We presented specific evidence of how our teachers and students use websites that are often blocked, such as YouTube and Facebook, in a powerful, constructivist way; we shared compelling examples of student projects; and we demonstrated the use of our acceptable use policy (AUP), which defines strict consequences for breaking the rules. Based on our testimony, the Commission reinstated individual district control statewide. We were elated, but wondered how other districts were making filtering decisions and what we could do to help students everywhere be free of the restrictions.

All schools want to do what's best for kids and select the level of filtering based on a desire to protect them. But taking your library and your classes online requires access, and access and network filtering policies are often in conflict. What to do? The filtering issue is contentious, with one side believing that access lets kids get to the real work and the other side feeling the responsibility to protect them from negative influences. How can schools decide?

Districts can begin by writing an AUP that holds students and faculty to ethical and responsible use. Writing it in such a way as not to mention specific Internet applications makes it possible to work with the same document over several years, whereas specifying technologies will mean rewriting annually—or more often—as new applications emerge. Once written, be sure to make teachers, students, and parents aware of the policy. Some schools make students and parents sign off on the document while others use an opt-out policy asking those who don't agree to sign and return it.

How open can a school filter be and still comply with the Children's Internet Protection Act (CIPA)? CIPA states that for schools and libraries to be eligible for E-rate funding, they must comply with the following regulations:

1. Filter obscene and harmful content in grades K–12
2. Monitor online activities by minors
3. Teach cybersafety and cyberbullying awareness as well as informing students of legal, ethical, and responsible use, particularly as it pertains to social networking

Districts often reference this mandate as justification for a restrictive filter, but with a bit of curriculum work and oversight of Internet use, students can be permitted broad access.

A closer read of the CIPA document ("Children's Internet Protection Act Guide," 2014) includes the term "harmful content," a concept that perplexes schools. There is no debating the fact that social networking sites such as Facebook can represent negative environments for kids. Chatrooms can open them up to unsavory connections, and sites such as YouTube can expose them to inappropriate content. But that is exactly why schools need to go there with them, to teach them the dangers and pitfalls, show them how to avoid them or how to handle a frightening, threatening, or distasteful situation. The fact is that schools can and should use these sites. Kids thrive on the social aspect, and social applications afford formidable learning opportunities. When used responsibly, social networking sites do not represent harmful content. On the contrary, they represent a unique window on the world.

What can schools do to construct the no-harm environment required by CIPA? They can create a scaffolded cybersafety curriculum for grades K through 12. At the K–5 level, lessons can be explicit and substantial. Once awareness is firmly established in young minds, librarians, technology integration teachers, and classroom teachers in grades 6–12 can supplement the curriculum by including a firmly stated cybersafety and cyberethics reminder as part of all Internet-based work. With today's emphasis on assessing soft skills, these reminders can be included in each project rubric, attaching a grade-point value to attributes including citizenship, personal accountability, and self-monitoring.

But what about filtering at the lower grade levels? In many cases, the filter can be set to provide age-appropriate content for different groups, thus permitting expanded access as students move to middle school and then high school. One district follows these guidelines: Students at the elementary level conduct Internet searches through Nettrekker and Google Safe Search. Discovery Education, open to grades K–12, has its own filtering system, making it possible to offer age-appropriate content in grades K–4. In middle school, Google and other Internet searches are taught and permitted. High school students have open access to the Internet with the exception of pornography and gaming sites. In this way, students and teachers are free to choose and use the best tools and applications for their classes. Encourage teachers and students to suggest new technologies. It keeps things fresh and engaging, and teaches flexibility, building confidence among users in their ability to transfer prior knowledge to new and emerging technologies.

If you're teaching in an environment with prohibitive filtering, don't hesitate to go to decision makers to demonstrate your need for more access. When you do, bring concrete evidence to demonstrate how working in currently blocked sites can enhance critical thinking, reinforce cybersafety considerations, let kids practice communications skills, and encourage creativity, thus playing a pivotal role in bringing 21st-century learning to prepare for future lives and work. If possible, bring a student or two who can speak to it as well.

If you're one of the decision makers, bring your stakeholders together to examine questions such as the following:

- How does filtering impact learning?
- What is gained and what is lost by filtering?
- Is filtering censorship, protection, or something else?
- Do filters keep students and teachers from significant and essential 21st-century tools?
- If the decision is to filter less aggressively, how are the gains worth the risks?
- What about student discipline?
- How does the AUP play an important role?
- What can one district do when faced with a strict state-imposed filter? What can one teacher do when faced with a district-imposed filter?
- Does the filter permit setting by grade level?

For many districts the real issue in determining filtering levels is around those social networking sites that always raise a red flag. Confused and concerned parents prefer that kids not be involved with sites that have the undeniable power to put students at risk, but they also acknowledge that students are going to those sites alone both at home and on mobile devices. When asked, parents often support the decision to allow access in school where education will positively impact student use and minimize misuse. Teachers can work with kids on reading and understanding the privacy settings that they often ignore and learning how to adjust them to protect themselves. It's important to let them know that privacy settings should be revisited often because they change routinely, meaning that today's settings might not protect you tomorrow. Ask kids to think carefully about what they upload and download, and constantly remind them that what they upload to one place often moves to another with or without their permission and sometimes with unwanted and potentially hurtful, embarrassing, and lasting consequences.

Although schools will often acknowledge the pros of in-school use of social networks, access remains contentious. Ironically—and not surprisingly—when students are told they can't go there, they immediately start trying to find a way to do just that. In fact, it doesn't take long to get around a filter. Try searching for "getting around the Facebook filter" in Google. In a blink, you'll find 457 million results! Instructions are straightforward and generally easy to follow, and successful students claim bragging rights for liberating their classmates! Given that outcome, there really is no point to limiting access. Why not return the focus to learning by letting kids navigate the social web, going there with them to ensure they know how to use it responsibly, ethically, and safely? Schools that have thrown open their filter report that when everything is available, students are free to think about learning. Remind kids of the AUP, but let them know that you respect them and trust them to do the right thing. It's important to teach students to separate school work from their personal social encounters. They should think of school as their "work" environment where they focus on building a professional profile that represents the best they have to offer while keeping more playful personal exchanges separate. Also, remind them to consider implications—both present and future—of each and every post they make.

The following are some of the ways that the top social sites can become educational resources.

# YouTube

- Seemingly infinite, authentic, relevant, and timely resources on all topics make research more appealing to this visual generation.
- Abounds with video tutorials. Teachers can flip the classroom by uploading their own videos for student use or search for those posted by others. Making your own "Public" videos lets people around the world benefit from your work.
- Personal YouTube channels let each user create favorites lists for each project, enabling easy retrieval of video resources. Note that Google Apps for Education gives each domain member a YouTube channel.
- Student-made videos can be uploaded in many formats. Marking them "Unlisted" will keep them out of search engines, but anyone with the link such as teachers and classmates will be able to view.
- Videos can be accessed from any computer or mobile device.
- Videos can be easily shared, and peer commenting is always available.
- Videos can be quickly embedded into web pages.
- VideoNot.es makes individual viewing and commenting on videos a useful tool for teachers in the flipped classroom. Entered notes are synchronized with the video on one screen. VideoNot.es can be accessed through and added to your Google Drive.

# Twitter

- Create project or class hashmark (#nchsabs = Absolutism project) for easy tracking of student posts.
- Excellent backchannel option when used as a chat room (must include selected class hashtag). Note: Tweets will be lost in heavy traffic if there's a major event going on. For example, don't try chatting when Ellen DeGeneres tweets a selfie with major stars from the Oscars or during the Super Bowl or World Cup Finals.
- Students enter questions, useful hints, good finds
- Library Twitter for announcements
- Quick how-tos
- Short answers to questions or links to longer answers
- Retweets of relevant links to share with the class or team
- Curation app: Tweets disappear quickly. Coupling Twitter with a curation app like Paper.li will turn tweets and retweets into a newspaper that updates daily as it pulls

feeds from Twitter based on registered project hashtags, allowing students to see information that classmates deemed valuable.

- The 140 character limit teaches students the valuable art of concise expression.

# Facebook

- Makes a unique Course Management Platform where students feel comfortable participating
- Lets teachers meet kids where they spend their time
- Subgroup or collaborative team formation is quick and easy.
- Easy communication with group or private messaging
- Create discussion forums, schedule chats, ask and answer questions. Students consistently demonstrate more critical thinking in a Facebook discussion forum than on a piece of paper in the classroom.
- Opportunities for peer review
- Collaboration on homework and projects; resources sharing
- Photo sharing and moving from home to school becomes a snap
- Post surveys for quick and efficient data collection. Students boast 400 responses in a school week.
- Post homework and quizzes
- Embed videos and other media
- Library Facebook to communicate library information, tech tips, publicity for upcoming library events
- Post forms to register for events such as author visits

## *What Is the Impact on Students?*

Schools that grant students access and strive to provide them with the experiences necessary to make responsible, ethical, safe, and legal decisions when using online resources will see the impact. When students are respected and trusted, they feel grown up and valued as partners in our learning. The classroom ceases to be teacher-centered as students conduct research and engage in higher-order thinking to solve problems and construct meaning in collaborative teams. Students and teachers appreciate the freedom to search the Internet, resulting in more relevant and current media embedded in their projects. Kids who are free to work as they wish will communicate and collaborate often without being asked. When you talk consistently to kids about safe and ethical use, they will begin to ask for opinions before posting and before copying and pasting someone else's intellectual property into their work. Encourage students to find new ways to achieve their goals with emerging technologies and let them do the work to learn and teach them to the entire class. Remind students that they are learning skills that they will be able to transfer to their own lives and to other curricular areas—and use the words trust and respect often.

## *What Is the Impact on Teachers?*

Teachers with open access to the Internet become risk takers empowered to innovate and assemble their own selection of online tools, opening the floodgates to new and innovative instructional practices. Teachers will no doubt report higher student engagement along with a decrease in computer-related discipline problems and increased proficiency in 21st-century skills, primarily around communication, collaboration, and digital literacy. Educators in these schools will quickly see that instruction becomes more student centered and, after a period of adjustment, are generally happy to share the teaching and learning with their students. Student-centered and project-based learning experiences need no longer be simulations but rather authentic, real-world work that involves primary sources, interactions with experts in the field, and actual data. You never know when one student's work will change the course of a life—theirs or yours!

Take the story of Jack Andraka who was mentioned in the chapter on visual literacy. At the age of 15, following the death of a family friend, this teenager developed a new way to detect pancreatic, ovarian, and lung cancers that costs three cents to produce and takes five minutes to run (Axelrod, 2013). Jack was limited by expensive access to scientific and medical publications but persevered with Google and Wikipedia until his work earned him lab access at Johns Hopkins University.

And in Bozeman, Montana, two high school amateur astrophysicists, Madeline Kelly and Hannah Cebulla, working with professors and experts at Harvard and CalTech, were invited to present their findings at the American Astronomical Society meeting in Washington, D.C. This was work done in conjunction with an after-school Astronomy Club with the help of their advisor, Lynn Powers (Swan, 2014).

None of these incredible young people earned high school credit for their work. It was driven by passion and fueled by access. Jack is now 17 and makes it a point in each speaking engagement to encourage the scientific and medical worlds to drop high-access fees and make their research available for more people like him to make world-changing breakthroughs. When presented with open access to the world, the real work of research, collaboration, creativity, discovery, development, and publishing can happen.

How do you know if the plan is working in your schools? The following are some of the things you should look for:

- Innovative instructional practices
- Increased student engagement
- Evidence of 21st-century communication, collaboration, and digital literacy skills
- Less student "hacking" and "damage" on school technology
- Increase in student-centered learning
- New relationships: student to student as well as student to teacher
- Authentic learning experiences that let kids make a difference in the world
- Students publishing their own work: writing, music, research, blogs, artwork, portfolios

There is no promise that this model of open filtering will be problem free, but you should expect a general shift in attitude and behavior as kids see that they no longer have to sneak around and be frustrated each time they hit a blocked site.

Food for thought from Harvard's white paper on *Copyright and Education*:

Rights holders are not the only parties responsible for limiting access to digital works. Educators also interfere with access to digital works. Institutional barriers to access, inadvertent and intentional, lock digital works within walled gardens. (Fisher, 2014)

What does your district or school do? Add your voice to a filtering survey at http://tinyurl.com/Yfilter.

# Conclusion

In 2008, Sharon Coatney wrote in *Teacher Librarian, Library Media Specialist: Not a Job for the Faint of Heart*, "The job is not for the fainthearted. It is difficult, time-consuming, exhausting, but hugely rewarding; so, we must find a way to do it all—not pick and choose what role we want to provide. We are both teachers and librarians—very special learning specialists in our schools—and we must somehow learn how to divide our time, work smarter, and do it all." These words are even more relevant today.

In our ever evolving, educational environment school librarians and technology integration teachers offer the 21st-century tools and knowhow that empower and challenge students to learn and to want to learn, appealing to their desire for the socialization and constant communication. They respond to this new norm of easy access, mobility, social media, and gadgets by personalizing learning and engaging students through

- Building connections and relationships
- Interactive leadership
- Promoting collaboration
- Demonstrating vision
- Transforming inquiry and problem solving
- Providing information on demand
- Energizing creativity and innovation
- Integrating cutting-edge technologies and new media
- Empowering accountability and motivation
- Taking responsible risks
- Analyzing data

As coteachers and instructional partners, they provide online and offline learning opportunities in multiple 21st-century literacies that foster curiosity and creativity. They guide learners in the effective and ethical use of technology and information, task identification and conceptualization, information seeking strategies, location and access, evaluation, comprehension, synthesis, citation, communication, and presentation. In addition to all this, they also embed higher-order thinking skills (HOTS) into performance-based learning activities so that students can meet not only the Pizza Hut challenge, but any challenge.

Librarians are able to do all this because they know students through casual conversations, reference queries, by examining student profiles, by working collaboratively with other faculty on individual education plans (IEPs), by progress monitoring, through ongoing assessment and constructive feedback, by looking at student work, by conferencing, by observation, and through school events and activities.

As advocates for open and free access to the Internet for the exchange of ideas and information and for lifelong learning, school librarians and technology integration teachers empower students to make judicious decisions about what, when, and how they learn. They afford students with the opportunities to make connections—to be creative thinkers.

Today, librarians do not pick and choose. They are school leaders, teachers, collaborators, guides, researchers, advocates, media specialists, knowledge brokers, assessors, communicators, writers, literacy coaches, reading instructors, literary reviewers, storytellers, technology integrators, trainers, collectors, administrators, managers, directors, catalogers, detectives, artists, curators, archivists, advertisers, raconteurs, connoisseurs, homework helpers, club advisors, mentors, analysts, problem solvers, designers, developers, negotiators, motivators, strategic planners, lecturers, publishers, photographers, website creators, analysts, database administrators, event planners, computer support specialists, tinkers, thinkers, and futurists.

Yes, they have heeded Coatney's advice. They do it all so that students can meet not only the Pizza Hut challenge, but any challenge. And because of this, it is the best of times to be a school librarian.

# Bibliography

AASL: American Association of School Librarians. (1998). *Information Power: Building Partnerships for Learning.* Chicago: American Library Association.

AASL: American Association of School Librarians. (2008). "7d. Benchmarks to Achieve by Grade 10." *Standards for the 21st Century Learner in Action.* Accessed December 11, 2010. http://aasl.ala.org/aaslstandindtf/index.php?title=Main_Page.

AASL: American Association of School Librarians. (2008). "Learning 4 Life: A National Plan for Implementation of Standards for 21st-century Learner and Empowering Learners: Guidelines for School Library Programs." Accessed February 6, 2011. http://www.ala.org/aasl/sites/ala.org.aasl/files/content/guidelinesandstandards/learning4life/document/l4lplan.pdf.

AASL: American Association of School Librarians. (2008). "Self-assessment Strategies (Stripling 4/4/08)." http://aasl.ala.org/aaslstandindtf/index.php?title=5._Self-Assessment_Strategies.

AASL: American Association of School Librarians. (2009). *Empowering Learners: Guidelines for School Library Media Programs.* Chicago: American Association of School Librarians.

AASL: American Association of School Librarians. (2009). *Standards for the 21st-century Learner in Action.* Chicago: ALA.

AASL: American Association of School Librarians. (2014). "AASL Governing Documents." Accessed April 4, 2014. http://www.ala.org/aasl/about/governing-docs.

AASL: American Association of School Librarians. (n.d.). "School Library Program Health and Wellness Toolkit: Advocacy." Accessed May 14, 2010. http://www.ala.org/aasl/advocacy/tools/toolkits/health-wellness.

AASL: American Association of School Librarians. (n.d). "English Language Arts. American Association of School Librarians (AASL)." American Library Association. Accessed October 5, 2014. http://www.ala.org/aasl/standards-guidelines/crosswalk/ela.

Abilock, Debbie. (2013). "NoodleTools." http://www.noodletools.com/debbie/literacies/visual/diglitnews.pdf.

Achieve, Inc. (2014). "Next Generation Science Standards for States by States." http://www.nextgenscience.org.

ALA: American Library Association. (1989). "Presidential Committee on Information Literacy: Final Report," Accessed June 7, 2011. http://www.ala.org/acrl/publications/whitepapers/presidential.

ALA: American Library Association. (2007). "Especially for Young People and Their Parents." Accessed June 7, 2011. http://www.ala.org/PrinterTemplate.cfm?Section=youngpeopleparents&Template=/ContentManagement/ContentDisplay.cfm&ContentID=164213.

ALA: American Library Association. (2007). "Online Safety Rules and Suggestions." Accessed June 11, 2011. http://www.ala.org/advocacy/intfreedom/censorshipfirstamendmentissues/censorshipschools#online.

ALA: American Library Association. (2007). "Standards for the 21st-Century Learner." Accessed June 7, 2011. http://www.ala.org/aasl/standards-guidelines/learning-standards.

ALA: American Library Association. (2008). "Code of Ethics of the American Library Association." Accessed May 3, 2011. http://www.ala.org/advocacy/proethics/codeofethics/codeethics.

ALA: American Library Association. (2010). "Questions and Answers: Access to Electronic Information, Services, and Networks: An Interpretation of the Library Bill of Rights." Accessed May 14, 2010. http://www.ala.org/Template.cfm?section=interpretations&Template=/ContentManagement/ContentDisplay.cfm&ContentID=31877.

ALA: American Library Association. (2011). "ACRL Visual Literacy Competency Standards for Higher Education." http://www.ala.org/acrl/standards/visualliteracy.

ALA: American Library Association. (2011). "Copyright." Accessed May 3, 2011. http://www.ala.org/advocacy/copyright.

ALA: American Library Association. (2011). "Information Power: Building Partnerships for Learning Mission and Goals of the School Library Media Program." Accessed June 12, 2011. http://www.ala.org/PrinterTemplate.cfm?Section=informationpower&Template=/ContentManagement/ContentDisplay.cfm&ContentID=19935.

ALA: American Library Association. (2011). "Teens and Social Media in School and Public Libraries: A Toolkit for Librarians and Library Workers." Accessed June 11, 2011. http://www.ala.org/yalsa/sites/ala.org.yalsa/files/content/professionaltools/Handouts/sn_toolkit11.pdf.

ALA: American Library Association. (2013). "Information Literacy Competency Standards for Higher Education." http://www.ala.org/acrl/standards/informationliteracycompetency.

ALA: American Library Association.(n.d). "Standard Three." Association of College & Research Libraries (ACRL)." Accessed October 6, 2014. http://www.ala.org/acrl/issues/infolit/standards/stnd3.

Allen, Rick. (2010). "Dawn of the New Literacies." ASCD Education Update 52, no. 8 (August). Accessed April 28, 2011. http://www.ascd.org/publications/newsletters/education-update/aug10/vol52/num08/Dawn-of-the-New-Literacies.aspx.

Alvy, Harvey, and Pam Robbins. (2010). Learning from Lincoln: Leadership Practices for School Success. Alexandria, VA: ASCD.

Anderson, Steven. 2014. "Blogging about the Web 2.0 Classroom." Blog. http://blog.web20classroom.org/.

Angelo, Thomas A. (1999). "Doing Assessment as If Learning Matters Most." AAHE Bulletin (May). Accessed July 2, 2011. http://www.aahea.org/aahea/articles/angelomay99.htm.

Annenberg Institute for School Reform. (n.d.). "Professional Learning Communities: Professional Development Strategies That Improve Instruction." Accessed March 31, 2014. http://annenberginstitute.org/pdf/proflearning.pdf

ARL: Association of Research Libraries. (2010). "Fair Use in the Electronic Age: Serving the Public Interest." Accessed May 3, 2011. http://old.arl.org/pp/ppcopyright/copyresources/fair_use_electronic.shtml.

Arnone, Marilyn P., and Rebecca Reynolds. (2009). "Empirical Support for the Integration of Dispositions In Action and Multiple Literacies Into AASL's Standards for the 21st Century Learner." *School Library Media Research* 12: 1–29. Accessed June 11, 2011. http://www.ala.org/aasl/sites/ala.org.aasl/files/content/aaslpubsandjournals/slr/vol12/SLMR_EmpiricalSupport_V12.pdf.

ASCD: Association for Supervision and Curriculum Development. (2011). "Classroom Tools—Decision Tree." Accessed February 25, 2014. http://www.ascd.org/ASCD/pdf/books/beersAT2011_decision_tree.pdf.

Association of American Publishers, Inc., National Association of College Stores, Inc., and Software and Information Industry Association, Inc. (2003). *Questions and Answers on Copyright for the Campus Community*, 6th ed. Washington, D.C.: Association of American Publishers.

Axelrod, Jim. (2013). "16-year-old finds a new way to detect cancer." http://www.cbsnews.com/news/16-year-old-finds-a-new-way-to-detect-cancer/.

Azzam, Amy M. (2009). "Teaching for the 21st Century: Why Creativity Now? A Conversation with Sir Ken Robinson." http://www.ascd.org/publications/educational leadership/sept09/vol67 /num01/Why-Creativity-Now%C2%A2-A-Conversation-with-Sir-Ken-Robinson.aspx.

Barrie, John M. (2008). "Catching the Cheats How Original." *The Biochemist Society Features: Ethics*. http://www.biochemist.org/bio/03006/0016/030060016.pdf.

Basromine, D. (2011). "WHITE PAPER: Plagiarism and the Web: Myths and Realities." *Study Mode*. http://www.studymode.com/essays/Turnitin-Whitepaper-Plagiarism-Web-684970.html.

Balard, Susan, and Kristin Fontichiaro. (2010). "More Than Shushing and Shelving." *Principal Leadership* (December): 50–54.

Begley, Sharon. (2010). "Your Brain Online: Does the Web Change How We Think?" *Newsweek*. Accessed April 29, 2011. http://www.newsweek.com/begley-does-internet-change-how-we-think-71085.

Bellanca, James A. *A Guide to Graphic Organizers: Helping Students Organize and Process Content for Deeper Learning*. (2007). Thousand Oaks, Calif: Corwin Press.

"Best Practices for Ensuring Originality in Written Work." (2014). Plagiarism.org. Accessed April 9, 2014. http://www.plagiarism.org/ask-the-experts/overview/.

Biegler, Samantha, and Danah Boyd. (n.d.). *Risky Behaviors and Online Safety: A 2010 Literature Review* (1–47). Edited by Harvard University, Beckman Center for Internet and Society. Accessed May 22, 2011. http://www.zephoria.org/files/2010SafetyLitReview.pdf.

Blachman, Nancy and Peek, Jerry (2013). "Interactive Online Google Tutorial and References." Accessed April 21, 2014. http://www.googleguide.com.

Black, Paul, Christine Harrison, Clare Lee, Bethan Marshall, and Dylan Wiliam. (2001). "'Working Inside the Black Box: Assessment for Learning in the Classroom." *Phi Delta Kappan* 86, no. 1 (September): 9–21. Accessed May 2, 2011. http://www.proquest.com.

Black, Paul, and Dylan Wiliam. (1998). "Inside the Black Box: Raising Standards through Classroom Assessment." *Phi Delta Kappa* (November): 139–144, 146–148. Accessed May 2, 2011. http://www.jstor.org/stable/20439383.

Blankstein, Alan M. (2010). *Failure Is Not an Option: 6 Principles for Making Student Success the Only Option*, 2nd ed. Thousand Oaks, CA: Corwin.

Booth, Char. (2010). "Build Your Own Instructional Literacy." *American Libraries* (June–July): 40–43.

Boss, Suzie. "Focus on Audience for Better PBL Results." (2014). Edutopia: The George Lucas Educational Foundation. http://www.edutopia.org/blog/focus-on- audience-for-better-pbl-results-suzie-boss.

Booz & Company, Inc. (2010). "The Rise of Generation C: Implications for the World of 2020." Accessed February 10, 2011. http://www.strategyand.pwc.com/global/home/what-we-think/reports-white-papers/article-display/rise-generation-implications-world-2020.

Boyd, Danah. (2008). "Teen Socialization Practices in Networked Publics." http://www.danah.org/papers/talks/MacArthur2008.html.

Britannica Editors. (2010). "The Decline of Creativity in the United States: 5 Questions for Educational Psychologist Kyung Hee Kim." http://www.britannica.com/blogs/2010/10/the-decline-of-creativity-in-the-united-states-5-questions-for-educational-psychologist-kyung-hee-kim/.

Bronson, Po, and Ashley Merryman. (2010). "The Creativity Crisis and the *Daily Beast*." http://www.thedailybeast.com/newsweek/2010/07/10/the-creativity-crisis.html.

Brookhart, Susan M. (2008). *How to Give Effective Feedback to Your Students*. Alexandria, VA: ASCD.

Brookhart, Susan M. (2010). *How to Assess Higher-Order Thinking Skills in Your Classroom*. Alexandria, VA: ASCD.

Brookhart, Susan M. (2013). *How to Create and Use Rubrics for Formative Assessment and Grading*. Alexandria, VA: ASCD.

Brookhart, Susan M. (2013). "Assessing Creativity." http://www.ascd.org/publications/educational-leadership/feb13/vol70/num05/Assessing-Creativity.aspx#interview.

"Brooklyn Collection." (2014). *Brooklyn Public Library*. http://www.bklynlibrary.org/brooklyncollection.

Brynjolfsson, Erik, and Andrew McAfee. (2014). *The Second Machine Age: Work, Progress, and Prosperity in a Time of Brilliant Technologies*. New York: W.W. Norton & Co.

Buffum, Austin, Mike Mattos, and Chris Weber. (2010). "The Why Behind RTI: Response to Intervention Flourishes When Educators Implement the Right Practices for the Right Reasons." *Educational Leadership* 68, no. 2 (October): 10–16. Accessed October 27, 2010. http://www.ascd.org/publications/educational-leadership/oct10/vol68/num02/The-Why-Behind-RTI.aspx.

Burk, Dan. (2002). "Copyright." *Encyclopedia.com*. http://www.encyclopedia.com/topic/copyright.aspx#3-1E1:copyright-full.

Bush, Gail, and Merrilee Andersen Kwieford. (2001). "Advocacy in Action." *Teacher Librarian* 28, no. 5 (June): 8+. Accessed May 28, 2010. http://eds.b.ebscohost.com/eds/detail/detail?vid=2&sid=731f083c-fa33-4361-8795-748823b7db3d%40sessionmgr198&hid=113&bdata=JnNpdGU9ZWRzLWxpdmUmc2NvcGU9c2l0ZQ%3d%3d#db=edsgcc&AN=edsgcl.76332731.

CCSS: Common Core State Standards Initiative. (2010). "Common Core State Standards for English Language Arts and Literacy in History/Social Studies, Science, and Technical Subjects." http://www.corestandards.org/assets/CCSSI_ELA%20Standards.pdf.

CCSS: Common Core State Standards Initiative. (2012). "Preparing America's Students for College and Careers." Accessed May 3, 2012. http://www.corestandards.org.

Center for International Scholarship in School Libraries~Rutgers University CISSL. (2009). "Evidence-Based Practice and School Improvement." Accessed May 14, 2010. http://cissl.rutgers.edu/joomla-license/evidence-based-practice-and-school-improvement/66-evidence-based-practice-articles.

Chen, Hsin-Yuan. (2009). "Online Reading Comprehension Strategies among General and Special Education Elementary and Middle School Students." PhD diss., Michigan State University. Accessed May 29, 2011. http://eric.ed.gov/?id=ED506429.

Chickering, A. W., and Z. F. Gamson. (2009). "Chickering & Gamson (1987): Seven Principles for Good Practice in Undergraduate Education." http://research.kinasevych.ca/2009/12/chickering-gamson-1987-seven-principles-for-good-practice-in-undergraduate-education

"Child's Internet Protection Act Guide." (2014). *FCC.* http://www.fcc.gov/guides/childrens-internet-protection-act.

Choose Responsibility.org. (n.d.). "John McCardell – Drinking age – Choose Responsibility." John McCardell – Drinking age – Choose Responsibility. Accessed October 6, 2014.

Church, Audrey P. (2008). "The Instructional Role of the Library Media Specialist as Perceived by Elementary School Principals." http://www.ala.org/aasl/sites/ala.org.aasl/files/content/aaslpubsandjournals/slr/vol11/SLMR_InstructionalRole_V11.pdf.

Church, Audrey P. (2010). "Secondary School Principals? Perceptions of the School Librarian's Instructional Role." http://www.ala.org/aasl/sites/ala.org.aasl/files/content/aaslpubsandjournals/slr/vol13/SLR_SecondarySchool_V13.pdf.

Churches, Andrew. (2011). "Bloom's Digital Taxonomy." http://www.techlearning.com/techlearning/archives/2008/04/andrewchurches.pdf.

Churches, Andrew. (2008). "Bloom's Taxonomy Bloom Digitally." Accessed June 10, 2010. http://www.techlearning.com/studies-in-ed-tech/0020/blooms-taxonomy-blooms-digitally/44988.

Clyde, Laurel A. (2002). "An Instructional Role for Librarians: An Overview and Content Analysis of Job Advertisements." *Australian Academic and Research Libraries* 33, no. 3 (September): 150–167. Accessed June 22, 2010. http://www.tandfonline.com/doi/abs/10.1080/00048623.2002.10755195#.VDVGcGddWSo.

Coatney, Sharon. (1998). "Information Power: Building Partnerships for Learning. Standards for School Library Media Program." *Teacher Librarian* 26, no. 1 (September): 9–10. Accessed May 28, 2010. http://eds.a.ebscohost.com/eds/detail/detail?vid=2&sid=753d089d-03f7-48d8-aebe-1918befe373d%40sessionmgr4001&hid=4110&bdata=JnNpdGU9ZWRzLWxpdmUmc2NvcGU9c2l0ZQ%3d%3d#db=edsgcc&AN=edsgcl.30462328.

Coatney, Sharon. (2008). "Library Media Specialist—Not a Job for the Faint of Heart." *Teacher Librarian* 35, no. 3 (February): 57. Accessed September 10, 2010. ProQuest Professional Collection.

Coiro, Julie. (2005). "Making Sense of Online Text." *EL: Educational Leadership* 63, no. 2 (October): 30–35. Accessed May 8, 2011. http://www.ascd.org/publications/educational-leadership/oct05/vol63/num02/Making-Sense-of-Online-Text.aspx.

Coiro, Julie. (2009). "Rethinking Online Reading Assessment." *Educational Leadership* (March): 59–63. Accessed May 14, 2010. http://www.ascd.org/publications/educational-leadership/mar09/vol66/num06/Rethinking-Online-Reading-Assessment.aspx.

Common Sense Media Inc. (2013). "New Research from Common Sense Media Reveals Mobile Media Use among Young Children Has Tripled in Two Years." http://www.commonsensemedia.org/about-us/news/press-releases/new-research-from-common-sense-media-reveals-mobile-media-use-among.

Connecticut State Department of Education. (2006). "Healthy and Balanced Living Curriculum Framework." Accessed September 8, 2010. http://www.sde.ct.gov/sde/LIB/sde/PDF/deps/student/Healthy&BalancedLiving.pdf.

Connecticut State Department of Education. (2011). "Information and Technology Literacy Framework K–12." Accessed April 30, 2011. http://www.sde.ct.gov/sde/lib/sde/pdf/dtl/technology/csde_2011_educational_technology_plan.pdf.

Connecticut State Department of Education. (2010). "Introduction: A Vision for Teaching and Learning in Connecticut Public Schools." Accessed June 12, 2011. http://www.sde.ct.gov/sde/lib/sde/pdf/educatorstandards/board_approved_cct_2-3-2010.pdf.

Connecticut State Department of Education. (2010). "2010 Common Core of Teaching: Foundational Skills." Accessed September 7, 2010. http://www.sde.ct.gov/sde/lib/sde/pdf/educatorstandards/board_approved_cct_2-3-2010.pdf.

Connecticut State Department of Education. (2013). "Section 2." Accessed October 12, 2014. http://www.sde.ct.gov/sde/cwp/view.asp?a=2618&q=333720.

Connecticut State Department of Education. (n.d.). "The Connecticut Plan: Academic and Personal Success for Every Middle and High School Students." Accessed November 10, 2010. http://www.sde.ct.gov/sde/lib/sde/pdf/pressroom/TheConnecticutPlan.pdf.

"Connie Yowell—Reimagining the Experience of Education." 2012. *Connected Learning*. http://connectedlearning.tv/connie-yowell-reimagining-experience-education.

Conzemius, Anne, and Jan O'Neill. (2002). *The Handbook for Smart School Teams*. Bloomington, IN: Solution Tree.

Copyright Advisory Network. (n.d.). "Copyright Advisory Network: A Community of Librarians, Copyright Leaders, Policy Wonks." Accessed December 7, 2010. http://www.librarycopyright.net.

Costa, Arthur L. (2008). *Learning and Leading with Habits of Mind*, Chapter 2, "Describing the Habits of Mind." Edited by Arthur L. Costa and Bena Kallick. Alexandria, VA: ASCD. http://www.ascd.org/publications/books/108008/chapters/Describing-the-Habits-of-Mind.aspx.

Council of Chief State officers, Student Achievement Partners, and Achieve. (2013). "TOOLKIT for Evaluating Alignment of Instructional and Assessment Materials to the Common Core State Standards." The Council of Chief State School Officers. Last modified July, 2013. http://www.ccsso.org/Documents/2013/Toolkit%20for%20Evaluating%20Alignment%20of%20Instructional%20and%20Assessment%20Materials.pdf.

Creighton, Theodore B. (2007). *Schools and Data: The Educator's Guide for Using Data to Improve Decision Making*. Thousand Oaks, CA: Corwin Press.

CSRIU: Center for Safe and Responsible Internet Use. (n.d.). "Mobilizing Educators, Parents, Students and Others to Combat Online Social Aggression." Accessed June 24, 2010. http://www.csriu.org.

Cutraro, Jennifer, and Katherine Schulten. (2013). "Mulling on Molly: Investigating the Dangers of a Club Drug." *New York Times*. learning.blogs.nytimes.com/2013/09/18/mulling-over-molly-investigating-the-dangers-of-a-club-drug/?_php=true&_type=blogs&_r=0.

Daly, James. (2004). "Life on the Screen: Visual Literacy in Education." *Edutopia*. http://www.edutopia.org/life-screen.

DeFranco, Francine, and Richard Bleiler. (2003). "Evaluating Library Instruction." Accessed June 10, 2011. http://www.arl.org/~doc/webbook.pdf.

Delaware Department of Education. (n.d.). "Leadership for Learning." Accessed February 7, 2011. http://www.doe.k12.de.us/dess/lfl/default.shtml.

Delisio, Ellen R. (2010). "Teaming Up to Lead Instruction." *Education Update* 52, no. 12 (December): 1.

Dewey, John. (1916). *Democracy and Education*. New York: MacMillan.

Dickinson, Gail K. (2010). "How Are You Acting in a Leadership Role in Your School?" http://www.librarymediaconnection.com/pdf/main/survey_results/1qs_November_December2009.pdf.

Digital Youth Research: Kids Informal Learning with Digital Media. (2008). "Final Report: Introduction." Accessed May 1, 2011. http://digitalyouth.ischool.berkeley.edu/introduction

Diigo. (2014). "Plans and Pricing." Accessed March 21, 2014. http://www.diigo.com/premium/pricing_table_details.

Diigo. (2014). "Special Offerings for Education." Accessed March 21, 2014. https://www.diigo.com/teacher_entry/educationupgrades

Diigo Blog. (2014). "What's New." Accessed March 21, 2014. http://blog.diigo.com/category/whats-new/

Diigo Help. (2014). "FAQ." Accessed March 21, 2014. http://help.diigo.com/teacher-account/faq

Diigo Help. (2014). "Getting Started." Accessed March 21, 2014. http://help.diigo.com/teacher-account/getting-started

Dole, Janice A., Jeffery D. Nokes, and Dina Drits. (2010). "Cognitive Strategy Instruction." Accessed November 10, 2010. http://www.ucrl.utah.edu/researchers/pdf/cognitive_strategy_instruction.pdf.

Donham, Jean. (2010). "Creating Personal Learning through Self-assessment." *Teacher Librarian* 37, no. 3: 14–22. Accessed June 22, 2010. http://eds.b.ebscohost.com/eds/detail/detail?vid=10&sid=eb84c311-ceb0-4b11-946f-32beafef2edd%40sessionmgr113&hid=113&bdata=JnNpdGU9ZWRzLWxpdmUmc2NvcGU9c2l0ZQ%3d%3d#db=edsgcc&AN=edsgcl.222556198.

DuFour, Richard. (2004). "Schools as Learning Communities: What Is a Professional Learning Community?" http://www.ascd.org/publications/educational-leadership/may04/vol61/num08/What-Is-a-Professional-Learning-Community%C2%A2.aspx.

Dumas, Alexandre. (1878). *The Three Musketeers*. London: George Routledge and Sons. https://play.google.com/store/books/details?id=KW0YAAAAYAAJ&rdid=book-KW0YAAAAYAAJ&rdot=1

eBiz. (2014). "Top 15 Most Popular Social Bookmarking Websites." eBizMBA—The eBusiness Guide. Accessed March 21, 2014. http://www.ebizmba.com/articles/social-bookmarking-websites.

edbarrows. (2009). "Planning through Performance." ebedbarrows. Accessed June 12, 2011. http://edbarrows.wordpress.com/page/3.

EduScapes. (n.d.). "Library Media Program: Accountability." Accessed May 14, 2010. http://eduscapes.com/sms/program/accountability.html.

EduScapes. (n.d.). "Library Media Program: Approach to Data Collection." Accessed May 14, 2010. http://eduscapes.com/sms/program/datacollect.html.

EduScapes. (n.d.). "Library Media Program: Data Sources." Accessed May 14, 2010. http://eduscapes.com/sms/program/data.html.

EduScapes. (n.d.). "Library Media Program: Evidence-based Decision Making." Accessed May 14, 2010. http://eduscapes.com/sms/program/evidence.html.

ERIC: University of Oregon. (1997). "Visionary Leadership." Accessed February 7, 2011. http://files.eric.ed.gov/fulltext/ED402643.pdf.

Everhart, Nancy. (2011). "100 Things Students Lose without a Library." http://www.studentsneedlibrariesinhisd.org/100-things-students-lose-without-a-library.html.

Farmer, Lesley. (2002). "Harnessing the Power in Information Power. (Information Literacy)." *Teacher Librarian* 29, no. 3 (February): 20–25. Accessed June 22, 2010. http://eds.b.ebscohost.com/eds/detail/detail?vid=7&sid=302dcc92-31cd-4d7d-b0a0-0cb23bb8dcce%40sessionmgr111&hid=113&bdata=JnNpdGU9ZWRzLWxpdmUmc2NvcGU9c2l0ZQ%3d%3d#db=edsgcc&AN=edsgcl.83516900.

Farr, Steven. (2010–2011). "Leadership, Not Magic." *EL: Educational Leadership* 68, no. 4 (December–January): 28–33. Accessed February 7, 2011. http://www.ascd.org/publications/educational-leadership/dec10/vol68/num04/Leadership,-Not-Magic.aspx.

Federal Communications Commission. (2014). "Children's Internet Protection Act." Accessed March 21, 2014. http://www.fcc.gov/guides/childrens-internet-protection-act.

Fisher, Douglas, and Nancy Frey. (2008). *Better Learning through Structured Teaching: A Framework for the Gradual Release of Responsibility.* Alexandria, VA: ASCD.

Fisher, Douglas, and Nancy Frey. (2010). *Enhancing RTI: How to Ensure Success with Effective Classroom Instruction and Intervention.* Alexandria, VA: ASCD.

Fisher III, William W. (2014). "The Digital Learning Challenge: Obstacles to Educational Uses of Content in the Digital Age—A Foundational White Paper." http://cyber.law.harvard.edu/media/files/copyrightandeducation.html#4_2_4

Fitzgibbons, Shirley A. (2000). "School and Public Library Relationships: Essential Ingredients in Implementing Educational Reforms and Improving Student Learning." *School Library Media Research* 3: 1–66. Accessed June 22, 2010. http://www.ala.org/aasl/sites/ala.org.aasl/files/content/aaslpubsandjournals/slr/vol3/SLMR_SchoolPublicLibRelationships_V3.pdf.

"Flickr: The Commons." (2014). http://www.flickr.com/commons.

"Flickr: The U.S. National Archives." (2014). http://www.flickr.com/usnationalarchives/.

Foundation for Critical Thinking. (2009). "The Role of Questioning in Thinking, Teaching, and Learning." Accessed May 1, 2011. http://www.criticalthinking.org/page.cfm?pageID=524.

Francis, Briana Hovendick, Keith Curry Lance, and Zeth Lietzau. (2010). "School Librarians Continue to Help Students Achieve Standards: The Third Colorado Study (2010)." Library Research Service. http://www.lrs.org/documents/closer_look/CO3_2010_Closer_Look_Report.pdf.

Frey, Carl Benedikt, and Michael A. Osborne. (2013). "The Future of Employment: How Susceptible Are Jobs to Computerization?" http://www.oxfordmartin.ox.ac.uk/downloads/academic/The_Future_of_Employment.pdf.

Friedrich, Roman, Michael Peterson, Alex Koster, and Sebastian Blum. (2010). "The rise of Generation C: Implications for the world of 2020." Strategy& (Formerly Booz & Company). Last modified March 26, 2010. http://www.strategyand.pwc.com/global/home/what-we-think/reports-white-papers/article-display/rise-generation-implications-world-2020.

Fry, Heather. (2009). *A Handbook for Teaching and Learning in Higher Education: Enhancing Academic Practice,* 3rd ed. New York: Routledge. Accessed April 29, 2011. http://books.google.com/?hl=en&lr=&id=L0bVuhl5OfMC&oi=fnd&pg=PA132&dq=assessing+student+learning&ots=EIlGcdOYcl&sig=LVh_Ff2rYpktkiCJA3k2CQe-3cw#v=onepage&q=assessing%20student%20learning&f=false

Fuchs, Douglas, and Lynn S. Fuchs. (2006). "Introduction to Response to Intervention: What, Why, and How Valid Is It?" *Reading Research Quarterly* 41, no. 1 (January–February): 93–99. Accessed May 13, 2010. https://www.uv.uio.no/forskning/om/helga-eng-forelesning/introduction-to-responsivenes-to-intervention.pdf.

Galalis, David. (2011). "Visual Literacy." https://mail.google.com/mail/u/0/#search/from%3A+david%40davidgalalis.com/1312063c108f6a68.

Galalis, David. (2014). "About David Galalis." http://www.davidgalalis.com/about-and-contact/.

Gangwer, Timothy. (2009). "Picture This: Visual Literacy Activities." http://visualteaching.ning.com/profiles/blogs/picture-this-visual-literacy

Garrett, Jeff. 2007. "Northwestern University Library Increases Access to Its Electronic Holdings Using Google Scholar Library Links." *Google Scholar's Library Links Program Case Study.* file:///C:/Users/Cathy.Swan/Downloads/google_scholar_northwestern_library.pdf.

The George Lucas Educational Foundation. (2010). "How to Use Twitter to Grow Your PLN." http://www.edutopia.org/blog/twitter-expanding-pln.

Georgia State University: University Library. (2014). "About Zotero." http://research.library.gsu.edu/zotero

Global Learning Centre. (n.d.). "Critical and Creative Thinking." Accessed March 10, 2014. http://www.glc.edu.au/Resources/Documents/Critical%20and%20Creative%20thinking.pdf.

Goleman, Daniel. (2013). *Focus: The Hidden Driver of Excellence*. New York: Harper.

Goleman, Daniel. (2013). "The Three Kinds of Focus Every Leader Needs." http://www.danielgoleman.info/three-kinds-focus-every-leader-needs/.

"Google: About Google News." (2013). http://news.google.com/intl/en_us/about_google_news.html.

"Google Advanced Search." (2014). Accessed March 21, 2014. https://www.google.com/advanced_search.

"Google Apps for Education." (2014). Accessed March 21, 2014. http://www.google.com/enterprise/apps/education/.

"Google Apps Script." (2014). *Google Developers*. https://developers.google.com/apps-script/reference/spreadsheet/.

"Google Books." (2012). http://books.google.com.

"Google Books History." (2007). Accessed March 21, 2014. http://books.google.com/googlebooks/about/history.html.

"Google Classroom: More Teaching, Less Tech-Ing." (2014). *Google for Education*. http://www.google.com/edu/classroom/.

"Google Drive." (2014). Accessed March 21, 2014. https://developers.google.com.

"Google Flu Trends." (2011). http://www.google.org/flutrends/about/how.html.

"Google for Education Learning Center." (2014). Accessed October 14, 2014. http://www.google.com/edu/training/.

"Google Images." 2014. *Wikipedia*. http://en.wikipedia.org/wiki/Google_Images.

"Google Play Books: My Books." 2014. https://play.google.com/books.

"Google Public Data Explorer." (2014). www.google.com/publicdata/directory.

"Google Public Data: Population in the U.S." (2014). http://www.google.com/publicdata/explore?ds=kf7tgg1uo9ude_.

"Google Scholar Library Support." (2014). *Google Scholar*. Accessed March 21, 2014. http://scholar.google.com/intl/en/scholar/libraries.html.

"Google Search." (2014). *Google*. http://www.google.com.

"Google Spreadsheet Service Google Apps Script." Accessed March 21, 2014. https://developers.google.com/apps-script/reference/spreadsheet/.

"Google Trends." (2014). Accessed April 3, 2014. http://www.google.com/trends/fetchComponent?q=tofu%2C%20seitan%2C%20tempeh%2C%20hummus&geo=US&cmpt=q&cid=TIMESERIES_GRAPH_0&export=5&w=0&h=0&nhf=1.

"Google Zeitgeist." (2013). Accessed March 21, 2014. http://scholar.google.com/zeitgeist

Gordon, Carol. (2007). "The Trouble with the Gold Standard: School Libraries and Research—Is Educational Research Tougher Than Medical Research?" *School Library Journal* 53, no. 10: 1–3.

Gordon, Carol A. (2009). "Raising Active Voices in School Libraries: Authentic Learning, Information Processing and Guided Inquiry." *Scan* 28, no. 3 (August): 34–41. Accessed June 22, 2010. http://www.curriculumsupport.education.nsw.gov.au/schoollibraries/assets/pdf/gordauthlea.pdf.

Gordon, Carol A. (2009). "Raising Active Voices in School Libraries: Authentic Learning, Information Procession and Guided Inquiry. Part 2: The Role of Reflection." *Scan* 28, no. 4 (November): 27–33. Accessed May 14, 2010. http://www.curriculumsupport.education.nsw. gov.au/schoollibraries/assets/pdf/gordauthrefl.pdf.

Gordon, Carol A. (2010). "The Culture of Inquiry in School Libraries." *School Libraries Worldwide* 16, no. 1 (January): 73–88. Accessed June 28, 2010. http:// http://www.iasl-online.org/pubs/ slw/jan2010.htm.

Guilford, J. P. (1973). *Characteristics of Creativity*. Accessed February 24, 2014. http://eric. ed.gov/?id=ED080171

Guthrie, Kathy L., and Sara Thompson. (2010). "Creating Meaningful Environments for Leadership Education." *Journal of Educational Leadership* 9, no. 2 (Summer): 50–57. Accessed February 7, 2011. http://www.leadershipeducators.org/resources/documents/jole/2010_summer/jole_9_2.pdf.

Hadro, Josh. (2010). "Consultant and Simmons Professor Discuss Leadership, Strategic Planning, and the Change Nature of Library Jobs." *Library Journal* (February 18): 1–4. Accessed June 23, 2010. http://www.libraryjournal.com/article/CA6719366.html?nid=2673&source=link& rid=17609399.

Hamilton, Laura, Richard Halverson, Sarnell S. Jackson, Ellen Mandinach, Jonathan A. Supovitz, and Jeffrey C. Wayman. (2009). "Using Student Achievement Data to Support Instructional Decision Making (NCEE 2009-4067)." Accessed October 5, 2010. http://ies. ed.gov/ncee/wwc/pdf/practice_guides/dddm_pg_092909.pdf.

Harada, Violet, and Jean Donham. (1998). "Information Power: Student Achievement Is the Bottom Line." *Teacher Librarian* 26, no. 1 (September): 14+. Accessed June 22, 2010. http:// eds.b.ebscohost.com/eds/detail/detail?vid=13&sid=f125b28d-14c4-4345-a55b-f985857188 61%40sessionmgr112&hid=113&bdata=JnNpdGU9ZWRzLWxpdmUmc2NvcGU9c2l0Z Q%3d%3d#db=f5h&AN=1284331.

Harada, Violet H. (n.d.). "Librarians as Learning Leaders: Cultivating Cultures of Inquiry." Accessed February 7, 2011. http://www2.hawaii.edu/~vharada/Harada-Learning-Leaders.pdf.

Hargittai, Eszter, Lindsay Fullerton, Ericka Menchen-Trevino, and Kristin Yates. (2010). "Trust Online: Young Adults' Evaluation of Web Content." *International Journal of Communication* 4: 468–492. Accessed April 30, 2011. http://ijoc.org/index.php/ijoc/article/view/636.

Hattwig, Denise, Joanna Burgess, Kaila Bussert, and Ann Medaille. (2011). "ACRL Visual Literacy Competency Standards for Higher Education." http://www.ala.org/acrl/standards/ visualliteracy.

Hay, Lyn, and Colleen Foley. (2009). "School Libraries Building Capacity for Student Learning in the 21C." *Scan* 28, no. 2: 17–25. Accessed June 22, 2010. http://www.curriculumsupport. education.nsw.gov.au/schoollibraries/assets/pdf/Schoollibraries21C.pdf.

Haycock, Kati. (1998). "Good Teaching Matters . . . a Lot." Center for Teaching and Learning: Teaching and the California's Future. Accessed May 15, 2010. http://www.cftl.org/ documents/K16.pdf.

Haycock, Ken. (2007). "What Works: Integrated Information Skills Instruction—Students Learn More and Produce Better Research Products Following Planned, Integrated Information Skills Instruction." *Emergency Librarian* 25, no. 7 (November–December): 29. Accessed June 22, 2010. http://web.b.ebscohost.com/ehost/detail/detail?sid=1cd1aae0-2110-442d- 89f8-f2590bfd1d4d%40sessionmgr114&vid=7&hid=125&bdata=JnNpdGU9ZWhvc3Qtb Gl2ZSSZzY29wZT1zaXRl#db=aph&AN=42116.

Heit, Ronda. (2008). "Using Web 2.0 to Extend the Walls of Your School Library." *Literacies, Learning, and Libraries: Exploring the Web 2.0 World* 1, no. 1: 23–25. Accessed May 14, 2010. http://albertaschoollibraries.pbworks.com/f/LLL-Vol1+No+1-2008.pdf.

Henderson, Carol C. (n.d.). "Libraries as Creatures of Copyright: Why Librarians Care about Intellectual Property Law and Policy." Accessed May 3, 2011. http://www.ala.org/advocacy/copyright/copyrightarticle/librariescreatures.

The Henry Kaiser Family Foundation. (2010). "Generation M: Media in the Lives of 8-to-18-Year Olds." A Kaiser Family Foundation Study: January 2010. Accessed April 21, 2010. http://kff.org/other/poll-finding/report-generation-m2-media-in-the-lives.

Hobbs, Renee. (2010). "Digital and Media Literacy: A Plan of Action: A White Paper on the Digital and Media Literacy: Recommendations of the Knight Commission on the Information Needs of Communities in a Democracy." Accessed June 7, 2011. http://www.knightcomm.org/wp-content/uploads/2010/12/Digital_and_Media_Literacy_A_Plan_of_Action.pdf.

Holum, Ann, and Jan Gahala. (2001). "Critical Issue: Using Technology to Enhance Literacy Instruction." Accessed April 30, 2011. http://www.ncrel.org/sdrs/areas/issues/content/cntareas/reading/li300.htm.

Honigsfeld, Andrea, and Maria Dove. (2013). *Common Core for the Not-so-Common Learner: English Language Arts Strategies.* Thousand Oaks, Calif: Corwin.

Howard, Jody K. (2010). "The Relationship between School Culture and the School Library Program: Four Case Studies." *School Library Research*, 13 (2010): 1–20 Accessed February 3, 2014. http://www.ala.org/aasl/sites/ala.org.aasl/files/content/aaslpubsandjournals/slr/vol13/SLR_RelationshipBetween.pdf.

"How to Find Plagiarism." (2005). *Plagiarism Today.* http://www.plagiarismtoday.com/stopping-internet-plagiarism/1-how-to-find-plagiarism/.

Hsieh, Pei-Hsuan, and Francis Dwyer. (2009). "The Instructional Effect of Online Reading Strategies and Learning Styles on Student Achievement." *Educational Technology and Society* 12, no. 2: 36–50. Accessed April 1, 2011. http://www.ifets.info/journals/12_2/4.pdf.

Hughes-Hassell, Sandra, Amanda Brasfield, and Debbie Dupree. (2012). "Making the Most of Professional Learning Communities." http://www.ala.org/aasl.

IASL: International Association of School Librarianship. (2003). "IASL Policy Statement on School Libraries." http://www.iasl-online.org/about/handbook/policysl.html.

IASL: International Association of School Librarianship. (2003). "International Association of School Librarianship." http://www.iasl-online.org/about/handbook/policysl.html.

Iddo, Gal. (2003). "Teaching for Statistical Literacy and Services of Statistics Agencies." *The American Statistician*, 57, no. 2: 80+. Accessed May 28, 2010. http://www.ifets.info/journals/12_2/4.pdf.

IDPF: International Digital Publishing Forum. (2014). "US Trade Wholesale Electronic Book Sales." Accessed October 9, 2014. http://idpf.org/about-us/industry-statistics.

Indiana University School of Medicine. (2007). "How Do You Define "Assessment?" Accessed April 28, 2011. http://medsci.indiana.edu/m620/reserves/def_assess.pdf.

iParadigms, LLC. (2014). "iThenticate: Prevent Plagiarism in Published Works." http://www.ithenticate.com/.

iParadigms, LLC. (2011). "Peermark: Streamline Peer Reviews." Turnitin.com. http://www.turnitin.com/en_us/features/peermark.

iParadigms, LLC. (2014). "Plagiarism.org : Learning Center : Plagiarism Definitions, Tips on Avoiding Plagiarism, Guidelines for Proper Citation, & Help Indentifying Plagiarism." Commercial. *plagiarismdotORG.* http://www.plagiarism.org/plag_article_what_is_plagiarism.html.

iParadigms. (2014). "Turnitin Originality Check: Reduce Plagiarism." Turnitin.com. http://www.turnitin.com/en_us/features/originalitycheck.

iParadigms, LLC. (2014). "WriteCheck for Students." Turnitin.com. http://turnitin.com/static/products/writecheck.php.

ISD, Malcolm, Inghram ISD, and Shiawassee READ. (2013). "Professional Learning Networks." http://www.21things4teachers.net/17---professional-learning-networks.html.

Ishan. (2011). "5 Freeware to Sync Bookmarks between Browsers." http://www.ilovefreesoftware.com/06/featured/5-freeware-to-sync-bookmarks-between-browsers.html.

ISTE: International Society for Technology in Education. (2009). "ISTE's U.S. Public Policy Principles and Federal and State Objectives." Accessed May 1, 2011. http://www.iste.org/docs/pdfs/109-09-us-public-policy-principles.

ISTE Wikispaces. (2014). "Creativity and Innovation." Accessed October 9, 2014. http://nets-implementation.iste.wikispaces.net/Creativity+and+Innovation.

ISTE Wikispaces. (2014). "Digital Citizenship." Accessed October 9, 2014. http://nets-implementation.iste.wikispaces.net/Digital+Citizenship.

Jang, Syh-Jong. (2009). "Exploration of Secondary Students' Creativity by Integrating Web-based Technology into an Innovative Science Curriculum." *Computers and Education* 52, no. 1: 247–255.

Jenkins, Henry, Katie Clinton, Ravi Purushotma, Alice J. Robison J. Robison, and Margaret Weigel. (2006). "Confronting the Challenges of Participatory Culture: Media Education for the 21st Century." http://digitallearning.macfound.org/atf/cf/%7BE45C7E0-A3E0-4B89-AC9C-E807E1B0AE4E%7D/JENKINS_WHITE_PAPER.PDF

John D. and Catherine T. MacArthur Foundation. (2008). "New Study Shows Time Spent Online Important for Teen Development." Accessed October 15, 2010. http://www.macfound.org/press/publications/study-shows-time-spent-online-important-for-teen-development.

Jukes, Ian, Ted McCain, and Lee Crockett. (2010). *Understanding the Digital Generation: Teaching and Learning in the New Digital Landscape*. Thousand Oaks, CA: Corwin.

Kelly, Frank S., Ted McCain, and Ian Jukes. (2009). *Teaching the Digital Generation: No More Cookie-Cutter High Schools*. Thousand Oaks, CA: Corwin.

Kelly, M. G. (Peggy), and Jon Haber. (2005). "Excerpted from National Educational Technology Standards for Students Resources for Student Assessment." Accessed June 11, 2011. http://www.iste.org/docs/excerpts/NETTAS-excerpt.pdf.

Ken Haycock and Associates. (2007). "Building Student Learning through School Libraries." *Teacher Librarian* 30, no. 1: 87–90.

Klopfer, Eric, Scot Osterweil, Jennifer Groff, and Jason Haas. (2009). "Using Technology in the Classroom Today: The Instructional Power of Digital Games, Social Networks and Simulations and How Teachers Can Leverage Them." Edited by The Education Arcade, Massachusetts Institute of Technology. Accessed June 11, 2011. http://education.mit.edu/papers/GamesSimsSocNets_EdArcade.pdf.

Knight Commission on the Information Needs of Communities in a Democracy. (2009). "Recommendation 6." Accessed April 28, 2011. http://www.knightcomm.org/recommendation6.

Koechlin, Carol, Esther Rosenfeld, and David V. Loertscher. (2010). *Building the Learning Commons: A Guide for School Administrators and Learning Leadership Teams*. Salt Lake City, UT: Hi Willow Research and Publishing.

Koechlin, Carol, and Sandi Zwaan. (2007). "Assignments Worth the Effort: Questions Are Key." *Teacher-Librarian* 34, no. 3 (February): 14–20. Accessed February 8, 2011. http://eds.b.ebscohost.com/eds/detail/detail?vid=4&sid=ca7d442a-df83-40de-b31c-b0937a94f33f%40sessionmgr114&hid=120&bdata=JnNpdGU9ZWRzLWxpdmUmc2NvcGU9c2l0ZQ%3d%3d#db=f5h&AN=23812161.

Koechlin, Carol, and Sandi Zwann. (2008). "Everyone Wins: Differentiation in the School Library." *Teacher Librarian* 35, no. 5 (June): 8–13. Accessed May 28, 2010. http://eds.b.ebscohost.com/eds/detail/detail?vid=8&sid=9afaa756-243e-46ed-aa3d-b86c6351ea8 7%40sessionmgr113&hid=126&bdata=JnNpdGU9ZWRzLWxpdmUmc2NvcGU9c2l0ZQ %3d%3d#db=f5h&AN=32753559.

Krueger, Keith R. (2011). "Recruiting and Supporting 21st-Century Education Technology Leaders." Accessed February 7, 2011. http://www.aasa.org/.aspx?id=11418.

Kuhlthau, Carol C. (1993). "Implementing a Process Approach to Information Skills: A Study Identifying Indicators of Success in Library Media Programs." *SLMQ* 22, no. 1 (Fall): 1–9. Accessed December 17, 2009. http://www.ala.org/aasl/sites/ala.org.aasl/files/content/ aaslpubsandjournals/slr/edchoice/SLMQ_ImplementingaProcessApproachtoInformation Skills_InfoPower.pdf.

Kuhlthau, Carol C., Jannica Heinstrom, and Ross J Todd. (2008). "The 'Information Search Process' Revisited: Is the Model Still Useful?" *iRinformationsearch* 13, no. 4 (December): 1–14. Accessed June 22, 2010. http://www.informationr.net/ir/13-4/paper355.html.

Kuhlthau, Carol C., Leslie K. Maniotes, and Ann K. Caspari. (2008). "Guided Inquiry: Learning in the 21st Century." Rutgers Center for International Scholarship in School Libraries. Accessed May 1, 2011. http://cissl.rutgers.edu/_inquiry/.html

Lamb, Annette. (2005). "Information Inquiry for Teachers." Accessed April 30, 2011. http://eduscapes.com/info/inquiry.html.

Lance, Keith Curry. (2002). "Impact of School Library Media Programs on Academic Achievement. (Proof of the Power)." *Teacher Librarian* 29, no. 3 (February): 29–35. Accessed May 29, 2010. http://web.b.ebscohost.com/ehost/detail/detail?vid=3&sid=03efbe11-268a-46f6-9298-0d77304c92e1%40sessionmgr114&hid=110&bdata=JnNpdGU9ZWhvc3QtbG l2ZSZzY29wZT1zaXRl#db=aph&AN=6190538.

Lance, Keith Curry. (2001). "Proof of the Power: Recent Research on the Impact of School Library Media Programs on the Academic Achievement of U.S. Public School Students." Accessed May 4, 2010. http://files.eric.ed.gov/fulltext/ED456861.pdf.

Lance, Keith Curry, Marcia J. Rodney, and Christine Hamilton-Pennell. (2005). "Powerful Libraries Make Powerful Learners: The Illinois Study." Illinois School Library Media Association. http://www.islma.org/pdf/ILStudy2.pdf.

Langer, Judith. (2000). "Literary Understandng and Literature Instruction: Reseach Report Series 2.11." University at Albany–SUNY. http://www.albany.edu/cela/reports/langer/ langerliteraryund.pdf.

Langer, Judith A. (1994). "A Response-Based Approach to Reading Literature." University at Albany–SUNY. http://www.albany.edu/cela/reports/langer/langerresponsebased.pdf.

Latrobe, Kathy. (2001). "A Case Study of One District's Implementation of Information Power." *School Library Media Research* 4: [0]1–23. Accessed May 27, 2010. http://www.ala. org/aasl/sites/ala.org.aasl/files/content/aaslpubsandjournals/slr/vol4/SLMR_ACaseStudy_ V4.pdf.

Learning Point Associates. (2004). "Critical Issue: Technology Leadership Enhancing Positive Educational Change." Accessed February 7, 2011. http://www.ncrel.org/sdrs/areas/issues/ educatrs/leadrshp/le700.htm.

Leclerc, M., A. C. Moreau, C. Dumouchel, and F. Sallafranque-St-Louis. (2012). "ERIC— Factors That Promote Progression in Schools Functioning as Professional Learning Community." *International Journal of Education Policy and Leadership*, 7, no. 7. http://eric. ed.gov/?id=EJ990980.

Lemov, Doug. (2010). *Teach Like a Champion: 49 Techniques That Put Students on the Path to College.* San Francisco: Jossey-Bass.

Lenhart, Amanda et al. (2010). "Teens, Cell Phones and Texting: Text Messaging Becomes Centerpiece Communication." Accessed April 10, 2011. http://www.pewinternet.org/2010/04/20/teens-and-mobile-phones.

Lerman, James, and Ronique Hicks. (2010). *Retool Your School: The Educator's Essential Guide to Google's Free Power Apps.* International Society for Technology in Education.

Leu, Donald J., Julie Coiro, Castek, Douglas K. Hartman, Laurie A. Henry, and David Reinking. (n.d.). "Research on Instruction and Assessment in the New Literacies of Online Reading Comprehension." Accessed September 6, 2010. http://newliteracies.uconn.edu/wp-content/uploads/sites/448/2014/07/Leu_et_al_Final_Chaptersinglespaced.pdf.

Leu, Donald J., W. Ian O'Byrne, Lisa Zawilinski, J. Greg McVerry, and Heidi Everett-Cacopardo. (2009). "Expanding the New Literacies Conversation." *Educational Researcher* 38, no. 4: 264–269. Accessed July 28, 2010. http://literacyachievementgap.pbworks.com/f/264.pdf.

Lewin, Larry. (2010). "Teaching Critical Reading with Questioning Strategies." *EL: Educational Leadership* 67, no. 6 (March). http://www.ascd.org/publications/educational-leadership/mar10/vol67/num06/Teaching-Critical-Reading-with-Questioning-Strategies.aspx.

"Library of Congress List of Collections." 2014. http://memory.loc.gov/ammem/dli2/html/list.html.

Loertscher, D., and C. Koechlin. (2012). "The Virtual Learning Commons and School Improvement." *Teacher Librarian* 39, no. 6: 20–24. http://lgdata.s3-website-us-east-1.amazonaws.com/docs/561/618934/The_Virtual_Learning_Commons_and_School_Improvement.pdf

Loertscher, David. (2006). "What Flavor Is Your School Library? The Teacher–Librarian as Learning Leader." *Teacher Librarian* 34, no. 2 (December): 8–13. Accessed May 28, 2010. http://tlplc.pbworks.com/f/What%20Flavor%20is%20your%20School%20Library.pdf.

Loertscher, David, Carol Koechlin, and Esther Rosenfeld. (2012). *The Virtual Learning Commons.* Salt Lake City, UT: Learning Commons Press.

Lou, Shi-Jer, Nai-Ci Chen, Huei-Yin Tsai, Kuo-Hung Tseng, and Ru-Chu Shih. (2012). "Using Blended Creative Teaching: Improving a Teacher Education Course on Designing Materials for YoungChildren." *Australasian Journal of Educational Technology* 28, no. 5: 776–792. http://www.ascilite.org.au/ajet/ajet28/lou.pdf.

Lowe, Carrie. (2001). "The Role of the School Library Media Specialists in the 21st Century." *Teacher Librarian* 29, no. 1: 30+. Accessed May 28, 2010. http://www.ericdigests.org/2001-3/21st.htm.

Madden, Mary, Amanda Lenhart, Maeve Duggan, and Urs Gasser. (2013). "Teens and Technology 2013." http://www.pewinternet.org/2013/03/13/teens-and-technology-2013.

Magiera, Jennie. (2011). "Teaching Like It's 2999: Schoology vs. Edmodo, Round 2—Also, why Schoology Solved My iPad Workflow woes." http://www.teachinglikeits2999.com/2013/02/schoology-vs-edmodo-round-2.html.

Marzano, Robert. (2006). *Classroom Assessment and Grading That Work.* Alexandria, VA: ASCD.

Marzano, Robert J., Debra J. Pickering, and Jane E. Pollock. (2001). *Classroom Instruction That Works: Research-based Strategies for Increasing Student Achievement.* Aurora, CO: McREL: Mid-continent Research for Education and Learning.

Marzano, Robert J., Timothy Waters, and Brian A. McNulty. (2005). *School Leadership That Works: From Research to Results.* Aurora, CO: McREL: Mid-continent Research for Education and Learning.

Mattei, Mario. (2011). "10 How To's for Visual Peacemaking." http://visualpeacemakers.org/blog/archive.

Metropolitan Life Insurance Company. (2013). "The MetLife Survey of American Teachers: Challenges for School Leadership." https://www.metlife.com/assets/cao/foundation/MetLife-Teacher-Survey-2012.pdf.

Michigan State University. (2004). "Best Practice Briefs: School Climate and Learning." http://outreach.msu.edu/bpbriefs/issues/brief31.pdf.

Moje, Elizabeth Birr, and Nicole Tysvaer. (2010). "Adolescent Literacy Development in Out-of-School Time: A Practitioner's Guide." Accessed April 30, 2011. http://carnegie.org/fileadmin/Media/Publications/PDF/tta_Moje.pdf.

Montiel-Overall, Patricia. (2005). "Toward a Theory of Collaboration for Teachers and Librarians."www.ala.org/aasl/aaslpubsandjournals/slmrb/slmrcontents/volume82005/theory.

Moreillon, Judi. (2013). "A Matrix for School Librarians: Aligning Standards, Inquiry, Reading, and Instruction." *School Library Monthly* 29, no. 4: 29–32. Accessed September 10, 2013. http://www.schoollibrarymonthly.com/articles/pdf/Moreillon2013-v29n4p29.pdf.

Moreillon, Judi, Michelle Luhtala, and Christina T. Russo. (2011). "Learning That Sticks: Engaged Educators + Engaged Learners." *School Library Monthly* 28, no. 1: 17–20.

Morse, Geoff. Interviewed by Cathy Swan, Skype. Northwestern University Library's Google Scholar's Live Links, May 17, 2011.

Mozilla. (2014). "How to Use Bookmarks to Save and Organize Your Favorite Websites." Accessed March 21, 2014. http://support.mozilla.com/en-US/kb/how-do-i-use-bookmarks.

Munoz, Caroline Lego, and Terri L. Towner. (2009). "Opening Facebook: How to Use Facebook in the College Classroom." Accessed November 22, 2010. http://carnegie.org/fileadmin/Media/Publications/PDF/tta_Moje.pdf.

Murray, Janet. (n.d.). "Applying Big6™ Skills, AASL Standards and ISTE NETS to Internet Research." Accessed May 27, 2010. http://www.janetsinfo.com/info.htm.

"National Archives." 2014. http://www.archives.gov/.

"National Archives Experience: Digital Vaults." 2014. http://digitalvaults.org/.

National Comprehensive Center for Teacher Quality. (n.d.). "Enhancing Leadership Quality TQ Source Tips and Tools: Emerging Strategies to Enhance Educator Quality." Accessed October 5, 2010. http://www.tqsource.org.

National Comprehensive Center for Teacher Quality. (n.d.). "Teacher Leadership as a Key to Education Innovation, August 2010." Accessed October 5, 2010. http://www.tqsource.org.

NCPS: New Canaan Public Schools. (2009). "Curriculum and Instruction." Accessed May 8, 2011. http://www2.newcanaan.k12.ct.us/education/school/school.php?sectiondetailid=34456.

NCPS: New Canaan Public Schools. (2009). "Responsive Teaching in the Differentiated Classroom." Accessed May 9, 2011. http://www2.newcanaan.k12.ct.us/education/components/docmgr/default.php?sectiondetailid=35683&fileitem=16466&catfilter=ALL.

NCPS: New Canaan Public Schools. (2009). "Sample Unit Organizer." Accessed May 9, 2011. http://www2.newcanaan.k12.ct.us/education/components/docmgr/default.php?sectiondetailid=35683&fileitem=16467&catfilter=ALL.

NCPS: New Canaan Public Schools. (2010). "Philosophy of Assessment." Accessed May 8, 2011. http://www2.newcanaan.k12.ct.us/education/components/scrapbook/default.php?sectionid=1201.

NCPS: New Canaan Public Schools. (2012). "Core Values, Beliefs and Expectations nchsneasc13." https://sites.google.com/a/ncps-k12.org/nchsneasc13/home/first-draft-of-core-expectations.

NCPS: New Canaan Public Schools. (n.d.). "Information Communication and Technologies: Enduring Understandings." Accessed May 7, 2011. http://www2.newcanaan.k12.ct.us/education/components/scrapbook/default.php?sectionid=1201.

NCPS: New Canaan Public Schools. (n.d.). "K–12 21st Century Learning Standards." Accessed May 8, 2011. http://www.newcanaan.k12.ct.us/education/components/layout/default.php?section id=20&linkid=nav-menu-container-1-129617&url_redirect=1.

NCPS: New Canaan Public Schools. (2013). "Library Mission & Philosophy." New Canaan High School Library. http://www.newcanaan.k12.ct.us/education/components/scrapbook/default.php?sectiond etailid=32925&.

NCTE: National Council of Teachers of English. (2008). "The NCTE Definition of 21st Century Literacies." Accessed April 28, 2011. http://www.ncte.org/positions/statements/21stcentdefinition.

NEA. (2012). "Preparing 21st Century Students for a Global Society: An Educator's Guide to the 'Four Cs.'" Accessed February 25, 2014. http://www.nea.org/assets/docs/A-Guide-to-Four-Cs.pdf.

The Nielsen Company. (2010). "14% Multi-tasked and Got Social on the Web during Super Bowl." Accessed April 10, 2011. http://www.nielsen.com/us/en/insights/news/2010/14-multi-tasked-and-got-social-on-the-web-during-super-bowl.html.

The Nielsen Company. (2009). "Women, Teens and Seniors Help Fuel 34% Mobile Web Spike." Accessed November 19, 2010. http://www.nielsen.com/us/en/insights/news/2009/mobile-web-up-34-percent-july-09.html.

Nolo Law for All, Stanford University Libraries, Justia, LawLibrary.com, and Onecle. (2010). "Measuring Fair Use: The Four Factors." Accessed May 30, 2011. http://fairuse.stanford.edu/overview/fair-use/four-factors.

North Central Regional Educational Laboratory. (1995). "Providing Hands-On, Minds-On, and Authentic Learning Experiences in Mathematics." http://www.ncrel.org/sdrs/areas/issues/content/cntareas/math/ma300.htm.

North Central Regional Educational Laboratory. (2000). "School Leadership in the 21st Century: Why and How It Is Important." Accessed June 24, 2011. http://files.eric.ed.gov/fulltext/ED470426.pdf.

November, Alan. (2014). "Web Literacy—Publisher of a Website." http://novemberlearning.com/educational-resources-for-educators/information-literacy-resources/5-find-the-publisher-of-a-web-site/.

NPR: National Public Radio. (2012). "Iraq Veteran Uses Rap to Treat His PTSD: NPR." http://www.npr.org/templates/story/story.php?storyId=152726726.

NYSED: New York State Education Department. (2013). "School Climate and Culture." http://www.p12.nysed.gov/dignityact/rgsection1.html.

NYSED: New York State Education Department. (2010). "CI&IT Curriculum, Instruction and Instructional Technology SLMPE Rubric." Accessed May 27, 2010. http://www.p12.nysed.gov/technology/library/SLMPE_rubric/AboutSLMPErubric.html.

NYU Libraries. (2014). "Applying Fair Use – Copyright – Research Guides at New York University." Home – Research Guides at New York University. http://guides.nyu.edu/content.php?pid=133679&sid=1146824.

Oakland Museum of California. (2014). "About the 'Picture This' Project" Accessed March 21, 2014. http://www.museumca.org/picturethis/about-picture-project.

Oakleaf, Megan, and Patricia L. Owen. (2010). "Closing the 12–13 Gap Together: School and College Libraries Supporting 21st Century Learners." *Teacher Librarian* 37, no. 4 (April): 52–59. Accessed May 28, 2010. http://meganoakleaf.info/oakleafowensyllabi.pdf.

O'Brennan , Lindsey, and Catherine Bradshaw. (2013). "Importance of School Climate." https://www.nea.org/assets/docs/15889_Bully_Free_Research_Brief-print.pdf

OCLC: Online Computer Library Center. (2010). "How Libraries Stack Up: 2010." Accessed December 7, 2010. http://www.oclc.org/content/dam/oclc/reports/pdfs/214109usf_how_libraries_stack_up.pdf.

O*NET. (n.d.). "O*NET Resource Center." Accessed March 10, 2014. http://www.onetcenter.org.

O'Reilly, Dennis. (2010). "Tools for Rooting Out Web Plagiarism, Copyright Violations." http://howto.cnet.com/8301-11310_39-20021945-285/tools-for-rooting-out-web-plagiarism-copyright-violations/

Pagani, Margherita. (2005). *Encyclopedia of Multimedia Technology and Networking*, Vol. 1. Hershey, PA: Ideas Group.

Parker, David. (2013). "The University in Transition: The 'Flipped' Library." http://edtechtimes.com/2013/08/26/the-university-in-transition-the-flipped-library.

Parker-Pope, Tara. (2009). "Weighing School Backpacks." http://well.blogs.nytimes.com/2009/07/21/weighing-school-backpacks.

Parness, Adam. (2007). "Welcome to Copyright Kids!" *Copyright Kids*. http://www.copyrightkids.org/.

Partnership for 21st Century Skills. (n.d.). "Framework for 21st Century Learning." Accessed May 14, 2010. http://www.21stcenturyskills.org.

Partnership for 21st Century Skills. (2009). "Learning Environments: A 21st Century Skills Implementation Guide." Accessed February 7, 2014. http://www.p21.org/storage/documents/p21-stateimp_learning_environments.pdf.

Partnership for 21st Century Skills. (n.d.). "Assessment of 21st Century Skills: The Current Landscape Pre-Publication Draft June 2005." Accessed October 6, 2006. http://www.21stcenturyskills.org.

Partnership for 21st Century Skills. (n.d.). "21st Century Learning Environments." Accessed May 2, 2011. http://www.p21.org/about-us/p21-framework/354-21st-century-learning-environments.

Partnership for 21st Century Skills. (n.d.). "Our Mission." Accessed May 1, 2011. http://www.p21.org/about-us/our-mission.

PBS and Grunwald Associates, LLC. (2009). "Digitally Inclined: Teachers Increasingly Value Media and Technology." Accessed May 1, 2011. http://www-tc.pbs.org/teachers/_files/pdf/annual-pbs-survey-report.pdf.

Pennsylvania Attorney General. (n.d.). "Cybersafety: Protecting Your Kids and Teens Online." Accessed May 3, 2011. http://www.pdsd.org/cms/lib6/PA01000989/Centricity/Domain/290/cybersafety.pdf.

Perez, Sarah. (2010). "So-Called 'Digital Natives' Not Media Savvy, New Study Shows." Accessed February 10, 2011. http://www.nytimes.com/external/readwriteweb/2010/07/29/29readwriteweb-so-called-digital-natives-not-media-savvy-n-74704.html?adxnnl=1&adxnnlx=1413025214-YGk4g218mJs5cQyFNT3Gpg.

Peters, Marybeth. (2000). "Statement of Marybeth Peters the Register of Copyrights before the Subcommittee on Courts and Intellectual Property Committee on the Judiciary." Accessed May 30, 2011. http://www.copyright.gov/docs/regstat61500.html.

Peterson, Kent. (1995). "Critical Issue: Building a Collective Vision." http://www.ncrel.org/sdrs/areas/issues/educatrs/leadrshp/le100.htm.

Petronzio, Matt. (2012). "Use These 10 Sites to Detect Plagiarism." Mashable. http://mashable.com/2012/08/29/plagiarism-online-services/.

"Picture This: California Perspectives on American History." (2014). *Picture This*. Accessed March 30. http://www.museumca.org/picturethis/about-picture-project

Pillai, Priya. (2009). "Creating an Online Community of Teachers and Librarians for Professional Development through Social Networking Tools." *ICAL 2009—Change Management:* 365–371. Accessed October 5, 2010. http://crl.du.ac.in/ical09/papers/index_files/ical-62_74_179_2_RV.pdf.

Plagiarism.org Facts and Stats (2014). http://www.plagiarism.org/resources/facts-and-stats.

Plagiarism.org: What is Plagiarism? (2014). http://www.plagiarism.org.

Plagiarism 101 (2014) http://www.plagiarism.org/plagiarism-101/overview.

"Plagiarism Solutions." (2011) http://www.plagiarism.org/plag_solutions.html.

"Plagiarism Definitions, Tips on Avoiding Plagiarism, Guidelines for Proper Citation, & Help Identifying Plagiarism." (2011). *plagiarismdotORG*. http://web.archive.org/web/20110714015905/http://www.plagiarism.org/plag_solutions.html.

Powell, Ronald R. (2006). "Evaluation Research: An Overview." *Library Trends* 55, no. 1 (Summer): 102–120. Accessed June 22, 2010. https://www.ideals.illinois.edu/bitstream/handle/2142/3666/Powell551.pdf.

Prensky, Marc. (2009). "H. Sapiens Digital: From Digital Immigrants and Digital Natives to Digital Wisdom." Accessed February 10, 2011. http://www.wisdompage.com/Prensky01.html.

Professional Development. "What Are the Characteristics of Good Professional Development Programs That Support 21st Century Skills?" (2007). *Route 21:Partnership for 21st Century Skills*. http://route21.p21.org/?option=com_content&view=category&layout=blog&id=3&Itemid=160&limitstart=4

Project Tomorrow. (2010). "Creating Our Future: Students Speak Up about Their Vision for 21st Century Learning." Accessed May 3, 2011. http://www.tomorrow.org/speakup/pdfs/SU09NationalFindingsStudents&Parents.pdf.

Project Tomorrow. (2010). "Unleashing the Future: Educators "Speak Up" about the Use of Emerging Technologies for Learning." Accessed May 3, 2011. http://www.tomorrow.org/speakup/pdfs/SU09UnleashingTheFuture.pdf.

"Public Domain Images." 2011. http://www.pdimages.com.

Puckett, Jason. (2011). *Zotero: A Guide for Librarians, Researchers and Educators*. Chicago: Association of College and Research Libraries.

Puckett, Jason. (2014). "Zotero: About Zotero." *Georgia State University: University Library*.http://research.library.gsu.edu/zotero.

Purcell, Kristen, Lee Rainie, Tom Rosentiel, and Amy Mitchell. (2011). "How Mobile Devices Are Changing Community Information Environments." Accessed April 29, 2011. http://www.pewinternet.org/2011/03/14/how-mobile-devices-are-changing-community-information-environments.

Purdue University Copyright Center. (2009). "Copyright Infringement Penalties." Purdue University. https://www.lib.purdue.edu/uco/CopyrightBasics/penalties.html.

Ray, Betty. (2010). "How to Use Twitter to Grow Your PLN." http://www.edutopia.org/blog/twitter-expanding-pln.

Refsnes Data. (2014). "Browser Statistics." http://www.w3schools.com/browsers/browsers_stats.asp.

Reid, Sheldon. (2010). "What Is the Legal Penalty for Plagiarism? | eHow.com". Blog. *eHow*. http://www.ehow.com/facts_6809837_legal-penalty-plagiarism_.html.

Riedel, Chris. (2012). "Digital Learning: What Kids Really Want" Accessed March 26, 2012. *THEJournal*.http://thejournal.com/articles/2012/02/01/digital-learning-what-kids-really-want.aspx.

Ribble, Mike, and Gerald Bailey. (2007). "Excerpted from Nine Elements of Digital Citizenship." Accessed May 1, 2007. http://www.iste.org/images/excerpts/digcit-excerpt.pdf.

Richtel, Matt. (2010). "Hooked on Gadgets, and Paying a Mental Price." Accessed June 9, 2010. http://www.nytimes.com/2010/06/07/technology/07brain.html?pagewanted=all&_r=0

RMIT University. (n.d.). "GP8: Communicate high expectations." Accessed February 3, 2014. http://www.rmit.edu.au/dsc/learningteaching/guidingprinciples/gp8.

Roberts, Donald F., Ulla G. Foehr, and Victoria Rideout. (2010). "Generation M: Media in the Lives of 8–18-year-olds—Report." http://kff.org/other/generation-m-media-in-the-lives-of/.

Robinson, Ken. "Ken Robinson: How Schools Kill Creativity | Talk Video | TED.com." *TED: Ideas worth spreading.* (2006). http://www.ted.com/talks/ken_robinson_says_schools_kill_creativity?About%20these%20ads.

Russo, Christina T., Michelle Luhtala, and Donna Sapienza. (2012). "Healthy Collaboration Is Good for All: Coteaching Team at New Canaan High School Helps Students Track Personal Wellness." *Knowledge Quest* 40, no. 4: 58–61.

Salkind, Neil J., ed. (2008). *Encyclopedia of Educational Psychology.* Los Angeles: Sage Publications.

Scheffers, Jenny, Michelle Bruce, and Bev Nix. (2006). "Teachers and Teacher–Librarians Supporting Higher-order Thinking Skills." *Scan* 25, no. 1 (February): 28–34. Accessed May 14, 2010. http://www.curriculumsupport.education.nsw.gov.au/schoollibraries/assets/pdf/sheffer scpptresearch.pdf.

Scholastic Inc. (2010). "New Study on Reading in the Digital Age: Parents Say Electronic, Digital Devices Negatively Affects Kids' Reading Time." Accessed May 3, 2011. http://mediaroom.scholastic.com/node/378.

Scholastic Inc. (2014). "BYOD to School?" Accessed April 21, 2014. http://www.scholastic.com/browse/article.jsp?id=3756757.

School of Communication American University. (n.d.)."Code of Best Practices in Fair Use of Media Literacy Education." Accessed May 21, 2010. http://www.centerforsocial media.org.

Shannon, Donna. (2002). "The Education and Competencies of School Library Media Specialists: A Review of the Literature." *School Library Media Research* 5: 1–19. Accessed May 14, 2010. http://www.ala.org/aasl/sites/ala.org.aasl/files/content/aaslpubsandjournals/slr/vol5/SLMR_EducationCompetencies_V5.pdf.

Simpson, Carol. (n.d.). "The School Librarian's Role in the Electronic Age." Accessed April 28, 2010. http://www.ericdigests.org/1997-3/librarian.html.

Skeldon, Paul. (2011). "Even Better Than the Real Thing: Commercial Opportunities for Companies Embracing Augmented Reality Are Vast, but Not Immediately Obvious." Accessed April 30, 2011. http://online.wsj.com/news/articles/SB10001424052748704739504576067780550250202?mod=_newsreel_4.

Slattery-Moschkau, Kathleen. (2011). "When 'Practical' Kills Us: Sir Ken Robinson at His Finest." http://www.huffingtonpost.com/kathleen-slatterymoschkau/work-motivation-when-prac_b_596599.html.

Smalley, Topsey N. (2004). "College Success: High School Librarians Make a Difference." *The Journal of Academic Librarianship* 30, no. 3 (April 17): 193–198. Accessed June 23, 2010. https://weloveschoollibraries.pbworks.com/f/Topsey+Smalley1.pdf.

SmartBrief, SmartBlogs. (2013). "How does #edchat connect educators?" http://smartblogs.com/education/2012/08/06/how-edchat-connect-educators-2.

Smarty, Ann. (2008). "Top Online Plagiarism Checkers—Protect Your Content." *Search Engine Journal.* http://www.searchenginejournal.com/top-online-plagiarism-checkers-protect-your-content/7931/.

Smith, Laurie, and Julie Evans. (2010). "Speak Up: Students Embrace Digital Resources for Learning." *Knowledge Quest* 39, no. 2 (November–December): 20–26.

Snyder, Lisa Gueldenzoph, and Mark J. Snyder. (2008). "Teaching Critical Thinking and Problem Solving." Accessed April 30, 2011. http://reforma.fen.uchile.cl/Papers/Teaching%20 Critical%20Thinking%20Skills%20and%20problem%20solving%20skills%20-%20 Gueldenzoph,%20Snyder.pdf.

"Social Bookmarking—Google Docs." (2011). Accessed July 10. https://docs.google.com/ document/d/1MGo88pPv-8IU1VI1Ru47hbUbjcT30taiSJiL5QgS6gU/edit?hl=en_US.

Spires, H. A., E. Wiebe, C. A. Young, K. Hollebrands, and J. K. Lee. (2012). "Current Practice: Toward a New Learning Ecology—Professional Development for Teachers in 1:1 Learning Environments." http://www.citejournal.org/vol12/iss2/currentpractice/article1.cfm.

Stronge, James H., Holly B. Richard, and Nancy Catano. (2008). "Instructional Leadership: Supporting Best Practice." Accessed February 3, 2014. http://www.ascd.org/publications/ books/108003/chapters/Instructional-Leadership@-Supporting-Best-Practice.aspx.

Swan, Cathy. (2012). "Selecting an Online CoursePlatform." *edWeb.net*. http://home.edweb. net/selecting-an-online-course-platform-2/.

Swan, Cathy. (2014). "Tech Tools for Assessing the 'Soft' Skills". Tech and Learning (February 26). http://www.techleaning.com/features/0039/tech-tools-for-assessing-the-"soft"-skills/54730.

Swift, Matthew. (2010). "Using ICT to Enhance Instructional Leadership." *Education Update* 52, no. 12 (December). Accessed May 5, 2011. http://www.ascd.org/publications/newsletters/ education-update/dec10/vol52/num12/Using-ICT-to-Enhance-Instructional-Leadership.aspx.

Tapscott, Don. (2009). *Grown Up Digital: How the Net generation Is Changing Your World.* New York: McGraw-Hill.

Teaching Channel. (n.d.). "Text Complexity: Simplifying Text Complexity and the Common Core." Teaching Channel. Accessed October 6, 2014. https://www.teachingchannel.org/ videos/simplifying-text-complexity.

"Teaching Copyright." (2014). *Teaching Copyright.org.* http://www.teachingcopyright.org/ curriculum/hs.

ThinkInspirationM. (2011). "Why I Need My High School Library." *YouTube.* (2011). http:// www.youtube.com/watch?v=HMb9d2rGydE.

Thurmond, Veronica, and Karen Wambach. (2004)."Understand Interaction." Accessed April 22, 2014. http://www.itdl.org/journal/Jan_04/article02.htm.

Todd, Ross. (2008). "The Evidence-based Manifesto for School Libraries." *School Library Journal* (April). Accessed April 1, 2010. http://www.slj.com/2008/04/librarians/ the-evidence-based-manifesto-for-school-librarian.

Todd, Ross. (2001). "Evidence Based Practices II: Getting into the Action." *Scan* 20, no. 1 (February): 1–8. Accessed June 22, 2010. http://www.curriculumsupport.education.nsw.gov. au/schoollibraries/assets/pdf/researchcolumns21-2.pdf.

Todd, Ross J. (2002). "School Librarian as Teachers: Learning Outcomes and Evidence-Based Practices." ERIC (ED 472 883). Accessed June 14, 2011. http://files.eric.ed.gov/fulltext/ ED472883.pdf.

Todd, Ross J. (2009). "School Libraries and Continuous Improvement." *Scan* 28, no. 2 (May): 16–25. Accessed May 14, 2010. http://www.curriculumsupport.education.nsw.gov.au/ schoollibraries/assets/pdf/Researchcolumn28-2.pdf.

Todd, Ross J. (2009). "School Libraries and Continuous Improvement: A Case Study." *Scan* 28, no. 2 (May): 26–31. Accessed May 14, 2010. http://www.curriculumsupport.education.nsw. gov.au/schoollibraries/assets/pdf/ToddContImp26-31Vol28-2.pdf.

Todd, Ross J., and Carol C. Kuhlthau. (2004). "Student Learning through Ohio School Libraries." Accessed May 14, 2010. http://webfiles.rbe.sk.ca/rps/terrance.pon/OELMAReport of Findings.pdf.

Todd, R, and C. Kuhlthau. (2005). "Student Learning through Ohio School Libraries, Part 1: How Effective School Libraries Help Students." *School Libraries Worldwide* 11, no. 1: 63–88.

Toffler Associates. (n.d.). "40 For the Next 40: A Sampling of the Drivers of Change That Will Shape Our World between Now and 2050." Accessed December 7, 2010. http://sandbox.purot.net/alfin-toffler-40-for-the-next-40--2010-12.pdf.

Tomlinson, Carol Ann. (1999). *The Differentiated Classroom: Responding to the Needs of All Learners.* Alexandria, VA: ASCD.

Tomlinson, Carol Ann. (2003). *Fulfilling the Promise of the Differentiated Classroom: Strategies and Tools for Responsive Teaching.* Alexandria, VA: ASCD.

Tomlinson, Carol Ann, Carolyn M. Callahan, Ellen M. Tomchin, Nancy Eiss, Marcia Imbeau, and Mary Landrum. (1997). "Becoming Architects of Communities of Learning: Addressing Academic Diversity in Contemporary Classrooms." *Exceptional Children* 63, no. 2 (Winter): 269–283.

Tomlinson, Carol Ann, and Jay McTighe. (2006). *Integrating Differentiated Instruction and Understanding by Design: Connecting Content and Kids.* Alexandria, VA: ASCD.

Trilling, Bernie, and Charles Fadel. (2009). *21st Century Skills: Learning for Life in Our Times.* San Francisco: Jossey-Bass.

Torrance, E. Paul. (1964). *Guiding Creative Talent,* 4th ed. Upper Saddle River, NJ: Prentice Hall. 21st Century Collaborative. (n.d.). "Visual Literacy | 21st Century Collaborative." Accessed March 22, 2014. http://www.21stcenturycollaborative.com/2005/10/visual-literacy.

"Turnitin: A Summary of the Effectiveness.pdf." (2011). Accessed July 9, 2011. http://turnitin.com/static/resources/documentation/turnitin/company/Turnitin_Summary_of_Effectiveness_hires.pdf.

Turnitin for Admissions. (2014). https://www.turnitinadmissions.com.

"Turnitin: Our Company." (2014). *Turnitin.* http://turnitin.com/en_us/about-us/our-company.

Turnitin. "White Paper: The Sources in Student Writing – Secondary Education." (2012). *Turnitin.com.* http://pages.turnitin.com/rs/iparadigms/images/Turnitin_WhitePaper_Sources_in_Student_Writing_SEC.pdf?mkt_tok=3RkMMJWWfF9wsRoks6vPZKXonjHpfsX67%2BolX6S1gYkz2EFye%2BLIHETpodcMT8tgPa%2BTFAwTG5toziV8R7nCJM1s0dkQWRHh

"Turnitin: WriteCheck for Students." Turntin.com. (2014). http://turnitin.com/static/products/writecheck.php.

21st Century Collaborative. (n.d.). "Visual Literacy | 21st Century Collaborative." Accessed March 22, 2014. http://www.21stcenturycollaborative.com/2005/10/visual-literacy.

Tyler, Ralph W. (1949). *Basic Principles of Curriculum and Instruction.* Chicago: University of Chicago Press.

Tyler, Ralph W. (1989). "Educational Evaluation: Classic Works of Ralph W. Tyler." http://books.google.com/books?id=dvQtruCTZHcC&pg=PR8&lpg=PR8&dq=ralph+w.+tyler+theory&source=bl&ots=HWJiHYcpXV&sig=oJUqriEDrGr86sn3UQQHGvtwbYY&hl=en&sa=X&ei=g80mU_7VMYjz0gG1xoD4Cw&ved=0CHkQ6AEwCTgK#v=onepage&q=ralph%20w.%20tyler%20theory&f=false.

Tyler, Ralph W., George F. Madaus, and Daniel L. Stufflebeam. (1989). *Educational Evaluation: Classic Works of Ralph W. Tyler.* Boston, MA: Kluwer Academic.

University of Oregon: Teaching Effectiveness Program. (2013). "Teaching Resources—Benefits of Collaborative Learning." http://tep.uoregon.edu/resources/librarylinks/articles/benefits.html.

U.S. Copyright Office. (2009). "Circular 21: Reproduction of Copyrighted Works by Educators and Librarians." Accessed May 3, 2011. http://www.copyright.gov/circs/circ21.pdf.

U.S. Copyright Office. (n.d.) "Copyright Law: Chapter 1, Subject Matter and Scope of Copyright, Circular 92." U.S. Copyright Office. Accessed October 7, 2014. http://www.copyright.gov/title17/92chap1.html.

U. S. Copyright Office. (n.d.). "Copyright in General (FAQ)."

U.S. Copyright Office. Accessed October 7, 2014. http://copyright.gov/help/faq/faq- general.html#protect.

USDA: United States Department of Agriculture. (2010). "MyPyramidTracker." Accessed April 28, 2011. http://www.mypyramidtracker.gov.

USDA: United States Department of Agriculture. (2011). "ChooseMyPlate." Accessed June 7, 2011. http://www.choosemyplate.gov.

USDA: United States Department of Agriculture. (2012). "Creative Class County Codes: Documentation." http://www.ers.usda.gov/data-products/creative-class-county-codes/documentation.aspx#.Uw4Be-NdVvA.

U.S. Department of Education. (2009). "Using Student Achievement Data to Support Instructional Decision Making." Accessed May 1, 2011. http://ies.ed.gov/ncee/wwc/pdf/practice_guides/dddm_pg_092909.pdf.

U.S. Department of Education. (2010). "Evaluation of Evidence-Based Practices in Online Learning: A Meta-Analysis and Review of Online Learning Studies." Accessed May 1, 2011. http://files.eric.ed.gov/fulltext/ED505824.pdf.

U.S. Department of Education. (2010). "Internet Safety." Accessed May 3, 2011. http://findit.ed.gov/search?utf8=%E2%9C%93&affiliate=ed.gov&query=internet+safety.

U.S. Department of Education. (2010). "National Educational Technology Plan." Accessed April 28, 2011. http://www2.ed.gov/about/offices/list/os/technology/plan/index.html.

U.S. Department of Education. (2011). "Assessment Measure What Matters." Accessed May 2, 2011. http://tech.ed.gov/netp/assessment-measure-what-matters.

U.S. Department of Education. (2007). "What Content-Area Teachers Should Know About Adolescent Literacy." National Institute for Literacy. Accessed April 2, 2010. https://lincs.ed.gov/publications/pdf/adolescent_literacy07.pdf.

U.S. Department of Education. (2006). "What Is Scientifically Based Research? A Guide for Teachers." Accessed June 21, 2010. https://lincs.ed.gov/publications/pdf/science_research.pdf.

Uso-Juan, Esther, and MaNoelia Ruiz-Madrid. (2009). "Reading Versus Online Text: A Study of EFL Learners' Strategic Reading Behavior." *International Journal of English Studies* 2, no. 9: 59–79. Accessed April 30, 2011. http://files.eric.ed.gov/fulltext/EJ878417.pdf.

U.S. Supreme Court. (1991). *Feist Publications, Inc. v. Rural Telephone Service Co., Inc.: Certiorari to the United States Court of Appeals for the Tenth Circuit.* United States Supreme Court. Accessed March 10, 2013. http://www.supremecourt.gov/opinions/boundvolumes/506bv.pdf.

Valdez, Gilbert. (2004). "Critical Issue: Technology Leadership: Enhancing Positive Educational Change." Accessed May 1, 2011. http://www.ncrel.org/sdrs/areas/issues/educatrs/leadrshp/le700.htm.

Van Scoyoc, Anna M. (2003). "Reducing Library Anxiety in First Year Students: The Impact of Computer-assisted Instruction and Bibliographic Instruction." *Reference and User Services Quarterly* 42, no. 4: 329+. Accessed May 28, 2010. http://www.jstor.org/discover/10.2307/20864059?uid=3739832&uid=2&uid=4&uid=3739256&sid=21104900414153.

Varlas, Laura. (2012). "It's Complicated: Common Core State Standards Focus on Text Complexity." *Education Update* 54, no. 4. Accessed August 12, 2013. http://www.ascd.org/publications/newsletters/education-update/apr12/vol54/num04/It's-Complicated.aspx.

Wagner, Tony. (2008). *The Global Achievement Gap.* New York: Basic Books.

Wagner, Tony, Robert Kegan, Lisa Lahey, Richard W. Lemons, Jude Garnier, Deborah Helsing, Annie Howell, and Harriett Thurber Rasmussen. (2006). *Change Leadership: A Practical Guide to Transforming Our Schools*. San Francisco: Jossey-Bass.

Warschauer, Mark, and Meei-Ling Liaw. (2010). "Emerging Technologies in Adult Literacy and Language Education." Accessed May 1, 2011. https://lincs.ed.gov/publications/pdf/technology_paper_2010.pdf.

Weiner, Sharon A. (2010). "The Learning Commons as a Locus for Information Literacy." http://docs.lib.purdue.edu/cgi/viewcontent.cgi?article=1176&context=lib_research.

Weiner, Sharon, Tomalee Doan, and Hal Kirkwood. (2010). "The Learning Commons as Locus for Information Literacy." http://docs.lib.purdue.edu/cgi/viewcontent.cgi?article=1161&context=lib_research.

Wesleyan University Library. (2014). "How to Write an Annotated Bibliography—LibGuides at Wesleyan University." http://libguides.wesleyan.edu/annotbib.

"What Is Plagiarism? Best Practices for Ensuring Originality in Written Work." (2014). Plagiarism.org. http://www.plagiarism.org/plagiarism-101/what-is-plagiarism/.

"What Is the Purpose of the WriteCheck Plagiarism and Grammar Checker?" (2014). *Experts123*. http://www.experts123.com/q/what-is-the-purpose-of-the-writecheck-plagiarism-and-grammar-checker.html.

Whitby, Tom. (n.d.). "Tom Whitby (tomwhitby) on Twitter." Accessed March 21, 2014. https://twitter.com/tomwhitby.

Wiggins, Grant. (2012). "On Assessing for Creativity: Yes You Can, and Yes You Should." http://grantwiggins.wordpress.com/2012/02/03/on-assessing-for-creativity-yes-you-can-and-yes-you-should.

Wiggins, Grant, and Jay McTighe. (2004). *Understanding by Design: Professional Development Workbook*. Alexandria, VA: ASCD.

Wiggins, Grant, and Jay McTighe. (2005). *Understanding by Design*, 2nd ed. Alexandria, VA: ASCD.

Wiggins, Grant, and Jay McTighe. (2007). *Schooling by Design: Mission, Action, and Achievement*. Alexandria, VA: ASCD.

"Wikimedia Commons." 2014. http://commons.wikimedia.org/wiki/Main_Page.

Wikipedia. (2014). "Google Books." http://en.wikipedia.org/w/index.php?title=Google_Images&oldid=594456587.

Wikipedia. (2014). "Google Images." http://en.wikipedia.org/w/index.php?title=Google_Images&oldid=594456587.

"Wikipedia: Public Domain Image Resources." (2014). http://en.wikipedia.org/wiki/Wikipedia:Public_domain_image_resources.

Wikipedia. (2013). "Ralph W. Tyler." http://en.wikipedia.org/wiki/Ralph_W._Tyler.

Wikipedia. (2014). "Torrance Tests of Creative Thinking." http://en.wikipedia.org/wiki/Torrance_Tests_of_Creative_Thinking.

Wikipedia. (2011). "Transliteracy." Accessed June 7, 2011. http://en.wikipedia.org/wiki/Transliteracy.

Wikipedia. (2014). "Zotero." http://en.wikipedia.org/w/index.php?title=Zotero&oldid=595959947.

Wolf, Gary. (1996). "Steve Jobs: The Next Insanely Great Thing." http://archive.wired.com/wired/archive/4.02/jobs_pr.html.

Wolf, Sara, Thomas Brush, and John Saye. (2003). "The Big Six Information Skills as a Metacognitive Scaffold: A Case Study of Six." Accessed May 14, 2010. http://www.ala.org/aasl/sites/ala.org.aasl/files/content/aaslpubsandjournals/slr/vol6/SLMR_BigSixInfoSkills_V6.pdf.

Wong, Venessa. (2013). "Q&A: 140 Seconds with Pizza Hut on Its 140-Second Job Interview." Accessed September 4, 2013. http://www.businessweek.com/articles/2013-03-07/q-and-a-140- seconds-with-pizza-hut-on-its-140-second-job-interview.

"WriteCheck FAQ." (2011). *WriteCheck* . http://en.writecheck.com/faq/.

"WriteCheck for Students: Formative Writing Tools for Students." (2014). *Turnitin.com*. http://turnitin.com/en_us/features/writecheck.

"Writing History." (2002). PBS NewsHour. http://www.pbs.org/newshour/bb/law-jan-june02-history_1-28/.

Young, Michael J, and Bokhee Yoon. (2000). "Estimating the Consistency and Accuracy of Classifications in a Standards-Referenced Assessment." Validating Standard -Referenced Science Assessment: CSE Technical Report 529. Accessed May 2, 2011. https://www.cse.ucla.edu/products/reports/TECH475.pdf.

Young, Robert D. (1991). "Risk-Taking in Learning, K-3." Accessed February 7, 2011. http://files.eric.ed.gov/fulltext/ED336207.pdf.

Youth Internet Safety Task Force. (2010). "Youth Internet Safety Task Force: Compilation of Current Research." Accessed May 8, 2011. http://www.atg.wa.gov///_Consumers/_Safety/%20Internet%20Research%20Compilation%20Sept-1-2010.pdf.

Zotero. (2009). "Quality concerns w/ distance ed." https://www.zotero.org/groups/blended_education__the_liberal_arts/items/BC737HBQ

Zotero. (2014). [Homepage]. https://www.zotero.org

Zotero. (2014). "Zotero Style Repository." https://www.zotero.org/styles.

Zotero. (2014). http://research.library.gsu.edu/zotero.

Zotero. (n.d.). "Creating Bibliographies." Accessed March 22, 2014. http://www.zotero.org/support/creating_bibliographies.

# Index